A History
of
Phallic Worship

A History
of
Phallic Worship

Two Volumes in One

A Discourse on the Worship of Priapus
by Richard Payne Knight

The Worship of the Generative Powers
by Thomas Wright

Dorset Press
New York

This edition published by Dorset Press,
a division of Marboro Books Corp.

1992 Dorset Press

ISBN 0-88029-977-0

Printed and bound in the United States of America

M 9 8 7 6 5 4 3 2 1

A DISCOURSE ON
THE WORSHIP OF PRIAPUS

AND ITS CONNECTION WITH THE
MYSTIC THEOLOGY OF THE ANCIENTS

BY
RICHARD PAYNE KNIGHT

TO WHICH IS ADDED

AN ACCOUNT OF THE REMAINS OF THE
WORSHIP OF PRIAPUS LATELY EXISTING
AT ISERNIA IN THE KINGDOM OF NAPLES

BY SIR WILLIAM HAMILTON, K. B.

WITH PLATES

VOLUME I

PREFACE

RICHARD PAYNE KNIGHT, one of the most distinguished patrons of art and learning in England during his time, a scholar of great attainments, an eminent antiquarian, member of the Radical party in Parliament, and a writer of great ability, was born at Wormesley Grange, in Herefordshire, in 1750. From an early age he devoted himself to the study of ancient literature, antiquities, and mythology. A large portion of his inherited fortune was expended in the collection of antiquities, especially, ancient coins, medals, and bronzes. His collection, which was continued until his death in 1820, was bequeathed to the British Museum, and accepted for that institution by a special act of Parliament. Its value was estimated at £50,000.

Among his works are an *Inquiry into the Principles of Taste; Analytical Essay on the Greek Alphabet; The Symbolical Language of Ancient Art;* and three poems; *The Landscape, the Progress of Civil Society, and The Romance of Alfred.*

The *Worship of Priapus* was originally printed in 1786. The bold utterances of Mr. Knight on a subject which until that time had been entirely tabooed, or had been treated in a way to hide rather than to discover the truth, shocked the sensibilities of the higher classes of English society, and the ministers and members of the various denominations of the Christian world. Rather than endure the storm of criticism, aroused by the publication, he suppressed during his lifetime all the copies of the book he could recall, consequently it became very scarce, and has continued so.

The numerous illustrations are engraved from antique coins, medals, stone carvings, etc., preserved in the Payne Knight collection in the British Museum. These are only to be found in museums and private collections scattered over Europe, and are practically inaccessible to the student; they are here engraved and fully described.

The present edition is published in the interest of science and scholarship. At a time when so many learned investigators are endeavouring to trace back religious beliefs and practices to their origin, it would seem that this is a branch of the subject which should not be ignored. The history of religions has been studied with more zeal and success during the nineteenth and twentieth centuries, than in all the ages which preceded them, and this book has now an interest fifty fold greater than when originally published.

The short account of the Remains of the Worship of Priapus in the Kingdom of Naples is from the letter of Sir William Hamilton, K.B., His Majesty's Minister at the Court of Naples, to Sir Joseph Banks, Bart., then President of the Royal Society.

ON THE WORSHIP OF PRIAPUS
IN THE KINGDOM OF NAPLES

SIR,   *Naples, Dec. 30, 1781.*

HAVING last year made a curious discovery, that in a Province of this Kingdom, and not fifty miles from its Capital, a sort of devotion is still paid to PRIAPUS, the obscene Divinity of the Ancients (though under another denomination), I thought it a circumstance worth recording; particularly, as it offers a fresh proof of the similitude of the Popish and Pagan Religion, so well observed by Dr. Middleton, in his celebrated Letter from Rome: and therefore I mean to deposit the authentic [1] proofs of this assertion in the British Museum, when a proper opportunity shall offer. In the meantime I send you the following account, which, I flatter myself, will amuse you for the present, and may in future serve to illustrate those proofs.

I had long ago discovered, that the women and

[1] A specimen of each of the *ex-voti* of wax, with the original letter from Isernia. See the Ex-voti, Plate I.

children of the lower class, at Naples, and in its neighbourhood, frequently wore, as an ornament of dress, a sort of Amulets, (which they imagine to be a preservative from the *mal occhii, evil eyes,* or enchantment) exactly similar to those which were worn by the ancient Inhabitants of this Country for the very same purpose, as likewise for their supposed invigorating influence; and all of which have evidently a relation to the Cult of Priapus. Struck with this conformity in ancient and modern superstition, I made a collection of both the ancient and modern Amulets of this sort, and placed them together in the British Museum, where they remain. The modern Amulet most in vogue represents a hand clinched, with the point of the thumb thrust betwixt the index and middle [1] finger; the next is a shell; and the third is a half-moon. These Amulets (except the shell, which is usually worn in its natural state) are most commonly made of silver, but sometimes of ivory, coral, amber, crystal, or some curious gem, or pebble. We have a proof of the hand above described having a connection with Priapus, in a most elegant small idol of bronze of that Divinity, now in the Royal Museum of Portici, and which was found in the ruins of Herculaneum: it has an enormous Phallus, and, with an

[1] See Plate II., Fig. 1.

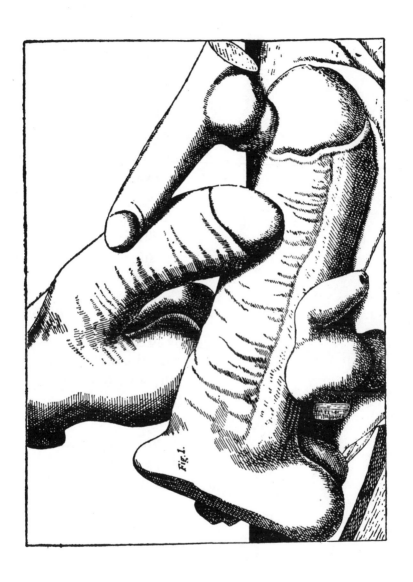

Fig.1.

PLATE I

EX VOTI OF WAX, FROM ISERNIA

arch look and gesture, stretches out its right hand
in the form above mentioned; [1] and which probably
was an emblem of consummation: and as a further
proof of it, the Amulet which occurs most frequently
amongst those of the Ancients (next to that which
represents the simple Priapus), is such a hand united
with the Phallus; of which you may see several specimens in my collection in the British Museum. One
in particular, I recollect, has also the half-moon
joined to the hand and Phallus; which half-moon is
supposed to have an allusion to the female *menses.*
The shell, or *concha veneris,* is evidently an emblem
of the female part of generation. It is very natural
then to suppose, that the Amulets representing the
Phallus alone, so visibly indecent, may have been
long out of use in this civilized capital; but I have
been assured, that it is but very lately that the Priests
have put an end to the wearing of such Amulets in
Calabria, and other distant Provinces of this
Kingdom.

A new road having been made last year from this
Capital to the Province of Abruzzo, passing through
the City of Isernia (anciently belonging to the Samnites, and very populous [2]), a person of liberal
education, employed in that work, chanced to be at

[1] In the first volume of the Bronzes of the Herculaneum.
[2] The actual population of Isernia is 5156.

17

Isernia just at the time of the celebration of the Feast
of the modern Priapus, St. Cosmo; and having been
struck with the singularity of the ceremony, so very
similar to that which attended the ancient Cult of
the God of the Gardens, and knowing my taste for
antiquities, told me of it. From this Gentleman's
report, and from what I learnt on the spot from the
Governor of Isernia himself, having gone to that city
on purpose in the month of February last, I have
drawn up the following account, which I have reason
to believe is strictly true. I did intend to have been
present at the Feast of St. Cosmo this year; but the
indecency of this ceremony having probably trans-
pired, from the country's having been more frequented since the new road was made, orders have
been given, that the *Great Toe* [1] of the Saint should
no longer be exposed. The following is the account
of the Fête of St. Cosmo and Damiano, as it actually
was celebrated at Isernia, on the confines of Abruzzo,
in the Kingdom of Naples, so late as in the year of
our Lord 1780.

On the 27th of September, at Isernia, one of the
most ancient cities of the Kingdom of Naples, situated in the Province called the Contado di Molise,
and adjoining to Abruzzo, an annual Fair is held,

[1] It appears the modern Priapi were so called at Isernia.

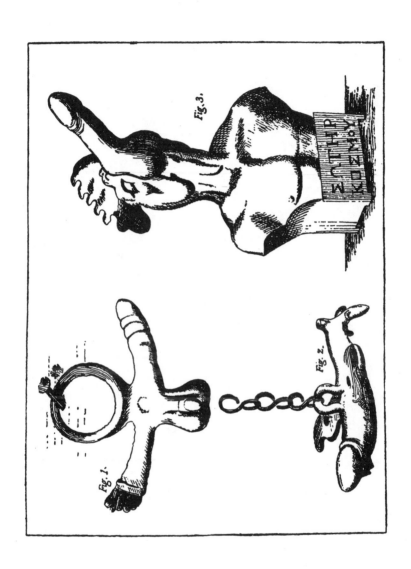

PLATE II

ANCIENT AND MODERN AMULETS

which lasts three days. The situation of this Fair is on a rising ground, between two rivers, about half a mile from the town of Isernia; on the most elevated part of which there is an ancient church, with a vestibule. The architecture is of the style of the lower ages; and it is said to have been a church and convent belonging to the Benedictine Monks in the time of their poverty. This church is dedicated to St. Cosmus and Damianus. One of the days of the Fair, the relicks of the Saints are exposed, and afterwards carried in procession from the cathedral of the city to this church, attended by a prodigious concourse of people. In the city, and at the fair, *ex-voti* of wax, representing the male parts of generation, of various dimensions, some even of the length of the palm, are publickly offered to sale. There are also waxen vows, that represent other parts of the body mixed with them; but of these there are few in comparison of the number of the Priapi. The devout distributers of these vows carry a basket full of them in one hand, and hold a plate in the other to receive the money, crying aloud, "St. Cosmo and Damiano!" If you ask the price of one, the answer is, *più ci metti, più meriti:* "The more you give, the more's the merit." In the vestibule are two tables, at each of which one of the canons of the church presides, this crying out, *Qui si riceveno le Misse, e Litanie:* "Here Masses and

21

Litanies are received;" and the other, *Qui si riceveno li Voti:* "Here the Vows are received." The price of a Mass is fifteen Neapolitan grains, and of a Litany five grains. On each table is a large bason for the reception of the different offerings. The Vows are chiefly presented by the female sex; and they are seldom such as represent legs, arms, &c., but most commonly the male parts of generation. The person who was at this fête in the year 1780, and who gave me this account (the authenticity of every article of which has since been fully confirmed to me by the Governor of Isernia), told me also, that he heard a woman say, at the time she presented a Vow, like that which is presented in Plate 1, Fig. i., *Santo Cosimo benedetto, cosi lo voglio:* "Blessed St. Cosmo, let it be like this;" another, *St. Cosimo, a te mi raccommendo:* "St. Cosmo, I recommend myself to you;" and a third, *St. Cosimo, ti ringrazio:* "St. Cosmo, I thank you." The Vow is never presented without being accompanied by a piece of money, and is always kissed by the devotee at the moment of presentation.

At the great altar in the church, another of its canons attends to give the holy unction, with the oil of St. Cosmo;[1] which is prepared by the same re-

[1] The cure of diseases by oil is likewise of ancient date; for

ceipt as that of the Roman Ritual, with the addition only of the prayer of the Holy Martyrs, St. Cosmus and Damianus. Those who have an infirmity in any of their members, present themselves at the great altar, and uncover the member affected (not even excepting that which is most frequently represented by the *ex-voti*); and the reverend canon anoints it, saying, *Per intercessionem beati Cosmi, liberet te ab omni malo. Amen.*

The ceremony finishes by the canons of the church dividing the spoils, both money and wax, which must be to a very considerable amount, as the concourse at this fête is said to be prodigiously numerous.

The oil of St. Cosmo is in high repute for its invigorating quality, when the loins, and parts adjacent, are anointed with it. No less than 1400 flasks of that oil were either expended at the altar in unctions, or charitably distributed, during this fête in the year 1780; and as it is usual for every one, who either makes use of the oil at the altar, or carries off a flask of it, to leave an alms for St. Cosmo, the ceremony of the oil becomes likewise a very lucrative one to the canons of the church.

Tertullian tells us, that a Christian, called Proculus, cured the Emperor Severus of a certain distemper by the use of oil; for which service the Emperor kept Proculus, as long as he lived, in his palace.

ON THE WORSHIP OF PRIAPUS

MEN, considered collectively, are at all times the same animals, employing the same organs, and endowed with the same faculties: their passions, prejudices, and conceptions, will of course be formed upon the same internal principles, although directed to various ends, and modified in various ways, by the variety of external circumstances operating upon them. Education and science may correct, restrain, and extend; but neither can annihilate or create: they may turn and embellish the currents; but can neither stop nor enlarge the springs, which, continuing to flow with a perpetual and equal tide, return to their ancient channels, when the causes that perverted them are withdrawn.

The first principles of the human mind will be more directly brought into action, in proportion to the earnestness and affection with which it contemplates its object; and passion and prejudice will acquire dominion over it, in proportion as its first principles are more directly brought into action. On all common subjects, this dominion of passion and prejudice is restrained by the evidence of sense and perception; but, when the mind is led to the contemplation of things beyond its comprehension, all such restraints vanish: reason has then nothing to oppose to the phantoms of imagination, which acquire terrors from their obscurity, and dictate uncontrolled, because unknown. Such is the case in all religious subjects, which, being beyond the reach of sense or reason, are always embraced or rejected with violence and heat. Men think they know, because they are sure they feel; and are firmly convinced, because strongly agitated. Hence proceed that haste and violence with which devout persons of all religions condemn the rites and doctrines of others, and the furious zeal and bigotry with which they maintain their own; while perhaps, if both were equally well understood, both would be found to have the same meaning, and only to differ in the modes of conveying it.

Of all the profane rites which belonged to the ancient polytheism, none were more furiously inveighed against by the zealous propagators of the Christian faith, than the obscene ceremonies performed in the worship of Priapus; which appeared not only contrary to the gravity and sanctity of religion, but subversive of the first principles of decency and good order in society. Even the form itself, under which the god was represented, appeared to them a mockery of all piety and devotion, and more fit to be placed in a brothel than a temple. But the forms and ceremonials of a religion are not always to be understood in their direct and obvious sense; but are to be considered as symbolical representations of some hidden meaning, which may be extremely wise and just, though the symbols themselves, to those who know not their true signification, may appear in the highest degree absurd and extravagant. It has often happened, that avarice and superstition have continued these symbolical representations for ages after their original meaning has been lost and forgotten; when they must of course appear nonsensical and ridiculous, if not impious and extravagant.

Such is the case with the rite now under consideration, than which nothing can be more monstrous and indecent, if considered in its plain and obvious meaning, or as a part of the Christian worship; but which will be found to be a very natural symbol of a very natural and philosophical system of religion, if considered according to its original use and intention.

What this was, I shall endeavour in the following sheets to explain as concisely and clearly as possible. Those who wish to know how generally the symbol, and the religion which it represented, once prevailed, will consult the great and elaborate work of Mr. D'Hancarville, who, with infinite learning and ingenuity, has traced its progress over the whole earth. My endeavour will be merely to show, from what original principles in the human mind it was first adopted, and how it was connected with the ancient theology: matters of very curious inquiry, which will serve, better perhaps than any others, to illustrate that truth, which ought to be present in every man's mind when he judges of the actions of others, *that in morals, as well as physics, there is no effect without an adequate cause.* If in doing this, I frequently find it necessary to differ in opinion with the learned author above-mentioned, it will be always with the utmost deference and respect; as it is to him that we are indebted for the only reasonable method of explaining the emblematical works of the ancient artists.

Whatever the Greeks and Egyptians meant by the symbol in question, it was certainly nothing ludicrous or licentious; of which we need no other proof, than its having been carried in solemn procession at the celebration of those mysteries in which the first principles of their religion, the knowledge of the God of Nature, the First, the Supreme, the Intellectual,[1] were

[1] Plut. *de Is. et Os.*

preserved free from the vulgar superstitions, and communicated, under the strictest oaths of secrecy, to the iniated (initiated); who were obliged to purify themselves, prior to their initiation, by abstaining from venery, and all impure food.[1] We may therefore be assured, that no impure meaning could be conveyed by this symbol; but that it represented some fundamental principle of their faith. What this was, it is difficult to obtain any direct information, on account of the secrecy under which this part of their religion was guarded. Plutarch tells us, that the Egyptians represented Osiris with the organ of generation erect, to show his generative and prolific power: he also tells us, that Osiris was the same Diety as the Bacchus of the Greek Mythology; who was also the same as the first begotten Love (Εϱως πϱωτογονος) of Orpheus and Hesiod.[2] This deity is celebrated by the ancient poets as the creator of all things, the father of gods and men;[3] and it appears, by the passage above referred to, that the organ of generation was the symbol of his great characteristic attribute. This is perfectly consistent with the general practice of the Greek artists, who (as will be made appear hereafter) uniformly represented the attributes of the deity by the corresponding proper-

[1] Plut. *de Is. et Os.*   [2] Ibid.   [3] Orph. *Argon.* 422.

ties observed in the objects of sight. They thus personified the epithets and titles applied to him in the hymns and litanies, and conveyed their ideas of him by forms, only intelligible to the initiated, instead of sounds, which were intelligible to all. The organ of generation represented the generative or creative attribute, and in the language of painting and sculpture, signified the same as the epithet παγγενετωζ, in the Orphic litanies.

This interpretation will perhaps surprise those who have not been accustomed to divest their minds of the prejudices of education and fashion; but I doubt not, but it will appear just and reasonable to those who consider manners and customs as relative to the natural causes which produced them, rather than to the artificial opinions and prejudices of any particular age or country. There is naturally no impurity or licentiousness in the moderate and regular gratification of any natural appetite; the turpitude consisting wholly in the excess or perversion. Neither are organs of one species of enjoyment naturally to be considered as subjects of shame and concealment more than those of another; every refinement of modern manners on this head being derived from acquired habit, not from nature: habit, indeed, long established; for it seems to have been as general in Homer's days as at present; but which certainly did not exist when the mystic symbols of the ancient worship were first adopted. As these symbols were intended to express abstract ideas by objects of sight, the contrivers of them naturally selected those objects whose characteristic properties seemed to have the greatest analogy with the Divine attributes which they wished to represent. In an age, therefore, when no prejudices of artificial decency existed, what more just and natural image could they find, by which to express their idea of the beneficent power of the great Creator, than that organ which endowed them with the power of procreation, and made them partakers, not only of the felicity of the Deity, but of his great characteristic attribute, that of multiplying his own image, communicating his blessings, and extending them to generations yet unborn?

In the ancient theology of Greece, preserved in the Orphic Fragments, this Deity, the Εϱως πϱωτογονος, or first-begotten Love, is said to have been produced, together with Æther, by Time, or Eternity (Κϱονος), and Necessity (Αναγχη), operating upon inert matter (Χαος). He is described as eternally begetting (αειγνητης); the Father of Night, called in later times, the lucid or splendid, (φανης), because he first appeared in splendour; of a double nature, (διφνης), as possessing the general power of creation and generation, both active and passive, both

31

male and female.[1]   Light is his necessary and pri-

[1] Orph. *Argon.*, ver. 12.   This poem of the Argonautic Expedition is not of the ancient Orpheus, but written in his name by some poet posterior to Homer; as appears by the allusion to Orpheus's descent into hell; a fable invented after the Homeric times.   It is, however, of very great antiquity, as both the style and manner sufficiently prove; and, I think, cannot be later than the age of Pisistratus, to which it has been generally attributed. The passage here referred to is cited from another poem, which, at the time this was written, passed for a genuine work of the Thracian bard: whether justly or not, matters little; for its being thought so at that time proves it to be of the remotest antiquity.   The other Orphic poems cited in this discourse are the Hymns, or Litanies, which are attributed by the early Christian and later Platonic writers to Onomacritus, a poet of the age of Pisistratus; but which are probably of various authors (See Brucker. *Hist. Crit. Philos.*, vol. i., part 2, lib. i., c. i.)   They contain, however, nothing which proves them to be later than the Trojan times; and if Onomacritus, or any later author, had anything to do with them, it seems to have been only in new-versifying them, and changing the dialect (See Gesner. *Proleg. Orphica*, p. 26).   Had he forged them, and attempted to impose them upon the world, as the genuine compositions of an ancient bard, there can be no doubt but that he would have stuffed them with antiquated words and obsolete phrases; which is by no means the case, the language being pure and worthy the age of Pisistratus.   These poems are not properly hymns, for the hymns of the Greeks contained the nativities and actions of the gods, like those of Homer and Callimachus; but these are compositions of a different kind, and are properly invocations or prayers used in the Orphic mysteries, and seem nearly of the same class as the Psalms of the Hebrews.   The reason why they are so seldom mentioned by any of the early writers, and so perpetually referred to by the later, is that they belonged to the mystic worship, where everything was kept concealed under the strictest oaths of secrecy.   But after the rise of Christianity, this sacred silence

was broken by the Greek converts, who revealed everything which they thought would depreciate the old religion or recommend the new; whilst the heathen priests revealed whatever they thought would have contrary tendency; and endeavoured to show, by publishing the real mystic creed of their religion, that the principles of it were not so absurd as its outward structure seemed to infer; but that, when stripped of poetical allegory and vulgar fable, their theology was pure, reasonable, and sublime (Gesner. *Proleg. Orphica*). The collection of these poems now extant, being probably compiled and versified by several hands, with some forged, and other interpolated and altered, must be read with great caution; more especially the Fragments preserved by the Fathers of the Church and Ammonian Platonics; for these writers made no scruple of forging any monuments of antiquity which suited their purposes; particularly the former, who, in addition to their natural zeal, having the interests of a confederate body to support, thought every means by which they could benefit that body, by extending the lights of revelation, and gaining proselytes to the true faith, not only allowable, but meritorious (See Clementina, Hom. vii., sec. 10. Recogn. lib. i., sec. 65. Origen, *apud Hieronom. Apolog.* i., *contra Ruf.* et Chrysostom. *de Sacerdot.*, lib. i. Chrysostom, in particular, not only justifies, but warmly commends, any frauds that can be practiced for the advantage of the Church of Christ). Pausanias says (lib. ix.), that the Hymns of Orpheus were few and short; but next in poetical merit to those of Homer, and superior to them in sanctity (θεολογικώτεροι) These are probably the same as the genuine part of the collection now extant; but they are so intermixed, that it is difficult to say which are genuine and which are not. Perhaps there is no surer rule for judging than to compare the epithets and allegories with the symbols and monograms on the Greek medals, and to make their agreement the test of authenticity. The medals were the public acts and records of the State, made under the direction of the magistrates, who were generally initiated into the mysteries. We may therefore be assured, that whatever theological and mythological allusions are found upon them were part of the ancient religion of Greece. It is from these that many of the Orphic Hymns and Fragments are proved to contain the pure theology or mystic faith of the ancients, which is called Orphic by Pausanias (lib. i., c. 39), and which is so unlike the vulgar religion, or poetical mythology, that one can scarcely imagine at first sight that it belonged to the same people; but which will nevertheless appear, upon accurate investigation, to be the source from whence it flowed, and the cause of all its extravagance.

The history of Orpheus himself is so confused and obscured by fable, that it is impossible to obtain any certain information concerning him. According to general tradition, he was a Thracian, and introduced the mysteries, in which a more pure system of religion was taught, into Greece (Brucker, vol. i., part 2, lib. i., c. i.) He is also said to have travelled into Egypt (Diodor. Sic. lib. i., p. 80); but as the Egyptians pretended that all foreigners received their sciences from them, at a time when all foreigners who entered the country were put to death or enslaved (Diodor. Sic. lib. i., pp. 78 et 107), this account may be rejected, with many others of the same kind. The Egyptians certainly could not have taught Orpheus the plurality of worlds, and true solar system, which appear to have been the fundamental principles of his philosophy and religion (Plutarch. *de Placit. Philos.*, lib. ii., c. 13. Brucker *in loc. citat.*) Nor could he have gained this knowledge from any people which history has preserved any memorials; for we know of none among whom science had made such a progress, that a truth so remote from common observation, and so contradictory to the evidence of unimproved sense, would not have been rejected, as it was by all the sects of Greek philosophy except the Pythagoreans, who rather revered it as an article of faith, than understood it as a discovery of science. Thrace was certainly inhabited by a civilized nation at some remote period; for, when Philip of Macedon opened the gold mines in that country, he found that they had been worked before with great expense and ingenuity, by a people well versed in mechanics, of whom no memorials whatever were then extant. Of these, probably, was Orpheus, as well as Thamyris, both of whose poems, Plato says, could be read with pleasure in his time.

mary attribute, co-eternal with himself, and with him brought forth from inert matter by necessity. Hence the purity and sanctity always attributed to light by the Greeks.[1] He is called the Father of Night, because by attracting the light to himself, and becoming the fountain which distributed it to the world, he produced night, which is called eternally-begotten, because it had eternally existed, although mixed and lost in the general mass. He is said to pervade the world with the motion of his wings, bringing pure light; and thence to be called the splendid, the ruling Priapus, and self-illumined (ανταυγης [2]). It is to be observed that the word Πριηπος, afterwards the name of a subordinate deity, is here used as a title relating to one of his attributes; the reasons for which I shall endeavour to explain hereafter. Wings are figuratively attributed to him as being the emblems of swiftness and incubation; by the first of which he pervaded matter, and by the second fructified the egg of Chaos. The egg was carried in procession at the celebration of the mysteries, because, as Plutarch says, it was the material of generation (νλη της γενεσεως [3]) containing the seeds and germs of life and motion, without being actually possessed of either.

[1] See Sophocl. *Œdip. Tyr.*, ver. 1436.
[2] Orph. Hym. 5.
[3] Symph. 1. 2.

For this reason, it was a very proper symbol of Chaos, containing the seeds and materials of all things, which, however, were barren and useless, until the Creator fructified them by the incubation of his vital spirit, and released them from the restraints of inert matter, by the efforts of his divine strength. The incubation of the vital spirit is represented on the colonial medals of Tyre, by a serpent wreathed around an egg; [1] for the serpent, having the power of casting his skin, and apparently renewing his youth, became the symbol of life and vigour, and as such is always made an attendant on the mythological deities presiding over health.[2] It is also observed, that animals of the serpent kind retain life more pertinaciously than any others except the Polypus, which is sometimes represented upon the Greek Medals,[3] probably in its stead. I have myself seen the heart of an adder continue its vital motions for many minutes after it has been taken from the body, and even renew them, after it has been cold, upon being moistened with warm water, and touched with a stimulus.

The Creator, delivering the fructified seeds of things from the restraints of inert matter by his divine

[1] See Plate XXI. Fig. 1.
[2] Macrob. Sat. i. c. 20.
[3] See Goltz, Tab. II. Figs. 7 and 8.

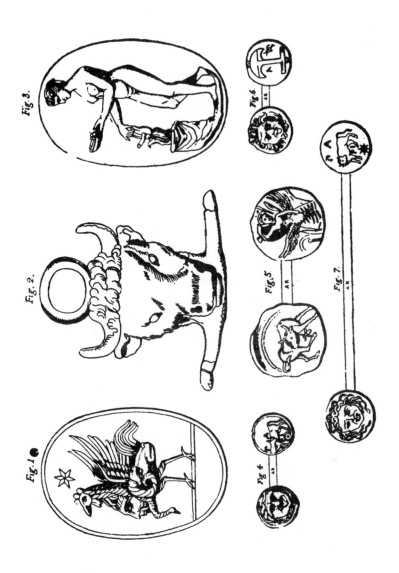

PLATE III

ANTIQUE GEMS AND GREEK MEDALS

strength, is represented on innumerable Greek medals by the Urus, or wild Bull, in the act of butting against the Egg of Chaos, and breaking it with his horns.[1] It is true, that the egg is not represented with the bull on any of those which I have seen; but Mr. D'Hancarville [2] has brought examples from other countries, where the same system prevailed, which, as well as the general analogy of the Greek theology, prove that the egg must have been understood, and that the attitude of the bull could have no other meaning. I shall also have occasion hereafter to show by other examples, that it was no uncommon practice, in these mystic monuments, to make a part of a group represent the whole. It was from this horned symbol of the power of the Deity that horns were placed in the portraits of kings to show that their power was derived from Heaven, and acknowledged no earthly superior. The moderns have indeed changed the meaning of this symbol, and given it a sense of which, perhaps, it would be difficult to find the origin, though I have often wondered that it has never exercised the sagacity of those learned gentle-

---

[1] See Plate IV. Fig. 1, and Recherches sur les Arts, vol. i. Pl. VIII. The Hebrew word *Chroub*, or *Cherub*, signified originally *strong* or *robust;* but is usually employed metaphorically, signifying a Bull. See Cleric. in *Exod.* c. XXV.

[2] Recherches sur les Arts, lib. i.

men who make British antiquities the subjects of their laborious inquiries. At present, it certainly does not bear any character of dignity or power; nor does it ever imply that those to whom it is attributed have been particularly favoured by the generative or creative powers. But this is a subject much too important to be discussed in a digression; I shall therefore leave it to those learned antiquarians who have done themselves so much honour, and the public so much service, by their successful inquiries into customs of the same kind. To their indefatigable industry and exquisite ingenuity I earnestly recommend it, only observing that this modern acceptation of the symbol is of considerable antiquity, for it is mentioned as proverbial in the Oneirocritics of Artemidorus; [1] and that it is not now confined to Great Britain, but prevails in most parts of Christendom, as the ancient acceptation of it did formerly in most parts of the world, even among that people from whose religion Christianity is derived; for it is a common mode of expression in the Old Testament, to say that the horns of any one shall be exalted, in order to signify that he shall be raised into power or pre-eminence; and when Moses descended from the Mount with the spirit of God still upon him, his head appeared horned. [2]

[1] Lib. i. c. 12.

[2] *Exod.* c. xxxiv. v. 35, ed. Vulgat. Other translators under-

Fig. 1.

Fig. 2.

Fig. 3.

Fig. 4.

Fig. 5.

PLATE IV

MEDALS POSSESSED BY PAYNE KNIGHT

To the head of the bull was sometimes joined the organ of generation, which represented not only the strength of the Creator, but the peculiar direction of it to the most beneficial purpose, the propagation of sensitive beings. Of this there is a small bronze in the Museum of Mr. Townley, of which an engraving is given in Plate III. Fig. 2.[1]

Sometimes this generative attribute is represented by the symbol of the goat, supposed to be the most salacious of animals, and therefore adopted upon the same principles as the bull and the serpent.[2] The choral odes, sung in honour of the generator Bacchus, were hence called τραγωδιαι, or songs of the goat; a title which is now applied to the dramatic dialogues anciently inserted in these odes, to break their uniformity . On a medal, struck in honour of Augustus, the goat terminates in the tail of a fish, to show the generative power incorporated with water. Under his feet is the globe of the earth, supposed to be fertilised by this union; and upon his back, the cornucopia, representing the result of this fertility.[3]

---

stand the expression metaphorically, and suppose it to mean radiated, or luminous.

[1] See Plate III.

[2] Τον δε τραγον αωεθεωσαν (οι Αιγνωτιοι) καθαωερ και ωαρα τοις Ελλησι τετιησθαι λεγκσι τον Πριαωον, δια το γεννητικον μοριον.   DIODOR. lib. i. p. 78.

[3] Plate x. Fig. 3.

Mr. D'Hancarville attributes the origin of all these symbols to the ambiguity of words; the same term being employed in the primitive language to signify God and a Bull, the Universe and a Goat, Life and a Serpent. But words are only the types and symbols of ideas, and therefore must be posterior to them, in the same manner as ideas are to their objects. The words of a primitive language, being imitative of the ideas from which they sprung, and of the objects they meant to express, as far as the imperfections of the organs of speech will admit, there must necessarily be the same kind of analogy between them as between the ideas and objects themselves. It is impossible, therefore, that in such a language any ambiguity of this sort could exist, as it does in secondary languages; the words of which, being collected from various sources, and blended together without having any natural connection, become arbitrary signs of convention, instead of imitative representations of ideas. In this case it often happens, that words, similar in form, but different in meaning, have been adopted from different sources, which, being blended together, lose their little difference of form, and retain their entire difference of meaning. Hence ambiguities arise, such as those above mentioned, which could not possibly exist in an original tongue.

The Greek poets and artists frequently give the personification of a particular attribute for the Deity himself; hence he is called Ταυροζοας, Ταυρωπος, Ταυρομορφος,[1] &c., and hence the initials and monograms of the Orphic epithets applied to the Creator, are found with the bull, and other symbols, on the Greek medals.[2] It must not be imagined from hence, that the ancients supposed the Deity to exist under the form of a bull, a goat, or a serpent: on the contrary, he is always described in the Orphic theology as a general pervading Spirit, without form, or distinct locality of any kind; and appears, by a curious fragment preserved by Proclus,[3] to have been no other than *attraction* personified. The self-created mind (νοος αντογενεθλος) of the Eternal Father is said to have spread the heavy bond of love through all things (πασιν ενεοπειρεν δεσμον περιζριθη Ερωτος), in order that they might endure for ever. This Eternal Father is Κρονος, time or eternity, personified; and so taken for the unknown Being that fills eternity and infinity. The ancient theologists knew that we could form no positive idea of infinity, whether of power, space, or time; it being

[1] Orph. Hymn. v. et xxix.

[2] Numm. Vet. Pop. et Urb. Tab. xxxix. Figs 19 et 20. They are on most of the medals of Marseilles, Naples, Thurium and many other cities.

[3] In *Tim.* iii., et *Frag. Orphic.*, ed. Gesner.

fleeting and fugitive, and eluding the understanding by a continued and boundless progression. The only notion we have of it is from the addition or division of finite things, which suggest the idea of infinite, only from a power we feel in ourselves of still multiplying and dividing without end. The Schoolmen indeed were bolder, and, by a summary mode of reasoning, in which they were very expert, proved that they had as clear and adequate an idea of infinity, as of any finite substance whatever. Infinity, said they, is that which has no bounds. This negation, being a positive assertion, must be founded on a positive idea. We have therefore a positive idea of infinity.

The Eclectic Jews, and their followers, the Ammonian and Christian Platonics, who endeavoured to make their own philosophy and religion conform to the ancient theology, held infinity of space to be only the immensity of the divine presence. Ὁ Θεος ἑαυτο τοπος εστι [1] was their dogma, which is now inserted into the Confessional of the Greek Church.[2] This infinity was distinguished by them from common space, as time was from eternity. Whatever is eternal or infinite, said they, must be absolutely indivisible; because division is in itself inconsistent with

---

[1] Philo. *de Leg. Alleg.* lib. 1. Jo Damasc *de Orth Fid.*
[2] Mosheim. Nota in Sec. xxiv. Cudw. *Syst. Intellect.*

infinite continuity and duration: therefore space and time are distinct from infinity and eternity, which are void of all parts and gradations whatever. Time is measured by years, days, hours, &c., and distinguished by past, present, and future; but these, being divisions, are excluded from eternity, as locality is from infinity, and as both are from the Being who fills both; who can therefore feel no succession of events, nor know any gradation of distance; but must comprehend infinite duration as if it were one moment, and infinite extent as if it were but a single point.[1] Hence the Ammonian Platonics speak of him as concentered in his own unity, and extended through all things, but participated of by none. Being of a nature more refined and elevated than intelligence itself, he could not be known by sense, perception, or reason; and being the cause of all, he must be anterior to all, even to eternity itself, if considered as eternity of time, and not as the intellectual unity, which is the Deity himself, by whose emanations all things exist, and to whose proximity or distances they owe their degrees of excellence or baseness. *Being* itself, in its most abstract sense, is derived from him; for that which is the cause and beginning of all *Being*, cannot be a part of that *All* which

[1] See Boeth. *de Consol. Philos.* lib. iv. prof. 6.

sprung from himself: therefore he is not *Being,* nor is *Being* his *Attribute;* for that which has an attribute cannot have the abstract simplicity of pure unity. All *Being* is in its nature finite; for, if it was otherwise, it must be without bounds every way; and therefore could have no gradation of proximity to the first cause, or consequent pre-eminence of one part over another: for, as all distinctions of time are excluded from infinite duration, and all divisions of locality from infinite extent, so are all degrees of priority from infinite progression. The mind *is* and *acts* in itself; but the abstract unity of the first cause is neither in itself, nor in another;—not in itself, because that would imply modification, from which abstract simplicity is necessarily exempt; nor in another, because then there would be an hypostatical duality, instead of absolute unity. In both cases there would be a locality of hypostasis, inconsistent with intellectual infinity. As all physical attributes were excluded from this metaphysical abstraction, which they called their first cause, he must of course be destitute of all moral ones, which are only generalized modes of action of the former. Even simple abstract truth was denied him; for truth, as Proclus says, is merely the relative to falsehood; and no relative can exist without a positive or correlative. The

Deity therefore who has no falsehood, can have no truth, in our sense of the word.[1]

As metaphysical theology is a study very generally, and very deservedly, neglected at present, I thought this little specimen of it might be entertaining, from its novelty, to most readers; especially as it is intimately connected with the ancient system, which I have here undertaken to examine. Those, who wish to know more of it, may consult Proclus on the Theology of Plato, where they will find the most exquisite ingenuity most wantonly wasted. No persons ever showed greater acuteness or strength of reasoning than the Platonics and Scholastics; but having quitted common sense, and attempted to mount into the intellectual world, they expended it all in abortive efforts which may amuse the imagination, but cannot satisfy the understanding.

The ancient Theologists showed more discretion; for, finding that they could conceive no idea of infinity, they were content to revere the Infinite Being in the most general and efficient exertion of his power, attraction; whose agency is perceptible through all matter, and to which all motion may, perhaps, be ultimately traced. This power, being personified, became the secondary Deity, to whom all

[1] Proclus *in Theolog. Platon.* lib. i. et ii.

adoration and worship were directed, and who is therefore frequently considered as the sole and supreme cause of all things. His agency being supposed to extend through the whole material world, and to produce all the various revolutions by which its system is sustained, his attributes were of course extremely numerous and varied. These were expressed by various titles and epithets in the mystic hymns and litanies, which the artists endeavoured to represent by various forms and characters of men and animals. The great characteristic attribute was represented by the organ of generation in that state of tension and rigidity which is necessary to the due performance of its functions. Many small images of this kind have been found among the ruins of Herculaneum and Pompeii, attached to the bracelets, which the chaste and pious matrons of antiquity wore round their necks and arms. In these, the organ of generation appears alone, or only accompanied with the wings of incubation,[1] in order to show that the devout wearer devoted herself wholly and solely to procreation, the great end for which she was ordained. So expressive a symbol, being constantly in her view, must keep her attention fixed on its natural object, and continually remind her of the gratitude she owed

[1] Plate II. Fig. 2, engraved from one in the British Museum.

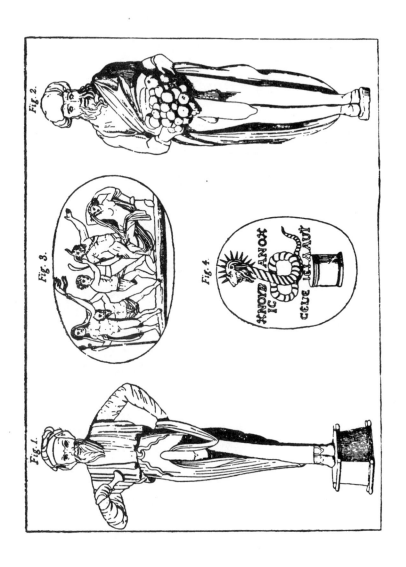

PLATE V

FIGURES OF PAN AND GEMS

the Creator, for having taken her into his service, made her a partaker of his most valuable blessings, and employed her as the passive instrument in the exertion of his most beneficial power.

The female organs of generation were revered [1] as symbols of the generative powers of nature or matter, as the male were of the generative powers of God. They are usually represented emblematically, by the Shell, or *Concha Veneris,* which was therefore worn by devout persons of antiquity, as it still continues to be by pilgrims, and many of the common women of Italy. The union of both was expressed by the hand mentioned in Sir William Hamilton's letter; [2] which being a less explicit symbol, has escaped the attention of the reformers, and is still worn, as well as the shell, by the women of Italy, though without being understood. It represented the act of generation, which was considered as a solemn sacrament, in honour of the Creator, as will be more fully shown hereafter.

The male organs of generation are sometimes found represented by signs of the same sort, which might properly be called the symbols of symbols. One of the most remarkable of these is a cross,

[1] August. *de Civ. Dei,* Lib. vi. c. 9.

[2] See Plate ii, Fig. 1. from one in the British Museum, in which both symbols are united.

in the form of the letter T,[1] which thus served as the emblem of creation and generation, before the church adopted it as the sign of salvation; a lucky coincidence of ideas, which, without doubt, facilitated the reception of it among the faithful. To the representative of the male organs was sometimes added a human head, which gives it the exact appearance of a crucifix; as it has on a medal of Cyzicus, published by M. Pellerin.[2] On an ancient medal, found in Cyprus, which, from the style of workmanship, is certainly anterior to the Macedonian conquest, it appears with the chaplet or rosary, such as is now used in the Romish churches;[3] the beads of which were used, anciently, to reckon time.[4] Their being placed in a circle, marked its progressive continuity; while their separation from each other marked the divisions, by which it is made to return on itself, and thus produce years, months, and days. The symbol of the creative power is placed upon them, because these divisions were particularly under his influence and protection; the sun being his visible image, and the centre of his power, from which his emanations

[1] Recherches sur les Arts, lib. i. c. 3.

[2] See Plate IX. Fig. 1.

[3] Plate IX. Fig. 2, from Pellerin. Similar medals are in the Hunter Collection, and are evidently of Phœnician work.

[4] Recherches sur les Arts, lib. i. c. 3.

extended through the universe. Hence the Egyptians, in their sacred hymns, called upon Osiris, as the being who dwelt concealed in the embraces of the sun;[1] and hence the great luminary itself is called Κοσμοκρατωζ (Ruler of the World) in the Orphic Hymns.[2]

This general emanation of the pervading Spirit of God, by which all things are generated and maintained, is beautifully described by Virgil, in the following lines:

> Deum namque ire per omnes
> Terrasque, tractusque maris, cœlumque profundum.
> Hinc pecudes, armenta, viros, genus omne ferarum,
> Quemque sibi tenues nascentum arcessere vitas.
> Scilicet huc reddi deinde, ac resoluta referri
> Omnia: nec morti esse locum, sed viva volare
> Sideris in numerum, atque alto succedere cœlo.[3]

The Ethereal Spirit is here described as expanding itself through the universe, and giving life and motion to the inhabitants of earth, water, and air, by a participation of its own essence, each particle of which returned to its native source, at the dissolution of the body which it animated. Hence, not only men, but all animals, and even vegetables, were supposed to be impregnated with some particles of the

[1] Plutarch. *de Is. et Osir.*
[2] See Hymn VII.
[3] Georgic. lib. iv. ver. 221.

Divine Nature infused into them, from which their various qualities and dispositions, as well as their powers of propagation, were supposed to be derived. These appeared to be so many emanations of the Divine attributes, operating in different modes and degrees, according to the nature of the beings to which they belonged. Hence the characteristic properties of animals and plants were not only regarded as representations, but as actual emanations of the Divine Power, consubstantial with his own essence.[1] For this reason, the symbols were treated with greater respect and veneration than if they had been merely signs and characters of convention. Plutarch says, that most of the Egyptian priests held the bull Apis, who was worshipped with so much ceremony, to be only an image of the Spirit of Osiris.[2] This I take to have been the real meaning of all the animal worship of the Egyptians, about which so much has been written, and so little discovered. Those animals or plants, in which any particular attribute of the Deity seemed to predominate, became the symbols of that attribute, and were accordingly worshipped as the images of Divine Providence, acting in that particular direction. Like many

[1] Proclus *in Theol. Plat.* lib. 1. pp. 56, 57.
[2] *De Is. et Os.*

PLATE VI

THE TAURIC DIANA

other customs, both of ancient and modern worship, the practice, probably, continued long after the reasons upon which it was founded were either wholly lost, or only partially preserved, in vague traditions. This was the case in Egypt; for, though many of the priests knew or conjectured the origin of the worship of the bull, they could give no rational account why the crocodile, the ichneumon, and the ibis, received similar honours. The symbolical characters, called hieroglyphics, continued to be esteemed by them as more holy and venerable than the conventional representations of sounds, notwithstanding their manifest inferiority; yet it does not appear, from any accounts extant, that they were able to assign any reason for this preference. On the contrary, Strabo tells us that the Egyptians of his time were wholly ignorant of their ancient learning and religion,[1] though impostors continually pretended to explain it. Their ignorance in these points is not to be wondered at, considering that the most ancient Egyptians, of whom we have any authentic accounts, lived after the subversion of their monarchy and destruction of their temples by the Persians, who used every endeavour to annihilate their religion; first, by command of Cambyses,[2] and then of Ochus.[3] What they

[1] Lib. xvii.   [2] Herodot. lib. iii.   Strabo, lib. xvii.
[3] Plutarch. de Is. et Os.

were before this calamity, we have no direct information; for Herodotus is the earliest traveller, and he visited this country when in ruins.

It is observable in all modern religions, that men are superstitious in proportion as they are ignorant, and that those who know least of the principles of religion are the most earnest and fervent in the practice of its exterior rites and ceremonies. We may suppose from analogy, that this was the case with the Egyptians. The learned and rational merely respected and revered the sacred animals, whilst the vulgar worshipped and adored them. The greatest part of the former being, as is natural to suppose, destroyed by the persecution of the Persians, this worship and adoration became general; different cities adopting different animals as their tutelar deities, in the same manner as the Catholics now put themselves under the protection of different saints and martyrs. Like them, too, in the fervency of their devotion for the imaginary agent, they forgot the original cause.

The custom of keeping sacred animals as images of the Divine attributes, seems once to have prevailed in Greece as well as Egypt; for the God of Health was represented by a living serpent at Epidaurus, even in the last stage of their religion. [1] In

[1] Liv. *Hist. Epitom.* lib. xi.

general, however, they preferred wrought images, not from their superiority in art, which they did not acquire until after the time of Homer,[1] when their theology was entirely corrupted; but because they had thus the means of expressing their ideas more fully, by combining several forms together, and showing, not only the Divine attribute, but the mode and purpose of its operation. For instance; the celebrated bronze in the Vatican has the male organs of generation placed upon the head of a cock, the emblem of the sun, supported by the neck and shoulders of a man. In this composition they represented the generative power of the Ερως, the Osiris, Mithras, or Bacchus, whose centre is the sun, incarnate with man. By the inscription on the pedestal, the attribute this personified, is styled *The Saviour of the World* (Σωτηζ κοσμψ); a title always venerable, under whatever image it be represented.[2]

The Egyptians showed this incarnation of the Deity by a less permanent, though equally expressive symbol. At Mendes a living goat was kept as the image of the generative power, to whom the women presented themselves naked, and had the honour of being publicly enjoyed by him. Herodotus saw the act

[1] When Homer praises any work of art, he calls it the work of Sidonians.
[2] See Plate II. Fig. 3.

openly performed (ες επιδειξιν ανθρωπων), and calls it a prodigy (τερας). But the Egyptians had no such horror of it; for it was to them a representation of the incarnation of the Deity, and the communication of his creative spirit to man. It was one of the sacraments of that ancient church, and was, without doubt, beheld with that pious awe and reverence with which devout persons always contemplate the mysteries of their faith, whatever they happen to be; for, as the learned and orthodox Bishop Warburton, whose authority it is not for me to dispute, says, *from the nature of any action morality cannot arise, nor from its effects;* [1] therefore, for aught we can tell, this ceremony, however shocking it may appear to modern manners and opinions, might have been intrinsically meritorious at the time of its celebration, and afforded a truly edifying spectacle to the saints of ancient Egypt. Indeed, the Greeks do not seem to have felt much horror or disgust at the imitative representation of it, whatever the historian might have thought proper to express at the real celebration. Several specimens of their sculpture in this way have escaped the fury of the reformers, and remained for the instruction of later times. One of these, found among the ruins of Herculaneum, and

[1] Div. Leg. book 1. c. 4.

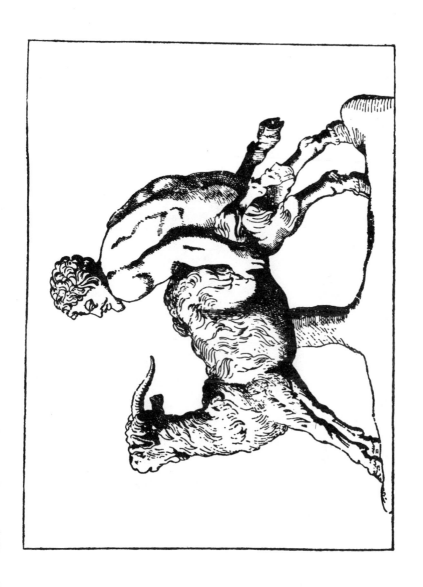

PLATE VII

GOAT AND SATYR, GREEK SCULPTURE

kept concealed in the Royal Museum of Portici, is well known. Another exists in the collection of Mr. Townley, which I have thought proper to have engraved for the benefit of the learned.[1] It may be remarked, that in these monuments the goat is *passive* instead of *active;* and that the *human symbol* is represented as incarnate with the *divine,* instead of the *divine* with the *human:* but this is in fact no difference; for the Creator, being of both sexes, is represented indifferently of either. In the other symbol of the bull, the sex is equally varied; the Greek medals having sometimes a bull, and sometimes a cow,[2] which, Strabo tells us, was employed as the symbol of Venus, the passive generative power, at Momemphis, in Egypt.[3] Both the bull and the cow are also worshipped at present by the Hindoos, as symbols of the male and female, or generative and nutritive, powers of the Deity. The cow is in almost all their pagodas; but the bull is revered with superior solemnity and devotion. At Tanjour is a monument of their piety to him, which even the inflexible perseverance, and habitual industry of the natives of that country, could scarcely have erected

[1] See Plate vii.

[2] See Plate iv. Fig. 1, 2, 3, and Plate iii. Fig. 4, engraved from medals belonging to me.

[3] Lib. xvii.

without greater knowledge in practical mechanics
than they now possess. It is a statue of a bull lying
down, hewn, with great accuracy, out of a single
piece of hard granite, which has been conveyed by
land from the distance of one hundred miles, although its weight, in its present reduced state, must
be at least one hundred tons.[1] The Greeks sometimes made their Taurine Bacchus, or bull, with a
human face, to express both sexes, which they signified by the initial of the epithet Διφνης placed under him.[2] Over him they frequently put the radiated
asterisk, which represents the sun, to show the Deity,
whose attribute he was intended to express.[3] Hence
we may perceive the reason why the Germans, who,
according to Cæsar,[4] worshipped the sun, carried a
brazen bull, as the image of their God, when they
invaded the Roman dominions in the time of
Marius;[5] and even the chosen people of Providence,
when they made unto themselves an image of the
God who was to conduct them through the desert,

[1] See Plate xxii. with the measurements, as made by Capt.
Patterson on the spot.

[2] See Plate iv. Fig. 2, from a medal of Naples in the Hunter
collection.

[3] See Plate iv. Fig. 2, and Plate xix. Fig. 4, from a medal of
Cales, belonging to me.

[4] *De B. G.*, lib. vi.

[5] Plut. *in Mario.*

and cast out the ungodly, from before them, made it in the shape of a young bull, or calf.[1]

The Greeks, as they advanced in the cultivation of the imitative arts, gradually changed the animal for the human form, preserving still the original character. The human head was at first added to the body of the bull;[2] but afterwards the whole figure was made human, with some of the features, and general character of the animal, blended with it.[3] Oftentimes, however, these mixed figures had a peculiar and proper meaning, like that of the Vatican Bronze; and were not intended as mere refinements of art. Such are the fawns and satyrs, who represent the emanations of the Creator, incarnate with man, acting as his angels and ministers in the work of universal generation. In copulation with the goat, they represent the reciprocal incarnation of man with the deity, when incorporated with universal matter: for the Deity, being both male and female, was both active and passive in procreation; first animating man by an emanation from his own essence, and then employing that emanation to reproduce, in conjunction with the common productive powers of nature,

[1] *Exod.* c. xxxii., with Patrick's *Commentary.*

[2] See the medals of Naples, Gela &c. Plate iv. Fig. 2. and Plate ix. Fig. ii, are specimens; but the coins are in all collections.

[3] See *Bronzi d'Herculano*, tom. v. Plate v.

which are no other than his own prolific spirit transfused through matter.

These mixed beings are derived from Pan, the principle of universal order; of whose personified image they partake. Pan is addressed in the Orphic Litanies as the first-begotten love, or creator incorporated in universal matter, and so forming the world.[1] The heaven, the earth, water, and fire are said to be members of him; and he is described as the origin and source of all things (παντοφνης γενετωζπατων), as representing matter animated by the Divine Spirit. Lycæan Pan was the most ancient and revered God of the Arcadians,[2] the most ancient people of Greece. The epithet Lycæan (Λνκαοις), is usually derived from λνκος, a wolf; though it is impossible to find any relation which this etymology can have with the deities to which it is applied; for the epithet Λνκαιος, or Λνκειος (which is only the different pronunciation of a different dialect), is occasionally applied to almost all the gods. I have therefore no doubt, but that it ought to be derived from the old word λνκος, or λνκη, light; from which came the Latin word *lux*.[3] In this sense it is a very proper epithet for the Divine Nature, of whose essence light was supposed

[1] Hymn. x.
[2] Dionys. *Antiq. Rom.* lib. i. c. 32.
[3] Macrob. *Sat.* xvii.

PLATE VIII

BRONZE STATUE OF CERES

to be. I am confirmed in this conjecture by a word in the *Electra* of Sophocles, which seems hitherto to have been misunderstood. At the opening of the play, the old tutor of Orestes, entering Argos with his young pupil, points out to him the most celebrated public buildings, and amongst them the Lycæan Forum, τψ λνκοκτονψ Θεψ, which the scholiast and translators interpret, *of the wolf-killing God,* though there is no reason whatever why this epithet should be applied to Apollo. But, if we derive the compound from λνκος, light, and εκτεινειν, to extend, instead of κτεινειν, to kill, the meaning will be perfectly just and natural; for *light-extending,* is of all others the properest epithet for the sun. Sophocles, as well as Virgil, is known to have been an admirer of ancient expressions, and to have imitated Homer more than any other Attic Poet; therefore, his employing an obsolete word is not to be wondered at. Taking this etymology as the true one, the Lycæan Pan of Arcadia is Pan *the luminous;* that is, the divine essence of light incorporated in universal matter. The Arcadians called him τον της νλης Κνριον, the lord of matter as Macrobius rightly translates it.[1] He was hence called Sylvanus by the Latins; *Sylvus* being, in the ancient Pelasgian and Æolian Greek, from which the

---

[1] Sat. i. c. 22.

Latin is derived, the same as ὕλη; for it is well known to all who have compared the two languages attentively, that the *Sigma* and *Vau* are letters, the one of which was partially, and the other generally omitted by the Greeks, in the refinement of their pronunciation and orthography which took place after the emigration of the Latian and Etruscan colonies. The Chorus in the *Ajax* of Sophocles address Pan by the title of 'Αλιπλαγκτος,[1] probably because he was worshipped on the shores of the sea; water being reckoned the best and most prolific of the subordinate elements,[2] upon which the Spirit of God, according to Moses, or the Plastic Nature, according to the Platonics, operating, produced life and motion on earth. Hence the ocean is said by Homer to be the source of all things;[3] and hence the use of water in baptism, which was to regenerate, and, in a manner, new create the person baptised; for the soul, supposed by many of the primitive Christians to be naturally mortal, was then supposed to become immortal.[4] Upon the same principle, the figure of Pan,[5]

---

[1] Ver. 703.

[2] Pindar. *Olymp.* i. ver i. Diodor. Sic. lib. i. p. ii.

[3] Il. Θ, ver. 246, and ζ, ver. 196.

[4] Clementina, *Hom.* xii. Arnob. *adv.* Gentes, lib. ii.

[5] See Plate v. Fig. i. The original is among the antiquities found in Herculaneum, now in the Museum of Portici.

is represented pouring water upon the organ of generation; that is, invigorating the active creative power
by the prolific element upon which it acted; for water
was considered as the essence of the passive principle, as fire was of the active; the one being of terrestrial, and the other of æthereal origin. Hence, St.
John the Baptist, who might have acquired some
knowledge of the ancient theology, through its re-
vivers, the Eclectic Jews, says: *I, indeed, baptise you
in water to repentance; but he that cometh after me,
who is more powerful than I am, shall baptise you in
the Holy Spirit, and in fire:* [1] that is, I only purify
and refresh the soul, by a communion with the terrestrial principle of life; but he that cometh after me,
will regenerate and restore it, by a communion with
the æthereal principle. [2] Pan is again addressed in
the Salaminian Chorus of the same tragedy of Sophocles, by the titles of author and director of the dances
of the gods (Θεων χοροποι' αναξ), as being the author
and disposer of the regular motions of the universe,
of which these divine dances were symbols, which
are said in the same passage to be (αυτοδαη) *self-*

[1] *Matth.* c. iii.

[2] It is the avowed intention of the learned and excellent work
of Grotius, to prove that there is nothing new in Christianity.
What I have here adduced, may serve to confirm and illustrate
the discoveries of that great and good man. *See de Veritate
Relig. Christ.* lib. iv, c. 12.

taught to him. Both the Gnossian and Nysian dances are here included,[1] the former sacred to Jupiter, and the latter to Bacchus; for Pan, being the principle of universal order, partook of the nature of all the other gods. They were personifications of particular modes of acting of the great all-ruling principle; and he, of his general law and pre-established harmony by which he governs the universe. Hence he is often represented playing on a pipe; music being the natural emblem of this physical harmony. According to Plutarch, the Jupiter Ammon of the Africans was the same as the Pan of the Greeks.[2] This explains the reason why the Macedonian kings assumed the horns of that god; for, though Alexander pretended to be his son, his successors never pretended to any such honour; and yet they equally assumed the symbols, as appears from their medals.[3] The case is, that Pan, or Ammon, being the universe, and Jupiter a title of the Supreme God (as will be shown hereafter), the horns, the emblems of his power, seemed the properest symbols of that supreme and universal dominion to which they all, as well as Alexander,

[1] Ver. 708.

[2] *De Is. et Os.*

[3] See Plate IV. Fig 4, engraved from one of Lysimachus, of exquisite beauty, belonging to me. Antigonus put the head of Pan upon his coins, which are not uncommon.

had the ambition to aspire. The figure of Ammon was compounded of the forms of the ram, as that of Pan was of the goat; the reason of which is difficult to ascertain, unless we suppose that goats were unknown in the country where his worship arose, and that the ram expressed the same attribute.[1] In a gem in the Museum of Charles Townley, Esq., the head of the Greek Pan is joined to that of a ram, on the body of a cock, over whose head is the asterisk of the sun, and below it the head of an aquatic fowl, attached to the same body.[2] The cock is the symbol of the sun, probably from proclaiming his approach in the morning; and the aquatic fowl is the emblem of water; so that this composition, apparently so whimsical, represents the universe between the two great prolific elements, the one the active, and the other the passive cause of all things.

The Creator being both male and female, the emanations of his creative spirit, operating upon universal matter, produced subordinate ministers of both sexes, and gave, as companions to the fauns and satyrs, the nymphs of the waters, the mountains and the woods, signifying the passive productive powers

[1] Pausanias (lib. ii.) says he knew the meaning of this symbol, but did not choose to reveal it, it being a part of the mystic worship.

[2] Plate III. Fig. I.

of each, subdivided and diffused. Of the same class are the Γενετνλλιδες, mentioned by Pausanias as companions to Venus,[1] who, as well as Ceres, Juno, Diana, Isis, &c., was only a personification of nature, or the passive principle of generation, operating in various modes. Apuleius invokes Isis by the names of the Eleusinian Ceres, Celestial Venus, and Proserpine; and, when the Goddess answers him, she describes herself as follows: "I am," says she, "nature, the parent of things, the sovereign of the elements, the primary progeny of time, the most exalted of the deities, the first of the heavenly Gods and Goddesses, the queen of the shades, the uniform countenance; who dispose, with my nod, the luminous heights of heaven, the salubrious breezes of the sea, and the mournful silence of the dead; whose single Deity the whole world venerates, in many forms, with various rites, and various names. The Egyptians, skilled in ancient learning, worship me with proper ceremonies, and call me by my true name, Queen Isis."[2]

According to the Egyptians, Isis copulated with her brother Osiris in the womb of their mother; from whence sprung Arueris, or Orus, the Apollo of the

[1] Lib. i.

[2] *Metamorph.* lib. xi.

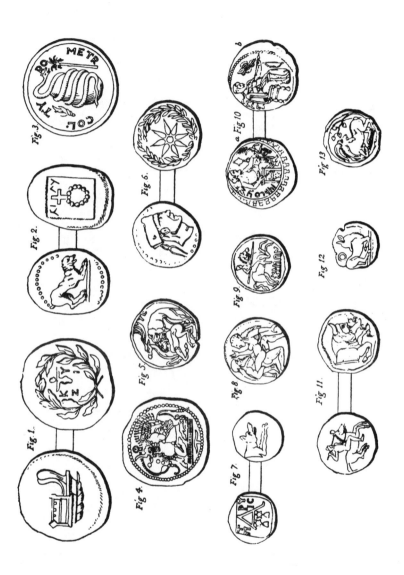

PLATE IX

COINS AND MEDALS

Greeks.[1] This allegory means no more than that the active and passive powers of creation united in the womb of night; where they had been implanted by the unknown father, Κρονος, or time, and by their union produced the separation or delivery of the elements from each other; for the name Apollo is only a title derived from απολνω, *to deliver from.*[2] They made the robes of Isis various in their colours and complicated in their folds, because the passive or material power appeared in various shapes and modes, as accommodating itself to the active; but the dress of Osiris was simple, and of one luminous colour, to show the unity of his essence, and universality of his power; equally the same through all things.[3] The luminous, or flame colour, represented the sun, who, in the language of the theologists, was the substance of his sacred power, and the visible image of his intellectual being.[4] He is called, in the Orphic Litanies, the chain which connects all things together (ο δ' ανεδραμε δεσμος απαντων),[5] as being the principle of attraction; and the deliverer (λνσιος),[6] as giving liberty to the innate powers of

[1] Plutarch, *de Is. et Os.*
[2] Damm. *Lex. Etym.*
[3] Plutarch. *de Is. et Os.*
[4] Ibid.
[5] Hymn. xlvi.
[6] Hymn. xlix. the initials of this epithet are with the bull on

nature, and thus fertilising matter. These epithets not only express the theological, but also the physical system of the Orphic school; according to which the sun, being placed in the centre of the universe, with the planets moving round, was, by his attractive force, the cause of all union and harmony in the whole; and, by the emanation of his beams, the cause of all motion and activity in the parts. This system is alluded to by Homer in the allegory of the golden chain, by which Jupiter suspends all things; [1] though there is every reason to believe that the poet himself was ignorant of its meaning, and only related it as he had heard it. The Ammonian Platonics adopted the same system of attraction, but changed its centre from the sun to their metaphysical abstraction or incomprehensible unity, whose emanations pervaded all things, and held all things together.[2]

Besides the Fauns, Satyrs, and Nymphs, the incarnate emanations of the active and passive powers of the Creator, we often find in the ancient sculptures

a medal of Naples belonging to me The bull has a human countenance, and has therefore been called a minotaur by antiquarians; notwithstanding he is to be found on different medals, accompanied with all the symbols both of Bacchus and Apollo, and with the initials of most of the epithets to be found in the Orphic Litanies.

[1] Il. Θ, ver. xix.

[2] Proclus in Theol. Plat. lib. i. c. 21.

certain androgynous beings possessed of the characteristic organs of both sexes, which I take to represent organized matter in its first stage; that is, immediately after it was released from chaos, and before it was animated by a participation of the ethereal essence of the Creator. In a beautiful gem belonging to R. Wilbraham, Esq.,[1] one of these androgynous figures is represented sleeping, with the organs of generation covered, and the egg of chaos broken under it. On the other side is Bacchus, the Creator, bearing a torch, the emblem of ethereal fire, and extending it towards the sleeping figure; whilst one of his agents seems only to wait his permission to begin the execution of that office, which, according to every outward and visible sign, he appears able to discharge with energy and effect. The Creator himself leans upon one of those figures commonly called *Sileni;* but which, from their heavy unwieldy forms, were probably intended as personifications of brute inert matter, from which all things are formed, but which, being incapable of producing anything of itself, is properly represented as the support of the creative power, though not actively instrumental in his work. The total baldness of this figure represents the exhausted, unproductive state of matter,

[1] See Plate v. Fig. 3.

when the generative powers were separated from it; for it was an opinion of the ancients, which I remember to have met with in some part of the works of Aristotle, to which I cannot at present refer, that every act of coition produced a transient chill in the brain, by which some of the roots of the hair were loosened; so that baldness was a mark of sterility acquired by excessive exertion. The figures of Pan have nearly the same forms with that which I have here supposed to represent inert matter; only that they are compounded with those of the goat, the symbol of the creative power, by which matter was fructified and regulated. To this is sometimes added the organ of generation, of an enormous magnitude, to signify the application of this power to its noblest end, the procreation of sensitive and rational beings. This composition forms the common Priapus of the Roman poets, who was worshipped among the other personages of the heathen mythology, but understood by few of his ancient votaries any better than by the good women of Isernia. His characteristic organ is sometimes represented by the artists in that state of tension and rigidity, which it assumes when about to discharge its functions,[1] and at other times in that state of tumid languor, which immediately

[1] Plate v. Fig. 1, from a bronze in the Museum at Portici.

succeeds the performance.[1] In the latter case he appears loaded with the productions of nature, the result of those prolific efforts, which in the former case he appeared so well qualified to exert. I have in Plate v. given a figure of him in each situation, one taken from a bronze in the Royal Museum of Portici, and the other from one in that of Charles Townley, Esq. It may be observed, that in the former the muscles of the face are all strained and contracted, so that every nerve seems to be in a state of tension; whereas in the latter the features are all dilated and fallen, the chin reposed on the breast, and the whole figure expressive of languor and fatigue.

If the explanation which I have given of these androgynous figures be the true one, the fauns and satyrs, which usually accompany them, must represent abstract emanations, and not incarnations of the creative spirit, as when in copulation with the goat. The Creator himself is frequently represented in a human form; and it is natural that his emanations should partake of the same, though without having any thing really human in their composition. It seems, however, to have been the opinion in some parts of Asia, that the Creator was really of a human form. The Jewish legislator says expressly, that God

[1] Plate v. Fig 2, from a bronze in the Museum of C. Townley, Esq.

made man in his own image, and, prior to the creation
of woman, created him *male and female*,[1] as he himself consequently was.[2] Hence an ingenious author
has supposed that these androgynous figures represented the first individuals of the human race, who,
possessing the organs of both sexes, produced children of each. This seems to be the sense in which
they were represented by some of the ancient artists;
but I have never met with any trace of it in any Greek
author, except Philo the Jew; nor have I ever seen
any monument of ancient art, in which the Bacchus,
or Creator in a human form, was represented with
the generative organs of both sexes. In the symbolical images, the double nature is frequently expressed
by some androgynous insect, such as the snail, which
is endowed with the organs of both sexes, and can
copulate reciprocally with either: but when the refinement of art adopted the human form, it was represented by mixing the characters of the male and
female bodies in every part, preserving still the distinctive organs of the male. Hence Euripides calls
Bacchus θηλυμορφος,[3] and the Chorus of Bachannals
in the same tragedy address him by masculine and

[1] Genes. c. i.

[2] Philo. *de. Leg. Alleg.* lib. ii.

[3] Bach. v. 358.

feminine epithets.[1] Ovid also says to him,

> ———Tibi, cum sine cornibus adstas,
> Virgineum caput est.[2]

alluding in the first line to his taurine, and in the second to his androgynous figure.

The ancient theologists were, like the modern, divided into sects; but, as these never disturbed the peace of society, they have been very little noticed. I have followed what I conceive to be the true Orphic system, in the little analysis which I have here endeavoured to give. This was probably the true catholic faith, though it differs considerably from another ancient system, described by Aristophanes; [3] which is more poetical, but less philosophical. According to this, Chaos, Night, Erebus, and Tartarus, were the primitive beings. Night, in the infinite breast of Erebus, brought forth an egg, from which sprung Love, who mixed all things together; and from thence sprung the heaven, the ocean, the earth, and the gods. This system is alluded to by the epithet Ωογενος, applied to the Creator in one of the Orphic Litanies: [4] but this could never have been a part of the orthodox

---

[1] Ω Βρομιε, Βρομιε, Πεδωνρθσνος ενοσι ποτνια. Vers. 504.

[2] *Metam.* lib. iv. v. 18.

[3] Ορνιθ. Vers. 693.

[4] Hymn v.

faith; for the Creator is usually represented as breaking the egg of chaos, and therefore could not have sprung from it. In the confused medleys of allegories and traditions contained in the Theogony attributed to Hesiod, Love is placed after Chaos and the Earth, but anterior to every thing else. These differences are not to be wondered at; for Aristophanes, supposing that he understood the true system, could not with safety have revealed it, or even mentioned it any otherwise than under the usual garb of fiction and allegory; and as for the author of the Theogony, it is evident, from the strange jumble of incoherent fables which he has put together, that he knew very little of it. The system alluded to in the Orphic verses quoted in the *Argonautics*, is in all probability the true one; for it is not only consistent in all its parts, but contains a physical truth, which the greatest of the modern discoveries has only confirmed and explained. The others seem to have been only poetical corruptions of it, which, extending by degrees, produced that unwieldly system of poetical mythology, which constituted the vulgar religion of Greece.

The fauns and satyrs, which accompany the androgynous figures on the ancient sculptures, are usually represented as ministering to the Creator by exerting their characteristic attributes upon them, as well as upon the nymphs, the passive agents of pro-

PLATE X.

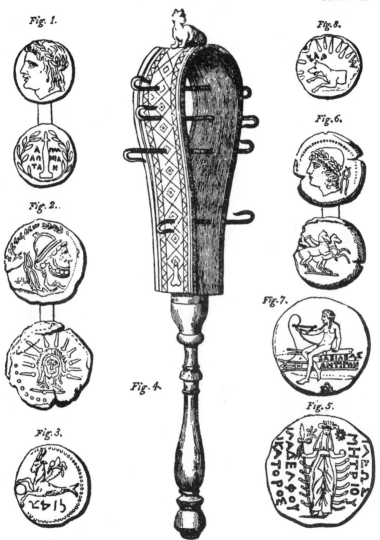

Fig. 1.

Fig. 2.

Fig. 3.

Fig. 4.

Fig. 8.

Fig. 6.

Fig. 7.

Fig. 5.

PLATE X

SYSTRUM, WITH VARIOUS MEDALS

creation: but what has puzzled the learned in these monuments, and seems a contradiction to the general system of ancient religion, is that many of these groups are in attitudes which are rather adapted to the gratification of disordered and unnatural appetites, than to extend procreation. But a learned author, who has thrown infinite light upon these subjects, has effectually cleared them from this suspicion, by showing that they only took the most convenient way to get at the female organs of generation, in those mixed beings who possessed both.[1] This is confirmed by Lucretius, who asserts, that this attitude is better adapted to the purposes of generation than any other.[2] We may therefore conclude, that instead of representing them in the act of gratifying any disorderly appetites, the artists meant to show their modesty in not indulging their concupiscence, but in doing their duty in the way best adapted to answer the ends proposed by the Creator.

On the Greek medals, where the cow is the symbol of the deity, she is frequently represented licking a calf, which is sucking her.[3] This is probably meant to show that the creative power cherishes and nour-

[1] *Recherches sur les Arts,* liv. i. c. 3.

[2] Lib. iv. v. 1260.

[3] See Plate iv. Fig. 3, from a medal of Dyrrachium, belonging to me.

ishes, as well as generates; for, as all quadrupeds lick their young, to refresh and invigorate them immediately after birth, it is natural to suppose, according to the general system of symbolical writing, that this action should be taken as an emblem of the effect it was thought to produce. On other medals the bull or cow is represented licking itself;[1] which, upon the same principle, must represent the strength of the deity refreshed and invigorated by the exertion of its own nutritive and plastic power upon its own being. On others again is a human head of an androgynous character, like that of the Bacchus διφνης, with the tongue extended over the lower lip, as if to lick something.[2] This was probably the same symbol, expressed in a less explicit manner; it being the common practice of the Greek artists to make a part of a composition signify the whole, of which I shall soon have occasion to give some incontestable examples. On a Parian medal published by Goltzius, the bull licking himself is represented on one side, accompanied by the asterisk of the sun, and on the other, the head with the tongue extended, having serpents, the emblems of life, for hair.[3] The same medal is in

[1] See Plate III. Fig. 5, from one of Gortyna, in the Hunter Collection; and Plate III. Fig. 4, from one of Parium, belonging to me.

[2] See Plate III. Fig. 4, and Plate III. Fig. 6, from Pellerin.

[3] Goltz. *Insul.* Tab. XIX. Fig. 8.

my collection, except that the serpents are not attached to the head, but placed by it as distinct symbols, and that the animal licking itself is a female accompanied by the initial of the word Θεος, instead of the asterisk of the sun. Antiquarians have called this head a Medusa; but, had they examined it attentively on any well-preserved coin, they would have found that the expression of the features means lust, and not rage or horror.[1] The case is, that antiquarians have been continually led into error, by seeking for explanations of the devices on the Greek medals in the wild and capricious stories of Ovid's *Metamorphoses*, instead of examining the first principles of ancient religion contained in the Orphic Fragments, the writings of Plutarch, Macrobius, and Apuleius, and the Choral Odes of the Greek tragedies. These principles were the subjects of the ancient mysteries, and it is to these that the symbols on the medals always relate; for they were the public acts of the states, and therefore contain the sense of nations, and not the caprices of individuals.

As M. D'Hancarville found a complete representation of the bull breaking the egg of chaos in the sculptures of the Japanese, when only a part of it appears on the Greek monuments; so we may find in a curi-

---

[1] See Plate III. Fig. 4.

ous Oriental fragment, lately brought from the sacred caverns of Elephanta, near Bombay, a complete representation of the symbol so enigmatically expressed by the head above mentioned. These caverns are ancient places of worship, hewn in the solid rock with immense labour and difficulty. That from which the fragment in question was brought, is 130 feet long by 110 wide, adorned with columns and sculptures finished in a style very different from that of the Indian artists.[1] It is now neglected; but others of the same kind are still used as places of worship by the Hindoos, who can give no account of the antiquity of them, which must necessarily be very remote, for the Hindoos are a very ancient people; and yet the sculptures represent a race of men very unlike them, or any of the present inhabitants of India. A specimen of these was brought from the island of Elephanta, in the Cumberland man-of-war, and now belongs to the museum of Mr. Townley. It contains several figures, in very high relief; the principal of which are a man and woman, in an attitude which I shall not venture to describe, but only observe, that the action, which I have supposed to be a symbol of refreshment and invigoration, is mutually applied by both to their respective organs of genera-

[1] *Archoel.* vol. viii. p. 289.

tion,[1] the emblems of the active and passive powers of procreation, which mutually cherish and invigorate each other.

The Hindoos still represent the creative powers of the deity by these ancient symbols, the male and female organs of generation; and worship them with the same pious reverence as the Greeks and Egyptians did.[2] Like them too they have buried the original principles of their theology under a mass of poetical mythology, so that few of them can give any more perfect account of their faith, than that they mean to worship one first cause, to whom the subordinate deities are merely agents, or more properly personified modes of action.[3] This is the doctrine inculcated, and very fully explained, in the *Bagvat Geeta;* a moral and metaphysical work lately translated from the Sanscrit language, and said to have been written upwards of four thousand years ago. Kreshna, or the deity become incarnate in the shape of man, in order to instruct all mankind, is introduced, revealing to his disciples the fundamental principles of true faith, religion, and wisdom; which are the exact counterpart of the system of emanations, so beautifully described in the lines of

[1] See Plate xi.

[2] Sonnerat, *Voyage aux Ines.* T. 1. p. 180.

[3] Niebuhr, *Voyages*, vol. II. p. 17.

Virgil before cited. We here find, though in a more mystic garb, the same one principle of life universally emanated and expanded, and ever partially returning to be again absorbed in the infinite abyss of intellectual being. This reabsorption, which is throughout recommended as the ultimate end of human perfection, can only be obtained by a life of inward meditation and abstract thought, too steady to be interrupted by any worldly incidents, or disturbed by any transitory affections, whether of mind or body. But as such a life is not in the power of any but a Brahman, inferior rewards, consisting of gradual advancements during the transmigrations of the soul, are held out to the soldier, the husbandman, and mechanic, accordingly as they fulfill the duties of their several stations. Even those who serve other gods are not excluded from the benefits awarded to every moral virtue; for, as the divine Teacher says, *If they do it with a firm belief, in so doing they involuntarily worship even me. I am he who partaketh of all worship, and I am their reward.*[1] This universal deity, being the cause of all motion, is alike the cause of creation, preservation, and destruction; which three attributes are all expressed in the mystic syllable *om*. To repeat this in silence, with firm

[1] *Bagvat Geeta*, p. 81.

PLATE XI

SCULPTURE FROM ELEPHANTA

devotion, and immoveable attention, is the surest means of perfection,[1] and consequent reabsorption, since it leads to the contemplation of the Deity, in his three great characteristic attributes.

The first and greatest of these, the creative or generative attribute, seems to have been originally represented by the union of the male and female organs of generation, which, under the title of the *Lingam,* still occupies the central and most interior recesses of their temples or pagodas; and is also worn, attached to bracelets, round their necks and arms.[2] In a little portable temple brought from the Rohilla country during the late war, and now in the British Museum, this composition appears mounted on a pedestal, in the midst of a square area, sunk in a block of white alabaster.[3] Round the pedestal is a serpent, the emblem of life, with his head rested upon his tail, to denote eternity, or the constant return of time upon itself, whilst it flows through perpetual duration, in regular revolutions and stated periods. From under the body of the serpent springs the lotus or water lily, the Nelumbo of Linnæus, which overspreads the whole of the area not occupied by the figures at the corners. This plant grows

---

[1] Bagvat Geeta p. 74.

[2] Sonnerat, *Voyage aux Indes,* liv. ii. p. 180. Planche. LIV.

[3] See Plate XII.

in the water, and, amongst its broad leaves, puts forth a flower, in the center of which is formed the seed-vessel, shaped like a bell or inverted cone, and punctuated on the top with little cavities or cells, in which the seeds grow.[1] The orifices of these cells being too small to let the seeds drop out when ripe, they shoot forth into new plants, in the places where they were formed; the bulb of the vessel serving as a matrice to nourish them, until they acquire such a degree of magnitude as to burst it open and release themselves; after which, like other aquatic weeds, they take root wherever the current deposits them. This plant therefore, being thus productive of itself, and vegetating from its own matrice, without being fostered in the earth, was naturally adopted as the symbol of the productive power of the waters, upon which the active spirit of the creator operated in giving life and vegetation to matter. We accordingly find it employed in every part of the northern hemisphere, where the symbolical religion, improperly called idolatry, does or ever did prevail. The sacred images of the Tartars, Japonese, and Indians, are almost all placed upon it; of which numerous instances occur in the publications of Kæmpfer, Chappe D'Auteroche, and Sonnerat. The upper part of the

[1] See Plate xx. Fig. 1.

base of the *Lingam* also consists of this flower, blended and composed with the female organ of generation which it supports: and the ancient author of the *Bagvat Geeta* speaks of the creator Brahma as sitting upon his lotus throne.[1] The figures of Isis, upon the Isiac Table, hold the stem of this plant, surmounted by the seed-vessel in one hand, and the cross,[2] representing the male organs of generation, in the other; thus signifying the universal power, both active and passive, attributed to that goddess. On the same Isiac Table is also the representation of an Egyptian temple, the columns of which are exactly like the plant which Isis holds in her hand, except that the stem is made larger, in order to give it that stability which is necessary to support a roof and entablature.[3] Columns and capitals of the same kind are still existing, in great numbers, among the ruins of Thebes, in Egypt; and more particularly upon those very curious ones in the island of Philæ, on the borders of Ethiopia, which are, probably, the most ancient monuments of art now extant; at least, if we except the neighbouring temples of Thebes. Both were certainly built when that city was the seat of wealth and empire, which it was, even to a

[1] Page 91.
[2] See Plate xviii. Fig. 2, from Pignorius.
[3] See Plate xviii. Fig. 1, from Pignorius.

proverb, during the Trojan war.[1] How long it had
then been so, we can form no conjecture; but that it
soon after declined, there can be little doubt; for,
when the Greeks, in the reign of Psammeticus (generally computed to have been about 530 years after
the Siege of Troy), first became personally acquainted with the interior parts of that country,
Memphis had been for many ages its capital, and
Thebes was in a manner deserted. Homer makes
Achilles speak of its immense wealth and grandeur,
as a matter generally known and acknowledged; so
that it must have been of long established fame, even
in that remote age. We may therefore fairly conclude, that the greatest part of the superb edifices
now remaining, were executed, or at least begun, before that time; many of them being such as could not
have been finished, but in a long term of years, even
if we suppose the wealth and power of the ancient
kings of Egypt to have equalled that of the greatest
of the Roman emperors. The finishing of Trajan's
column in three years, has been justly thought a very
extraordinary effort; for there must have been, at
least, three hundred good sculptors employed upon
it: and yet, in the neighbourhood of Thebes, we find
whole temples of enormous magnitude, covered with

[1] Hom. *Iliad. i*, ver. 381.

figures carved in the hard and brittle granite of the Libyan mountains, instead of the soft marbles of Paros and Carrara. Travellers, who have visited that country have given us imperfect accounts of the manner in which they are finished; but, if one may judge by those upon the obelisc of Rameses, now lying in fragments at Rome, they are infinitely more laboured than those of Trajan's Column. An eminent sculptor, with whom I examined that obelisc, was decidedly of opinion, that they must have been finished in the manner of gems, with a graving tool; it appearing impossible for a chisel to cut red granite with so much neatness and precision. The age of Rameses is uncertain; but the generality of modern chronologers suppose that he was the same person as Sesostris, and reigned at Thebes about 1500 years before the Christian æra, and about 300 before the Siege of Troy. Their dates are however merely conjectural, when applied to events of this remote antiquity. The Egyptian priests of the Augustan age had a tradition, which they pretended to confirm by records written in hieroglyphics, that their country had once possest the dominion of all Asia and Ethiopia, which their king Ramses, or Rameses, had conquered.[1] Though this account may be exagge-

[1] Tacit, *Ann.* lib. ii. c. 60.

rated, there can be no doubt, from the buildings still remaining, but that they were once at the head of a great empire; for all historians agree that they abhorred navigation, had no sea-port, and never enjoyed the benefits of foreign commerce, without which, Egypt could have no means of acquiring a sufficient quantity of superfluous wealth to erect such expensive monuments, unless from tributary provinces; especially if all the lower part of it was an uncultivated bog, as Herodotus, with great appearance of probability, tells us it anciently was. Yet Homer, who appears to have known all that could be known in his age, and transmitted to posterity all he knew, seems to have heard nothing of their empire or conquests. These were obliterated and forgotten by the rise of new empires; but the renown of their ancient wealth still continued, and afforded a familiar object of comparison, as that of the Mogul does at this day, though he is become one of the poorest sovereigns in the world.

But far as these Egyptian remains lead us into unknown ages, the symbols they contain appear not to have been invented in that country, but to have been copied from those of some other people, still anterior, who dwelt on the other side of the Erythræan ocean. One of the most obvious of them is the hooded snake, which is a reptile peculiar to the

PLATE XII

INDIAN TEMPLE, SHOWING THE LINGAM

south-eastern parts of Asia, but which I found represented, with great accuracy, upon the obelisc of
Rameses, and have also observed frequently repeated
on the Isiac Table, and other symbolical works of
the Egyptians. It is also distinguishable among the
sculptures in the sacred caverns of the island of
Elephanta; [1] and appears frequently added, as a
characteristic symbol, to many of the idols of the
modern Hindoos, whose absurd tales concerning its
meaning are related at length by M. Sonnerat; but
they are not worth repeating. Probably we should
be able to trace the connexion through many more
instances, could we obtain accurate drawings of the
ruins of Upper Egypt.

By comparing the columns which the Egyptians
formed in imitation of the Nelumbo plant, with each
other, and observing their different modes of decorating them, we may discover the origin of that order
of architecture which the Greeks called Corinthian,
from the place of its supposed invention. We first
find the plain bell, or seed-vessel, used as a capital,
without any further alteration than being a little
expanded at bottom, to give it stability.[2] In the next
instance, the same seed-vessel is surrounded by the

[1] Niebuhr, *Voyage*, vol. ii.
[2] See Plate xix. Fig. 6, from Norden.

leaves of some other plant;[1] which is varied in different capitals according to the different meanings intended to be expressed by these additional symbols. The Greeks decorated it in the same manner, with the leaves of the acanthus, and other sorts of foliage; whilst various other symbols of their religion were introduced as ornaments on the entablature, instead of being carved upon the walls of the cell, or shafts of the columns. One of these, which occurs most frequently, is that which the architects call the honey-suckle, but which, as Sir Joseph Banks (to whom I am indebted for all that I have said concerning the Lotus) clearly shewed me, must be meant for the young shoots of this plant, viewed horizontally, just when they have burst the seed-vessel, and are upon the point of falling out of it. The ornament is variously composed on different buildings; it being the practice of the Greeks to make vegetable, as well as animal monsters, by combining different symbolical plants together, and blending them into one; whence they are often extremely difficult to be discovered. But the specimen I have given, is so strongly characterised, that it cannot easily be mistaken.[2] It appears on many Greek medals with the animal symbols and personified attributes of the Deity; which first led me

[1] See Plate xix. Fig. 7, from Norden.
[2] Plate xix. Fig. 3, from the Ionian Antiquities, Ch. ii. Pl. xiii.

to imagine that it was not a mere ornament, but had some mystic meaning, as almost every decoration employed upon their sacred edifices indisputably had.

The square area, over which the Lotus is spread, in the Indian monument before mentioned, was occasionally floated with water; which, by means of a forcing machine, was first thrown in a spout upon the *Lingam.* The pouring of water upon the sacred symbols, is a mode of worship very much practised by the Hindoos, particularly in their devotions to the Bull and the *Lingam.* Its meaning has been already explained, in the instance of the Greek figure of Pan, represented in the act of paying the same kind of worship to the symbol of his own procreative power.[1] The areas of the Greek temples were, in like manner, in some instances, floated with water; of which I shall soon give an example. We also find, not unfrequently, little portable temples, nearly of the same form, and of Greek workmanship: the areas of which were equally floated by means of a fountain in the middle, and which, by the figures in relief that adorn the sides, appear evidently to have been dedicated to the same worship of Priapus, or the *Lingam.*[2] The square area is likewise impressed upon many

[1] See Plate v. Fig. 1.
[2] See Plate xiv. from one in the collection of Mr. Townley.

ancient Greek medals, sometimes divided into four, and sometimes into a greater number of compartments.[1] Antiquarians have supposed this to be merely the impression of something put under the coin, to make it receive the stroke of the die more steadily; but, besides that it is very ill adapted to this purpose, we find many coins which appear, evidently, to have received the stroke of the hammer (for striking with a balance is of late date) on the side marked with this square. But what puts the question out of all doubt, is, that impressions of exactly the same kind are found upon the little Talismans, or mystic pastes, taken out of the Egyptian Mummies, which have no impression whatever on the reverse.[2] On a little brass medal of Syracuse, we also find the asterisc of the Sun placed in the centre of the square, in the same manner as the *Lingam* is on the Indian monument.[3] Why this quadrangular form was adopted, in preference to any other, we have no means of discovering, from any known

[1] See Plate XIII. Fig. 1, from one of Selinus, and Fig. 3, from one of Syracuse, belonging to me.

[2] See Plate XIII. Fig. 2, from one in the collection of Mr. Townley.

[3] See Plate XIII. Fig. 3. The medal is extremely common, and the quadrangular impression is observable upon a great number of the more ancient Greek medals, generally with some symbol of the Deity in the centre. See those of Athens, Lyttus, Maronea, &c.

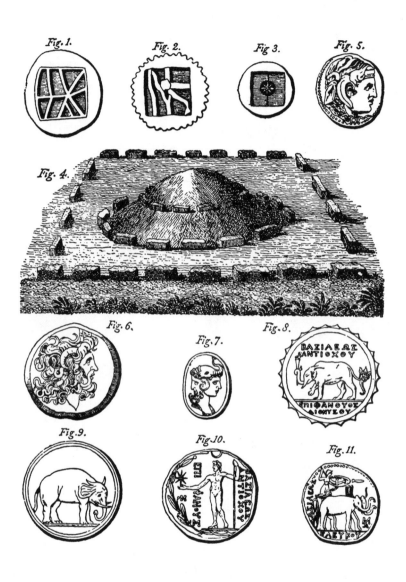

Fig. 1.

Fig. 2.

Fig 3.

Fig. 5.

Fig. 4.

Fig. 6.

Fig. 7.

Fig. 8.

Fig. 9.

Fig. 10.

Fig. 11.

PLATE XIII

CELTIC TEMPLE AND GREEK MEDALS

Greek or Egyptian sculptures; but from this little Indian temple, we find that the four corners were adapted to four of the subordinate deities, or personified modes of action of the great universal Generator, represented by the symbol in the middle, to which the others are represented as paying their adorations, with gestures of humility and respect.[1]

What is the precise meaning of these four symbolical figures, it is scarcely possible for us to discover, from the small fragments of the mystic learning of the ancients which are now extant. That they were however intended as personified attributes, we can have no doubt; for we are taught by the venerable authority of the *Bagvat Geeta,* that all the subordinate deities were such, or else canonised men, which these figures evidently are not. As for the mythological tales now current in India, they throw the same degree of light upon the subject, as Ovid's Metamorphoses do on the ancient theology of Greece; that is, just enough to bewilder and perplex those who give up their attention to it. The ancient author before cited is deserving of more credit; but he has said very little upon the symbolical worship. His work, nevertheless, clearly proves that its principles were precisely the same as those of the Greeks and

[1] See Plate xii.

Egyptians, among whose remains of art or literature, we may, perhaps, find some probable analogies to aid conjecture. The elephant is, however, a new symbol in the west; the Greeks never having seen one of those animals before the expedition of Alexander,[1] although the use of ivory was familiar among them even in the days of Homer. Upon this Indian monument the head of the elephant is placed upon the body of a man with four hands, two of which are held up as prepared to strike with the instruments they hold, and the other two pointed down as in adoration of the *Lingam*. This figure is called Gonnis and Pollear by the modern Hindoos; but neither of these names is to be found in the *Geeta*, where the deity only says, *that the learned behold him alike in the reverend Brahman perfected in knowledge, in the ox, and in the elephant.* What peculiar attributes the elephant was meant to express, the ancient writer has not told us; but, as the characteristic properties of this animal are strength and sagacity, we may conclude that his image was intended to represent ideas somewhat similar to those which the Greeks represented by that of Minerva, who was worshipped as the goddess of force and wisdom, of war and counsel. The Indian Gonnis is indeed male, and Minerva fe-

[1] Pausan. lib. i. c. 12.

male; but this difference of sexes, however important it may be in a physical, is of very little consequence in metaphysical beings, Minerva being, like the other Greek deities, either male or female, or both.[1] On the medals of the Ptolemies, under whom the Indian symbols became familiar to the Greeks through the commerce of Alexandria, we find her repeatedly represented with the elephant's skin upon her head, instead of a helmet; and with a countenance between male and female, such as the artist would naturally give her, when he endeavoured to blend the Greek and Indian symbols, and mould them into one.[2] Minerva is said by the Greek mythologists to have been born without a mother from the head of Jupiter, who was delivered of her by the assistance of Vulcan. This, in plain language, means no more than that she was a pure emanation of the divine mind, operating by means of the universal agent fire, and not, like others of the allegorical personages, sprung from any of the particular operations of the deity upon external matter. Hence she is said to be next in dignity to her father, and to be endowed with all his attributes; [3] for, as wisdom is the most exalted quality of the mind, and the divine mind the perfection of

[1] Αρσεν και θηλνς εφνς.   Orph. ειςΑθην·
[2] See Plate xiii. Fig. 5, engraved from one belonging to me.
[3] Hor. lib. i. Od. 12. Callimach. εις Αθην·

wisdom, all its attributes are the attributes of wisdom, under whose direction its power is always exerted. Strength and wisdom therefore, when considered as attributes of the deity, are in fact one and the same. The Greek Minerva is usually represented with the spear uplifted in her hand, in the same manner as the Indian Gonnis holds the battle-axe.[1] Both are given to denote the destroying power equally belonging to divine wisdom, as the creative or preserving. The statue of Jupiter at Labranda in Caria held in his hand the battle-axe, instead of thunder; and on the medals of Tenedos and Thyatira, we find it represented alone as the symbol of the deity, in the same manner as the thunder is upon a great variety of other medals. *I am the thunderbolt,* says the deity in the *Bagvat Geeta;*[2] and when we find this supposed engine of divine vengeance upon the medals, we must not imagine that it is meant for the weapon of the supreme god, but for the symbol of his destroying attribute. What instrument the Gonnis holds in his other hand, is not easily ascertained, it being a little injured by the carriage. In one of those pointed downwards he holds the Lotus flower, to denote that he has the direction of the passive powers

[1] See Plate XIII. Fig. II, from a medal of Seleucus I. belonging to me.

[2] Page 86.

of production; and in the other, a golden ring or disc, which, I shall soon shew, was the symbol by which many nations of the East represented the sun. His head is drawn into a conical, or pyramidal form, and surrounded by an ornament which evidently represents flames; the Indians, as well as the Greeks, looking upon fire as the essence of all active power; whence perpetual lamps are kept burning in the holy of holies of all the great pagodas in India, as they were anciently in the temple of Jupiter Ammon, and many others both Greek and Barbarian; [1] and the incarnate god in the *Bagvat Geeta* says, *I am the fire residing in the bodies of all things which have life.*[2] Upon the forehead of the Gonnis is a crescent representing the moon, whose power over the waters of the ocean caused her to be regarded as the sovereign of the great nutritive element, and whose mild rays, being accompanied by the refreshing dews and cooling breezes of the night, made her naturally appear to the inhabitants of hot countries as the comforter and restorer of the earth. *I am the moon* (says the deity in the Bagvat Geeta) *whose nature it is to give the quality of taste and relish, and to cherish the herbs and plants of the field.*[3] The light of the sun, moon,

[1] See Plut. *de Orac. defect.*
[2] Page 113.
[3] Page 113.

and fire, were however all but one, and equally emanations of the supreme being. *Know,* says the deity
in the same ancient dialogue, *that the light which
proceedeth from the sun, and illuminateth the world,
and the light which is in the moon and in the fire, are
mine. I pervade all things in nature, and guard them
with my beams.*[1] In the figure now under consideration a kind of pre-eminence seems to be given to the
moon over the sun; proceeding probably from the
Hindoos not possessing the true solar system, which
must however have been known to the people from
whom they learnt to calculate eclipses, which they
still continue to do, though upon principles not understood by themselves. They now place the earth
in the centre of the universe, as the later Greeks did,
among whom we also find the same preference given
to the lunar symbol; Jupiter being represented, on a
medal of Antiochus VIII., with the crescent upon his
head, and the asterisc of the sun in his hand.[2] In a
passage of the *Bagvat Geeta* already cited we find the
elephant and bull mentioned together as symbols of
the same kind; and on a medal of Seleucus Nicator
we find them united by the horns of the one being
placed on the head of the other.[3] The later Greeks

[1] See Plut. *de Orac. defect.*

[2] Plate XIII. Fig. 10, from one belonging to me.

[3] See Plate XIII. Fig. 9, and Gesner, *Num. Reg. Syr.* Tab. VIII.
Fig. 23.

also sometimes employed the elephant as the universal symbol of the deity; in which sense he is represented on a medal of Antiochus VI. bearing the torch, the emblem of the universal agent, fire, in his proboscis, and the cornucopia, the result of its exertion, in his tail.[1]

On another corner of the little Indian pagoda, is a figure with four heads, all of the same pointed form as that of the Gonnis. This I take to represent Brahma, to whom the Hindoos attribute four mouths, and say that with them he dictated the four Beads, or Veads, the mystic volumes of their religion.[2] The four heads are turned different ways, but exactly resemble each other. The beards have been painted black, and are sharp and pointed, like those of goats, which the Greeks gave to Pan, and his subordinate emanations, the Fauns and Satyrs. Hence I am inclined to believe, that the Brahma of the Indians is the same as the Pan of the Greeks; that is, the creative spirit of the deity transfused through matter, and acting in the four elements represented by the four heads. The Indians indeed admit of a fifth element, as the Greeks did likewise; but this is never classed with the rest, being of an ætherial and more

[1] See Plate xiii. Fig. 8, and Gesner, *Num. Reg. Syr.* Tab. viii. Fig. i.

[2] *Bagvat Geeta*, Note 41.

exalted nature, and belonging peculiarly to the deity. *Some call it heaven, some light, and some æther,* says Plutarch.[1] The Hindoos now call it *Occus,* by which they seem to mean pure ætherial light or fire.

This mode of representing the allegorical personages of religion with many heads and limbs to express their various attributes, and extensive operation, is now universal in the East,[2] and seems anciently not to have been unknown to the Greeks, at least if we may judge by the epithets used by Pindar and other early poets.[3] The union of two symbolical heads is common among the specimens of their art now extant, as may be seen upon the medals of Syracuse, Marseilles, and many other cities. Upon a gem of this sort in the collection of Mr. Townley, the same ideas which are expressed on the Indian pagoda by the distinct figures Brahma and Gonnis, are expressed by the united heads of Ammon and Minerva. Ammon, as before observed, was the Pan of the Greeks, and Minerva is here evidently the same as the Gonnis, being represented after the Indian manner, with the elephant's skin on her head, instead of a helmet.[4] Both these heads appear separate upon

[1] Ei apud Delph.

[2] See Kæmpfer, Chappe D'Auteroche, Sonnerat, &c.

[3] Such as ἑκατογκεφαλος, εκατοντακανος, εκατογχειρος, &c.

[4] See Plate XIII. Fig. 7.

different medals of the Ptolemies,[1] under one of whom this gem was probably engraved, Alexandria having been for a long time the great centre of religions, as well as of trade and science.

Next to the figure of Brahma on the pagoda is the cow of plenty, or the female emblem of the generative or nutritive power of the earth; and at the other corner, next to the Gonnis, is the figure of a woman, with a head of the same conic or pyramidal form, and upon the front of it a flame of fire, from which hangs a crescent.[2] This seems to be the female personification of the divine attributes represented by the Gonnis or Pollear; for the Hindoos, like the Greeks, worship the deity under both sexes, though they do not attempt to unite both in one figure. *I am the father and the mother of the world,* says the incarnate god in the *Bagvat Geeta.*[3] *Amongst cattle,* adds he in a subsequent part, *I am the cow Kamadhook. I am the prolific Kandarp, the god of love.*[4] These two sentences, by being placed together, seem to imply some relation between this *god of love* and the *cow Kamadhook;* and, were we to read the words without punctuation, as they are in all ancient or-

1 See Plate xii. Fig. 5 and 6.
2 See Plate xii.
3 Page 80.
4 Page 86.

thography, we should think the author placed the god of love amongst the cattle; which he would naturally do, if it were the custom of his religion to represent him by an animal symbol. Among the Egyptians, as before observed, the cow was the symbol of Venus, the goddess of love, and passive generative power of nature. On the capitals of one of the temples of Philæ we still find the heads of this goddess represented of a mixed form; the horns and ears of the cow being joined to the beautiful features of a woman in the prime of life; [1] such as the Greeks attributed to that Venus, whom they worshipped as the mother of the prolific god of love, Cupid, who was the personification of animal desire or concupiscence, as the Orphic love, the father of gods and men, was of universal attraction. The Greeks, who represented the mother under the form of a beautiful woman, naturally represented the son under the form of a beautiful boy; but a people who represented the mother under the form of a cow, would as naturally represent the son under the form of a calf. This seems to be the case with the Hindoos, as well as with the Egyptians; wherefore Kandarp may be very properly placed among the cattle.

By following this analogy, we may come to the

[1] See Plate xviii. Fig. 3.

PLATE XIV

PORTABLE TEMPLE DEDICATED TO PRIAPUS OR THE LINGAM

true meaning of a much-celebrated object of devotion, recorded by another ancient writer, of a more venerable character. When the Israelites grew clamorous on account of the absence of Moses, and called upon Aaron to make them a god to go before them, he set up a golden calf; to which the people sacrificed and feasted, and then rose up (as the translator says) *to play;* but in the original the term is more specific, and means, in its plain direct sense, that particular sort of play which requires the concurrence of both sexes,[1] and which was therefore a very proper conclusion of a sacrifice to Cupid, though highly displeasing to the god who had brought them out of Egypt. The Egyptian mythologists, who appeared to have invented this secondary deity of love, were probably the inventors likewise of a secondary Priapus, who was the personification of that particular generative faculty, which springs from animal desire, as the primary Priapus was of the great generative principle of the universe. Hence, in the allegories of the poets, this deity is said to be a son of Bacchus and Venus; that is, the result of the active and passive generative powers of nature. The story of his being the son of a Grecian conqueror, and born at Lampsacus, seems to be a corruption of this allegory.

[1] *Exod.* xxxii.

Of all the nations of antiquity the Persians were the most simple and direct in the worship of the creator. They were the puritans of the heathen world, and not only rejected all images of god or his agents, but also temples and altars, according to Herodotus,[1] whose authority I prefer to any other, because he had an opportunity of conversing with them before they had adopted any foreign superstitions.[2] As they worshipped the ætherial fire without any medium of personification or allegory, they thought it unworthy of the dignity of the god to be represented by any definite form, or circumscribed to any particular place. The universe was his temple, and the all-pervading element of fire his only symbol. The Greeks appear originally to have held similar opinions; for they were long without statues;[3] and Pausanias speaks of a temple at Sicyon, built by Adrastus,[4] who lived an age before the Trojan war; which consisted of columns only, without wall or roof, like the Celtic temples of our Northern ancestors, or the Pyrætheia of the Persians, which were

[1] Lib. i.

[2] Hyde, Anquetil, and other modern writers, have given us the operose superstitions of the present Parsees for the simple theism of the ancient Persians.

[3] Pauson, lib. vii. and ix.

[4] Lib. ii.

124

circles of stones, in the centre of which was kindled
the sacren fire,[1] the symbol of the god. Homer frequently speaks of places of worship consisting of an
area and altar only (τεμενοε Βωμος τε), which were
probably inclosures like these of the Persians, with
an altar in the centre. The temples dedicated to the
creator Bacchus, which the Greek architects called
hypaethral, seem to have been anciently of the same
kind; whence probably came the title περικιονιον
(*surrounded with columns*) attributed to that god
in the Orphic litanies.[2] The remains of one of these
are still extant at Puzzuoli near Naples, which the
inhabitants call the Temple of Serapis: but the ornaments of grapes, vases, &c. found among the ruins,
prove it to have been of Bacchus. Serapis was indeed the same deity worshipped under another form,
being equally a personification of the sun.[3]   The
architecture is of the Roman times; but the ground
plan is probably that of a very ancient one, which
this was made to replace; for it exactly resembles
that of a Celtic temple in Zeeland, published in
Stukeley's *itinerary*.[4] The ranges of square buildings which inclose it are not properly parts of the

[1] Strab. lib. xv.
[2] Hymn. 46.
[3] Diodor. Sic. lib. i.   Macrob. *Sat.* lib. i. c. 20.
[4] See Plate xv. Fig. 1 and 2, and Plate xiii. Fig. 4.

temple, but apartments of the priests, places for victims and sacred utensils, and chapels dedicated to subordinate deities introduced by a more complicated and corrupt worship, and probably unknown to the founders of the original edifice.[1] The portico, which runs parallel with these buildings,[2] inclosed the *temenos*, or area of sacred ground, which in the *pyræthia* of the Persians was circular, but is here quadrangular, as in the Celtic temple in Zeeland, and the Indian pagoda before described. In the centre was the holy of holies, the seat of the god, consisting of a circle of columns raised upon a basement, without roof or walls, in the middle of which was probably the sacred fire, or some other symbol of the deity.[3] The square area in which it stood, was sunk below the natural level of the ground,[4] and, like that of the little Indian pagoda, appears to have been occasionally floated with water, the drains and conduits being still to be seen,[5] as also several fragments of sculpture representing waves, serpents, and various aquatic animals, which once adorned the basement.[6] The Bacchus περικιονιος here worshipped, was,

[1] Plate xv. Fig. 2, *a—a.*
[2] Plate xv. Fig. 2, *b—b.*
[3] See Plate xv. Fig. i, *a*, and Fig. 2, *c.*
[4] See Plate xv. Fig. i, *b—b.*
[5] See Plate xv. Fig. i, *c—c.*
[6] See Plate xvii. Fig. i.

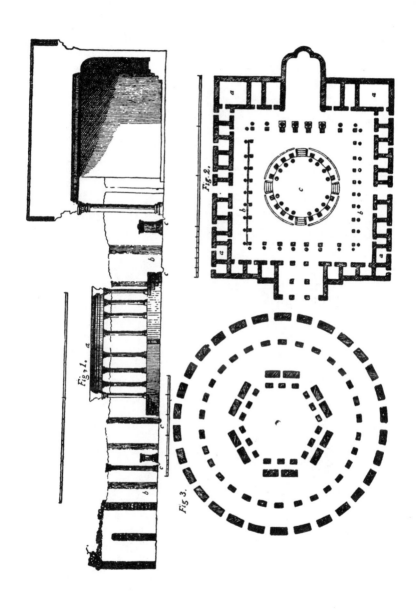

PLATE XV

TEMPLE DEDICATED TO BACCHUS AT PUZZUOLI

as we learn from the Orphic hymn above cited, the sun in his character of extinguisher of the fires which once pervaded the earth. This he was supposed to have done by exhaling the waters of the ocean, and scattering them over the land, which was thus supposed to have acquired its proper temperature and fertility. For this reason the sacred fire, the essential image of the god, was surrounded by the element which was principally employed in giving effect to the beneficial exertions of his great attribute.

These Orphic temples were, without doubt, emblems of that fundamental principle of the mystic faith of the ancients, the solar system; fire, the essence of the deity, occupying the place of the sun, and the columns surrounding it as the subordinate parts of the universe. Remains of the worship of fire continued among the Greeks even to the last, as appears from the sacred fires kept in the interior apartment, or holy of holies, of almost all their temples, and places of worship: and, though the Ammonian Platonics, the last professors of the ancient religion, endeavoured to conceive something beyond the reach of sense and perception, as the essence of their supreme god; yet, when they wanted to illustrate and explain the modes of action of this metaphysical abstraction, who was more subtle than intelligence itself, they do it by images and comparisons of light and fire.[1]

From a passage of Hecatæus, preserved by Diodorus Siculus, I think it is evident that Stonehenge, and all the other monuments of the same kind found in the North, belonged to the same religion, which appears, at some remote period, to have prevailed over the whole northern hemisphere. According to that ancient historian, *the Hyperboreans inhabited an island beyond Gaul, as large as Sicily, in which Apollo was worshipped in a circular temple considerable for its size and riches.*[2] Apollo, we know, in the language of the Greeks of that age, can mean no other than the sun, which, according to Cæsar, was worshipped by the Germans, when they knew of no other deities except fire and the moon.[3] The island I think can be no other than Britain, which at that time was only known to the Greeks by the vague reports of Phœnician mariners, so uncertain and obscure, that Herodotus, the most inquisitive and credulous of historians, doubts of its existence.[4] The circular temple of the sun being noticed in such

[1] See Proclus. *in Theol. Platon.* lib. i. c. 19.

[2] Ναον αξιολογον, αναθημασι πολλοις κεκοσ μημενον, σφαιροειδη τωσχηματι. Diod. Sic. lib. ii.

[3] *De B. Gal.* lib. vi.

[4] Lib. iii. c. 15.

Fig.1.

Fig.2.

PLATE XVI
ORNAMENT FROM PUZZUOLI TEMPLE

slight and imperfect accounts, proves that it must have been something singular and important; for, if it had been an inconsiderable structure, it would not have been mentioned at all; and, if there had been many such in the country, the historian would not have employed the singular number. Stonehenge has certainly been a circular temple, nearly the same as that already described of the Bacchus περικιονιος at Puzzuoli, except that in the latter the nice execution, and beautiful symmetry of the parts, are in every respect the reverse of the rude but majestic simplicity of the former; in the original design they differ but in the form of the area.[1] It may therefore be reasonably supposed, that we have still the ruins of the identical temple described by Hecatæus, who, being an Asiatic Greek, might have received his information from some Phœnician merchant, who had visited the interior parts of Britain when trading there for tin. Macrobius mentions a temple of the same kind and form upon Mount Zilmissus in Thrace,

[1] See Plate xv. Fig. 2 and 3. I have preferred Webb's plan of Stonehenge to Stukeley's and Smith's, after comparing each with the ruins now existing. They differ materially only in the cell, which Webb supposes to have been a hexagon, and Stukeley a section of an ellipsis. The position of the altar is merely conjectural; wherefore I have omitted it; and I much doubt whether either be right in their plans of the cell, which seems, as in other Druidical temples, to have been meant for a circle, but incorrectly executed.

dedicated to the sun under the title of Bacchus Sebazius.[1] The large obeliscs of stone found in many parts of the North, such as those at Rudstone,[2] and near Boroughbridge in Yorkshire,[3] belong to the same religion; obeliscs being, as Pliny observes, sacred to the sun, whose rays they represented both by their form and name.[4] An ancient medal of Apollonia in Illyria, belonging to the Museum of the late Dr. Hunter, has the head of Apollo crowned with laurel on one side, and on the other an obelisc terminating in a cross, the least explicit representation of the male organs of generation.[5] This has exactly the appearance of one of those crosses, which were erected in church-yards and cross roads for the adoration of devout persons, when devotion was more prevalent than at present. Many of these were undoubtedly erected before the establishment of Christianity, and converted, together with their worshippers, to the true faith. Anciently they represented the generative power of light, the essence of God; *for God is light, and never but in unapproached light dwelt from*

[1] *Sat.* lib. i. c. 18.

[2] *Archaeologia*, vol. v.

[3] Now called the Devil's Arrows. See Stukeley's *Itin.* vol. i. Table xc.

[4] *Hist. Nat.* lib. xxxvi. sec. 14.

[5] Plate x. Fig. i, and *Nummi Pop. & Urb.* Table x. Fig. 7.

eternity, says Milton, who in this, as well as many other instances, has followed the Ammonian Platonics, who were both the restorers and corrupters of the ancient theology. They restored it from the mass of poetical mythology, under which it was buried, but refined and sublimated it with abstract metaphysics, which soared as far above human reason as the poetical mythology sunk below it. From the ancient solar obeliscs came the spires and pinnacles with which our churches are still decorated, so many ages after their mystic meaning has been forgotten. Happily for the beauty of these edifices, it was forgotten; otherwise the reformers of the last century would have destroyed them, as they did the crosses and images; for they might with equal propriety have been pronounced heathenish and prophane.

As the obelisc was the symbol of light, so was the pyramid of fire, deemed to be essentially the same. The Egyptians, among whom these forms are the most frequent, held that there were two opposite powers in the world, perpetually acting contrary to each other, the one creating, and the other destroying: the former they called Osiris, and the latter Typhon.[1] By the contention of these two, that mix-

[1] Plutarch. *de Is. & Os.*

ture of good and evil, which, according to some verses of Euripides quoted by Plutarch,[1] constituted the harmony of the world, was supposed to be produced. This opinion of the necessary mixture of good and evil was, according to Plutarch, of immemorial antiquity, derived from the oldest theologists and legislators, not only in traditions and reports, but in mysteries and sacrifices, both Greek and barbarian.[2] Fire was the efficient principle of both, and, according to some of the Egyptians, that ætherial fire which concentred in the sun. This opinion Plutarch controverts, saying that Typhon, the evil or destroying power, was a terrestrial or material fire, essentially different from the ætherial. But Plutarch here argues from his own prejudices, rather than from the evidence of the case; for he believed in an original evil principle coeternal with the good, and acting in perpetual opposition to it; an error into which men have been led by forming false notions of good and evil, and considering them as self-existing inherent properties, instead of accidental modifications, variable with every circumstance with which causes and events are connected. This error, though adopted by individuals, never formed a part either of the the-

[1] Plutarch. de Is. & Os.
[2] Ibid. Ed. Reiskii.

ology or mythology of Greece. Homer, in the beautiful allegory of the two casks, makes Jupiter, the supreme god, the distributor of both good and evil.[1] The name of Jupiter, Ζευς, was originally one of the titles or epithets of the sun, signifying, according to its etymology, *aweful* or *terrible;*[2] in which sense it is used in the Orphic litanies.[3] Pan, the universal substance, is called the horned Jupiter (Ζευς ο κεραστης); and in an Orphic fragment preserved by Macrobius[4] the names of Jupiter and Bacchus appear to be only titles of the all-creating power of the sun.

Αγλαε Ζεν, Λιοννσε, πατεζ ποντον, πατεζ αιης,

'Ηλιε παγγενετοζ.

In another fragment preserved by the same author,[5] the name of Pluto, Αιδης, is used as a title of the same deity; who appears therefore to have presided over the dead as well as over the living, and to have been the lord of destruction as well as creation and preservation. We accordingly find that in one of the Orphic litanies now extant, he is expressly called the giver of life, and the destroyer.[6]

[1] *Il. w,* v. 527.
[2] Damm. *Lex. Etymol.*
[3] Hymn. x. v. 13.
[4] *Sat.* lib. i. c. 23.
[5] *Sat.* lib. i. c. 8 .
[6] Hymn. lxxii. *Ed. Gesn.*

The Egyptians represented Typhon, the destroying power, under the figure of the hippopotamus or river-horse, the most fierce and destructive animal they knew;[1] and the Chorus in the *Bacchae* of Euripides invoke their inspirer Bacchus to appear under the form of a bull, a many-headed serpent, or flaming lion;[2] which shews that the most bloody and destructive, as well as the most useful of animals, was employed by the Greeks to represent some personified attribute of the god. M. D'Hancarville has also observed, that the lion is frequently employed by the ancient artists as a symbol of the sun;[3] and I am inclined to believe that it was to express this destroying power, no less requisite to preserve the harmony of the universe than the generating. In most of the monuments of ancient art where the lion is represented, he appears with expressions of rage and violence, and often in the act of killing and devouring some other animal. On an ancient sarcophagus found in Sicily he is represented devouring a horse,[4] and on the medals of Velia in Italy, devouring a deer;[5] the former, as sacred to Neptune, represented

---

[1] Plutarch. *de Is. & Os.*
[2] V. 1015.
[3] *Recherches sur les Arts.* See also Macrob. *Sat.* i. c. 21.
[4] Houel, *Voyage de la Sicile.* Plate xxxvi.
[5] Plate ix. Fig. 5, engraved from one belonging to me.

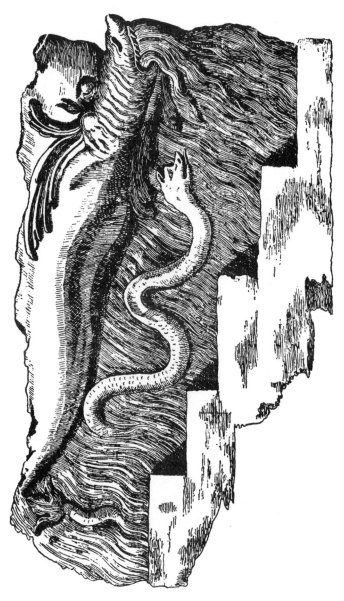

PLATE XVII
ORNAMENT FROM PUZZUOLI TEMPLE

the sea; and the latter, as sacred to Diana, the produce of the earth; for Diana was the fertility of the earth personified, and therefore is said to have received her nymphs or productive ministers from the ocean, the source of fecundity.[1] The lion, therefore, in the former instance, appears as a symbol of the sun exhaling the waters; and in the latter, as withering and putrifying the produce of the earth. On the frieze of the Temple of Apollo Didymæus, near Miletus, are monsters composed of the mixt forms of the goat and lion, resting their fore feet upon the lyre of the god, which stands between them.[2] The goat, as I have already shewn, represented the creative attribute, and the lyre, harmony and order; therefore, if we admit that the lion represented the destroying attribute, this composition will signify, in the symbolical language of sculpture, the harmony and order of the universe preserved by the regular and periodical operations of the creative and destructive powers. This is a notion to which men would be naturally led by observing the common order and progression of things. The same heat of the sun, which scorched and withered the grass in summer, ripened the fruits in autumn, and cloathed the earth

[1] Callimach. *Hymn ad Dian.* v. 13. *Genitor Nympharum Oceanus.* Catullus *in Gell.* v. 84.
[2] *Ionian Antiquities*, vol. i. c. 3. Plate IX.

with verdure in the spring. In one season it dried up the waters from the earth, and in another returned them in rain. It caused fermentation and putrefaction, which destroy one generation of plants and animals, and produce another in constant and regular succession. This contention between the powers of creation and destruction is represented on an ancient medal of Acanthus, in the museum of the late Dr. Hunter, by a combat between the bull and lion.[1] The bull alone is represented on other medals in exactly the same attitude and gesture as when fighting with the lion;[2] whence I conclude that the lion is there understood. On the medals of Celenderis, the goat appears instead of the bull in exactly the same attitude of struggle and contention, but without the lion;[3] and in a curious one of very ancient but excellent workmanship, belonging to me, the ivy of Bacchus is placed over the back of the goat, to denote the power which he represents.[4]

The mutual operation which was the result of this contention was signified, in the mythological tales of the poets, by the loves of Mars and Venus, the one

[1] Plate IX. Fig. 4, & *Nummi Vet. Pop. & Urb.* Table I. Fig. 16.
[2] Plate IX. Fig. 12, from one of Aspendus in the same Collection. See *Nummi Vet. Pop. & Urb.* Table VIII. Fig. 20.
[3] *Nummi Vet. Pop. & Urb.* Table XVI. Fig. 13.
[4] Plate IX. Fig. 13.

the active power of destruction, and the other the passive power of generation. From their union is said to have sprung the goddess *Harmony,* who was the physical order of the universe personified. The fable of Ceres and Proserpine is the same allegory inverted; Ceres being the prolific power of the earth personified, and hence called by the Greeks *Mother Earth* (Γη or Λη-μητηζ). The Latin name Ceres also signifying *Earth,* the Roman C being the same originally, both in figure and power as the Greek Γ,[1] which Homer often uses as a mere guttural aspirate, and adds it arbitrarily to his words, to make them more solemn and sonorous.[2] The guttural aspirates and hissing terminations more particularly belonged to the Æolic dialect, from which the Latin was derived; wherefore we need not wonder that the same word, which by the Dorians and Ionians was written Εϱα and Εϱε, should by the Æolians be written Γεϱες or Ceres, the Greeks always accommodating their orthography to their pronunciation. In an ancient bronze at Strawberry Hill this goddess is represented sitting, with a cup in one hand, and various sorts of fruits in the other; and the bull, the emblem of the power of the Creator, in her lap.[3] This composition

[1] See S. C. Marcian, and the medals of Gela and Agrigentum.
[2] As in the word εϱιδψπος, usually written by him εϱιγδψπος.
[3] See Plate VIII.

shews the fructification of the earth by the descent of the creative spirit in the same manner as described by Virgil:—

> Vere tument terræ, et genitalia semina poscunt;
> Tum pater omnipotens fœcundis imbribus æther
> Conjugis in gremium lætæ descendit, & omnes
> Magnus alit, magno commixtus corpore, fœtus.[1]

Æther and water are here introduced by the poet as the two prolific elements which fertilize the earth, according to the ancient system of Orphic philosophy, upon which the mystic theology was founded. Proserpine, or Ηερσιφονεια, the daughter of Ceres, was, as her Greek name indicates, the goddess of destruction, in which character she is invoked by Althæa in the ninth Iliad; but nevertheless we often find her on the Greek medals crowned with ears of corn, as being the goddess of fertility as well as destruction.[2] She is, in fact, a personification of the heat or fire that pervades the earth, which is at once the cause and effect of fertility and destruction, for it is at once the cause and effect of fermentation, from which both proceed. The Libitina, or goddess of death of the Romans, was the same as the Persiphoneia of the Greeks; and yet, as Plutarch observes,

[1] *Georgic.* lib. ii. .v. 324.

[2] Plate IV. Fig. 5, from a medal of Agathocles, belonging to me. The same head is upon many others, of Syracuse, Metapontum, &c.

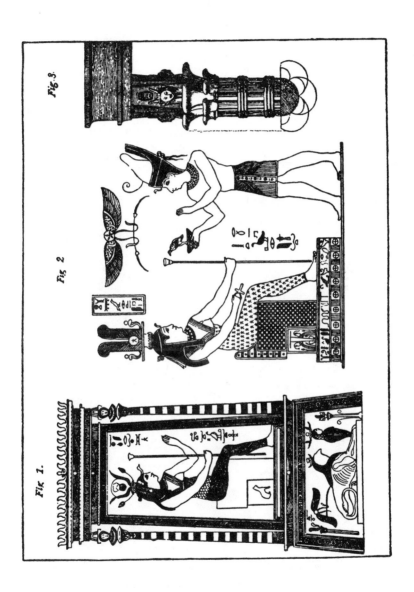

PLATE XVIII

EGYPTIAN FIGURES AND ORNAMENTS

the most learned of that people allowed her to be the same as Venus, the goddess of generation.[1]

In the Gallery at Florence is a collossal image of the organ of generation, mounted on the back parts of a lion, and hung round with various animals. By this is represented the co-operation of the creating and destroying powers, which are both blended and united in one figure, because both are derived from one cause. The animals hung round show likewise that both act to the same purpose, that of replenishing the earth, and peopling it with still rising generations of sensitive beings. The Chimæra of Homer, of which the commentators have given so many whimsical interpretations, was a symbol of the same kind, which the poet probably, having seen in Asia, and not knowing its meaning (which was only revealed to the initiated) supposed to be a monster that had once infested the country. He describes it as composed of the forms of the *goat*, the *lion*, and the *serpent*, and breathing *fire* from its mouth.[2] These are the symbols of the *creator*, the *destroyer*, and the *preserver*, united and animated by *fire*, the divine essence of all *three*.[3] On a gem, published in the

[1] In Numa.

[2] *Il.* ζ. v. 223.

[3] For the natural properties attributed by the ancients to fire, see Plutarch, *in Camillo*, Plin. *Hist. Nat.* lib. xxxvi. c. 68.

Memoirs of the Academy of Cortona,[1] this union of the destroying and preserving attributes is represented by the united forms of the lion and serpent crowned with rays, the emblems of the cause from which both proceed. This composition forms the Chnoubis of the Egyptians.

Bacchus is frequently represented by the ancient artists accompanied by tigers, which appear, in some instances, devouring clusters of grapes, the fruit peculiarly consecrated to the god, and in others drinking the liquor pressed from them. The author of the *Recherches sur les Arts* has in this instance followed the common accounts of the Mythologists, and asserted that tigers are really fond of grapes;[2] which is so far from being true, that they are incapable of feeding upon them, or upon any fruit whatever, being both externally and internally formed to feed upon flesh only, and to procure their food by destroying other animals. Hence I am persuaded, that in the ancient symbols, tigers, as well as lions, represent the destroying power of the god. Sometimes his chariot appears drawn by them; and then they represent the powers of destruction preceding the powers of generation, and extending their operation, as putrefaction precedes, and increases vegetation. On

[1] Vol. iv. p. 32. See also Plate v. Fig. 4, copied from it.
[2] Liv. i. c. 3.

a medal of Maronea, published by Gesner,[1] a goat is coupled with the tiger in drawing his chariot; by which composition the artist has shewn the *general active* power of the deity, conducted by his two great attributes of creation and destruction. On the Choragic monument of Lysicrates at Athens, Bacchus is represented feeding a tiger; which shows the active power of destruction.[2] On a beautiful cameo in the collection of the Duke of Marlborough, the tiger is sucking the breast of a nymph; which represents the same power of destruction, nourished by the passive power of generation.[3] In the museum of Charles Townley, Esq., is a group, in marble, of three figures;[4] the middle one of which grows out of a vine in a human form, with leaves and clusters of grapes springing out of its body. On one side is the Bacchus διφνης, or creator of both sexes, known by the effeminate mold of his limbs and countenance; and on the other, a tiger, leaping up, and devouring the grapes which spring from the body of the personified vine, the hands of which are employed in receiving

[1] Table xliii. Fig. 26.

[2] Stuart's *Athens*, vol. i. c. 4, Plate x.

[3] See Plate xxiii. engraved merely to show the composition, it not being permitted to make an exact drawing of it.

[4] See Plate xxi. Fig. 7.

another cluster from the Bacchus. This composition represents the vine between the creating and destroying attributes of god; the one giving it fruit, and the other devouring it when given. The tiger has a garland of ivy round his neck, to show that the destroyer was co-essential with the creator, of whom ivy, as well as all other ever-greens, was an emblem representing his perpetual youth and viridity.[1]

The mutual and alternate operation of the two great attributes of creation and destruction, was not confined by the ancients to plants and animals, and such transitory productions, but extended to the universe itself. Fire being the essential cause of both, they believed that the conflagration and renovation of the world were periodical and regular, proceeding from each other by the laws of its own constitution, implanted in it by the creator, who was also the destroyer and renovator;[2] for, as Plato says, all things arise from one, and into one are all things resolved.[3] It must be observed, that, when the ancients speak of creation and destruction, they mean only formation

[1] Strabo, lib. xv. p. 712.

[2] Brucker, *Hist. Crit. Philos.* vol. i. part 2, lib. i. Plutarch *de Placit. Philos.* lib. ii. c. 18. Lucretius, lib. v. ver. 92. Cic. *de Nat. Deor.* lib. ii.

[3] Εξ ἑνος τα παντα γενεσθαι, και εις τ' ἁυτον αναλυεσθαι, in Phæd. The same dogma is still more plainly inculcated by the ancient Indian author before cited, see *Bagvat Geeta*, Lect. ix.

and dissolution; it being universally allowed, through all systems of religion, or sects of philosophy, that *nothing could come from nothing, and that no power whatever could annihilate that which really existed.* The bold and magnificent idea of a creation from nothing was reserved for the more vigorous faith, and more enlightened minds of the moderns,[1] who need seek no authority to confirm their belief; for, as that which is self-evident admits of no proof, so that which is in itself impossible admits of no refutation.

The fable of the serpent Pytho being destroyed by Apollo, probably arose from an emblematical composition, in which that god was represented as the destroyer of life, of which the serpent was a symbol. Pliny mentions a statue of him by Praxiteles, which was much celebrated in his time, called Σαυροκτων (*the Lizard-killer.*)[2] The lizard, being supposed to live upon the dews and moisture of the earth, is employed as the symbol of humidity in general; so that the god destroying it, signifies the same as the lion devouring the horse. The title Apollo, I

[1] The word in *Genesis* upon which it is founded, conveyed no such sense to the ancients; for the Seventy translated it εποιησε, which signifies *formed*, or *fashioned*.

[2] *Hist. Nat.* lib. xxxiv. c. 8. Many copies of it are still extant. Winkleman has published one from a bronze of Cardinal Albani's. *Monum. Antichi. inediti*, Plate xl.

am inclined to believe, meant originally the Destroyer, as well as the Deliverer; for, as the ancients
supposed destruction to be merely dissolution, the
power which delivered the particles of matter from
the bonds of attraction, and broke the δεσμον περιβριϑη
ερωτος, was in fact the destroyer.[1] It is, probably,
for this reason, that sudden death, plagues, and epi-
demic diseases, are said by the poets to be sent by
this god; who is, at the same time, described as the
author of medicine, and all the arts employed to
preserve life. These attributes are not joined merely
because the destroyer and preserver were essentially
the same; but because disease necessarily precedes
cure, and is the cause of its being invented. The
God of Health is said to be his son, because the health
and vigour of one being are supported by the decay
and dissolution of others which are appropriated to
its nourishment. The bow and arrows are given to
him as symbols of his characteristic attributes, as
they are to Diana, who was the female personification of the destructive, as well as the productive and
preserving powers. Diana is hence called the triple
Hecate, and represented by three female bodies

[1] The verb λυω, from which Apollo is derived, signifies in
Homer both to *free* and to dissolve or destroy, *Il. a, ver.* 20;
Il, i, ver. 25. Macrobius derives the title from απολλυμι, to
destroy; but this word is derived from λυω Sat. lib. i. c. 17.

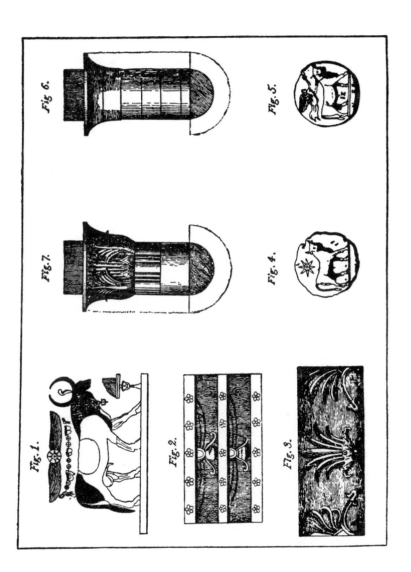

PLATE XIX

EGYPTIAN FIGURES AND ORNAMENTS

joined together. Her attributes were however worshippd separately; and some nations revered her under one character, and others under another. Diana of Ephesus was the productive and nutritive power, as the many breasts and other symbols on her statues imply; [1] whilst Βριμω, the *Tauric* or *Scythic* Diana, apears to have been the destructive, and therefore was appeased with human sacrifices, and other bloody rites.[2] She is represented sometimes standing on the back of a bull,[3] and sometimes in a chariot drawn by bulls; [4] whence she is called by the poets Ταυροπολα [5] and Βοων ελατειρα.[6]. Both compositions show the passive power of nature, whether creative or destructive, sustained and guided by the general active power of the creator, of which the sun was the centre, and the bull the symbol.

It was observed by the ancients, that the destructive power of the sun was exerted most by day, and the creative by night: for it was in the former season that he dried up the waters, withered the herbs, and

[1] Hieron. *Comment. in* Paul *Epist. ad Ephes.*

[2] Pausan. lib. iii. c. 16.

[3] See a medal of Augustus, published by Spanheim. *Not. in* Callim. *Hymn. ad Dian.* ver. 113.

[4] Plate vi., from a bronze in the museum of C. Townley, Esq.

[5] Sophoclis *Ajax,* ver. 172.

[6] *Nonni* Dionys, lib. i. the title Ταυοοπολος was sometimes given to Apollo, Eustath. *Schol in* Dionys. Περιηγησ., ver. 609.

produced disease and putrefaction; and in the latter, that he returned the exhalations in dews, tempered with the genial heat which he had transfused into the atmosphere, to restore and replenish the waste of the day. Hence, when they personified the attributes, they revered the one as the *diurnal,* and the other as the *nocturnal* sun, and in their mystic worship, as Macrobius says,[1] called the former Apollo, and the latter Dionysus or Bacchus. The mythological personages of Castor and Pollux, who lived and died alternately, were allegories of the same dogma; hence the two asteriscs, by which they are distinguished on the medals of Locri, Argos, and other cities.

The pæans, or war-songs, which the Greeks chanted at the onset of their battles,[2] were originally sung to Apollo,[3] who was called Pæon; and Macrobius tells us,[4] that in Spain, the sun was worshipped as Mars, the god of war and destruction, whose statue they adorned with rays, like that of the Greek Apollo. On a Celtiberian or Runic medal found in Spain, of barbarous workmanship, is a head surrounded by

[1] Sat. lib. 1. c. 18.

[2] Thucyd. lib. vii.

[3] Homer. *Il. a,* v. 472.

[4] Sat. lib. 1. c. 19.

obeliscs or rays, which I take to be of this deity.[1] The hairs appear erect, to imitate flames, as they do on many of the Greek medals; and on the reverse is a bearded head, with a sort of pyramidal cap on, exactly resembling that by which the Romans conferred freedom on their slaves, and which was therefore called the cap of liberty.[2] On other Celtiberian medals is a figure on horseback, carrying a spear in his hand, and having the same sort of cap on his head, with the word Helman written under him,[3] in characters which are something between the old Runic and Pelasgian; but so near to the latter, that they are easily understood.[4] This figure seems to be of the same person as is represented by the head with the cap on the preceding medal, who can be no other than the angel or minister of the deity of death, as the name implies; for Hela or Hel, was, among the

[1] Plate x Fig. 2, engraven from one belonging to me. I have since been confirmed in this conjecture by observing the characters of Mars and Apollo mixt on Greek coins. On a Mamertine one belonging to me is the head with the youthful features and laurel crown of Apollo; but the hair is short, and the inscription on the exergue denotes it to be Mars. See Plate xvi. Fig 2.

[2] It may be seen with the dagger on the medals of Brutus.

[3] See Plate ix. Fig. 9, from one belonging to me.

[4] The first is a mixture of the Runic *Hagle* and Greek H. The second is the Runic *Laugur*, which is also the old Greek Λ, as it appears on the vase of the Calydonian Boar in the British Museum. The other three differ little from the common Greek.

Northern nations, the goddess of death,[1] in the same manner as Persiphoneia or Brimo was among the Greeks. The same figure appears on many ancient British medals, and also on those of several Greek cities, particularly those of Gela, which have the Taurine Bacchus or Creator on the reverse.[2] The head which I have supposed to be the Celtiberian Mars, or destructive power of the diurnal sun, is beardless like the Apollo of the Greeks, and, as far as can be discovered in such barbarous sculpture, has the same androgynous features.[3] We may therefore reasonably suppose, that, like the Greeks, the Celtiberians personified the destructive attribute under the different genders, accordingly as they applied it to the sun, or subordinate elements; and then united them, to signify that both were essentially the same. The Helman therefore, who was the same as the Μοιραγητης or Διακτωζ of the Greeks, may with equal propriety be called the minister of *both* or *either*. The spear in his hand is not to be considered merely as the implement of destruction, but as the symbol of power and command, which it was in Greece and Italy, as well as all over the North. Hence ευθυνειν

---

[1] Edda. Fab. xvi. *D'Hancarville, Recherches sur les Arts*, liv. ii. c. i.

[2] See Plate ix. Fig. ii, from one belonging to me.

[3] See Plate x. Fig. 2.

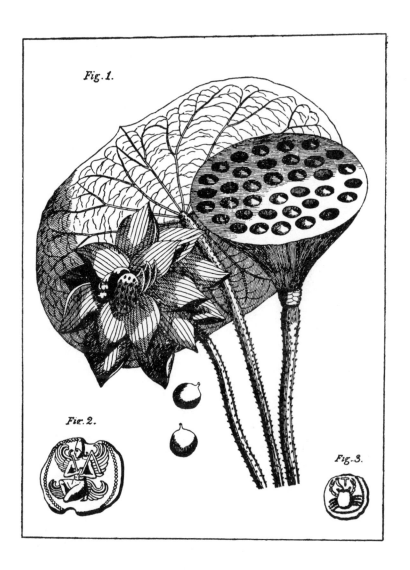

Fig. 1.

Fig. 2.

Fig. 3.

PLATE XX

THE LOTUS AND MEDALS OF MELITA

δορι *was to govern,*[1] and *venire sub hastâ,—to be sold as a slave.* The ancient Celtes and Scythians paid divine honors to the sword, the battle-axe, and the spear; the first of which was the symbol by which they represented the supreme god: hence to swear by the edge of the sword was the most sacred and inviolable of oaths.[2] Euripides alludes to this ancient religion when he calls a sword ορκιον ξιφος; and Æschylus shows clearly, that it once prevailed in Greece, when he makes the heroes of the Thebaid swear by the point of the spear (ομνυσι δ'αιχμην[3]). Homer sometimes uses the word αρης to signify the God of War, and sometimes a weapon: and we have sufficient proof of this word's being of Celtic origin in its affinity with our Northern word *War;* for, if we write it in the ancient manner, with the Pelasgian *Vau,* or Æolian *Digamma,* Φαρης (*Wares*), it scarcely differs at all.

Behind the bearded head, on the first-mentioned Celtiberian medal is an instrument like a pair of fire-tongs, or blacksmith's pincers;[4] from which it seems that the personage here represented is the same as the 'Ηφαιστος or Vulcan of the Greek and Roman

---

[1] Eurip. *Hecuba.*

[2] Mallet, *Introd. à l'Hist. de Danemarc,* c. 9.

[3] ' Επταοπι Θη Βας. v. 535.

[4] Plate x. Fig. 2.

mythology. The same ideas are expressed somewhat more plainly on the medals of Æsernia in Italy, which are executed with all the refinement and elegance of Grecian art.[1] On one side is Apollo, the diurnal sun, mounting in his chariot; and on the other a beardless head, with the same cap on, and the same instrument behind it, but with the youthful features and elegant character of countenance usually attributed to Mercury, who, as well as Vulcan, was the God of Art and Mechanism; and whose peculiar office it also was to conduct the souls of the deceased to their eternal mansions, from whence came the epithet Διακτωζ, applied to him by Homer. He was, therefore, in this respect, the same as the Helman of the Celtes and Scythians, who was supposed to conduct the souls of all who died a violent death (which alone was accounted truly happy) to the palace of Valhala.[2] It seems that the attributes of the deity which the Greeks represented by the mythological personages of Vulcan and Mercury, were united in the Celtic mythology. Cæsar tells us that the Germans worshipped Vulcan, or fire, with the sun and moon; and I shall soon have occasion to show that the Greeks held fire to be the real con-

[1] See Plate x. Fig. 6, from one belonging to me.
[2] Mallet, *Hist. de Danemarc. Introd.* c. 9.

ductor of the dead, and emancipator of the soul. The Æsernians, bordering upon the Samnites, a Celtic nation, might naturally be supposed to have adopted the notions of their neighbours, or, what is more probable, preserved the religion of their ancestors more pure than the Hellenic Greeks. Hence they represented Vulcan, who, from the inscription on the exergue of their coins, appears to have been their tutelar god, with the characteristic features of Mercury, who was only a different personification of the same deity.

At Lycopolis in Egypt the destroying power of the sun was represented by a wolf; which, as Macrobius says, was worshipped there as Apollo.[1] The wolf appears devouring grapes in the ornaments of the temple of Bacchus περικιονιος at Puzzuoli;[2] and on the medals of Cartha he is surrounded with rays, which plainly proves that he is there meant as a symbol of the sun.[3] He is also represented on most of the coins of Argos,[4] where I have already shown that the diurnal sun Apollo, the light-extending god, was peculiarly worshipped. We may therefore conclude, that this animal is meant for one of the mys-

[1] *Sat.* lib. i. c. 17.
[2] Plate xvi. Fig. i.
[3] Plate x, Fig. 8, from one belonging to me.
[4] Plate ix, Fig. 7, from one belonging to me.

tic symbols of the primitive worship, and not, as some antiquarians have supposed, to commemorate the mythological tales of Danaus or Lycaon, which were probably invented, like many others of the same kind, to satisfy the inquisitive ignorance of the vulgar, from whom the meaning of the mystic symbols, the usual devices on the medals, was strictly concealed. In the Celtic mythology, the same symbol was employed, apparently in the same sense, Lok, the great destroying power of the universe, being represented under the form of a wolf.[1]

The Apollo Didymæus, or *double Apollo,* was probably the two personifications, that of the *destroying,* and that of the creating power, united; whence we may perceive the reason why the ornaments before described should be upon his temple.[2] On the medals of Antigonus, king of Asia, is a figure with his hair hanging in artificial ringlets over his shoulders, like that of a woman, and the whole composition, both of his limbs and countenance, remarkable for extreme delicacy, and feminine elegance.[3] He is sitting on the prow of a ship, as god of the waters; and we should, without hesitation, pronounce him to be

[1] Mallet, *Introd. à l'Hist. de Danemarc.*
[2] See *Ionian Antiq.* vol. i. c. 3, Pl. IX.
[3] See Plate x. Fig. 7, from one belonging to me. Similar figures are on the coins of most of the Seleucidæ.

the Bacchus διφυης, were it not for the bow that he carries in his hand, which evidently shows him to be Apollo. This I take to be the figure under which the refinement of art (and more was never shown than in this medal) represented the Apollo Didymæus, or union of the creative and destructive powers of both sexes in one body.

As fire was the primary essence of the active or male powers of creation and generation, so was water of the passive or female. Appian says, that the goddess worshipped at Hierapolis in Syria was *called by some* Venus, *by others* Juno, *and by others held to be the cause which produced the beginning and seeds of things from humidity.*[1] Plutarch describes her nearly in the same words;[2] and the author of the treatise attributed to Lucian[3] says, *she was Nature, the parent of things, or the creatress.* She was therefore the same as Isis, who was the prolific material upon which both the creative and destructive attributes operated.[4] As water was her terrestrial essence, so was the moon her celestial image, whose attractive power, heaving the waters of the ocean, naturally led men to associate them. The moon was

[1] *De Bell oParthico.*
[2] *In Crasso.*
[3] *De Dea Syriâ.*
[4] Plutarch. *de Is. & Os.*

also supposed to return the dews which the sun ex-
haled from the earth; and hence her warmth was
reckoned to be moistening, as that of the sun was
drying.[1] The Egyptians called her the Mother of the
World, because she sowed and scattered into the air
the prolific principles with which she had been impregnated by the sun.[2] These principles, as well as
the light by which she was illumined, being supposed to emanate from the great fountain of all life
and motion, partook of the nature of the being from
which they were derived. Hence the Egyptians attributed to the moon, as well as to the sun, the active
and passive powers of generation,[3] which were both,
to use the languages of the scholastics, *essentially* the
same, though *formally* different. This union is represented on a medal of Demetrius the second, king of
Syria,[4] where the goddess of Hierapolis appears with
the male organs of generation sticking out of her
robe, and holding the thyrsus of Bacchus, the emblem
of fire, in one hand, and the terrestrial globe, representing the subordinate elements, in the other. Her
head is crowned with various plants, and on each
side is an asterisc representing (probably) the diur-

[1] *Calor solis arefacit, lunaris humectat.* Macrob. *Sat.* VII. c. 10.
[2] Plutarch. *de Is. & Os.*
[3] Ibid.
[4] Plate x. Fig. 5, from Haym. *Tes. Brit.* p. 70.

nal and nocturnal sun, in the same manner as when placed over the caps of Castor and Pollux.[1] This is not the form under which she was represented in the temple at Hierapolis, when the author of the account attributed to Lucian visited it; which is not to be wondered at, for the figures of this universal goddess, being merely emblematical, were composed according to the attributes which the artists meant particularly to express. She is probably represented here in the form under which she was worshipped in the neighbourhood of Cyzicus, where she was called Αρτεμις Πριαπινη, the *Priapic Diana*.[2] In the temple at Hierapolis the active powers imparted to her by the Creator were represented by immense images of the male organs of generation placed on each side of the door. The measures of these must necessarily be corrupt in the present text of Lucian; but that they were of an enormous size we may conclude from what is related of a man's going to the top of one of them every year, and residing there seven days, in order to have a more intimate communication with the deity, while praying for the prosperity of Syria.[3] Athenæus relates, that Ptolemy Philadelphus had one of 120 cubits long carried in

[1] See Plate IX. Fig. 7.
[2] Plutarch. *in Lucullo*.
[3] Lucian. *de Dea Syriâ*.

procession at Alexandria,[1] of which the poet might justly have said—

> Horrendum protendit Mentula contum
> Quanta queat vastos Thetidis spumantis hiatus;
> Quanta queat priscamque Rheam, magnamque parentem
> Naturam, solidis naturam implere medullis,
> Si foret immensos, quot ad astra volantia currunt,
> Conceptura globos, et tela trisulca tonantis,
> Et vaga concussum motura tonitrua mundum.

This was the real meaning of the enormous figures at Hierapolis:—they were the generative organs of the creator personified, with which he was supposed to have impregnated the heavens, the earth, and the waters. Within the temple were many small statues of men with these organs disproportionably large. These were the angels or attendants of the goddess, who acted as her ministers of creation in peopling and fructifying the earth. The statue of the goddess herself was in the sanctuary of the temple; and near it was the statue of the creator, whom the author calls Jupiter, as he does the goddess, Juno; by which he only means that they were the supreme deities of the country where worshipped. She was borne by lions, and he by bulls, to show that nature, the passive productive power of matter, was sustained by anterior destruction, whilst the ætherial spirit, or active productive power, was sustained by his own

[1] *Deipnos. lib.*

strength only, of which the bulls were symbols.[1] Between both was a third figure, with a dove on his head, which some thought to be Bacchus.[2] This was the Holy Spirit, the first-begotten love, or plastic nature, (of which the dove was the image when it really deigned to descend upon man,[3]) proceeding from, and consubstantial with *both;* for all *three* were but personifications of *one.* The dove, or some fowl like it, appears on the medals of Gortyna in Crete, acting the same part with Dictynna, the Cretan Diana, as the swan is usually represented acting with Leda.[4] This composition has nearly the same signification as that before described of the bull in the lap of Ceres, Diana being equally a personification of the productive power of the earth. It may seem extraordinary, that after this adventure with the dove, she should still remain a virgin; but mysteries of this kind are to be found in all religions. Juno is said to have renewed her virginity every year by bathing

---

[1] The *active* and *passive* powers of creation are called *male* and *female* by the Ammonian Platonics. See Proclus *in Theol. Platon.* lib. i. c. 28.

[2] Lucian, *de Dea Syriâ.*

[3] Matth. ch. iii. ver. 17.

[4] See Plate III. Fig. 5. Καλψσι δε την Αρτεμιν Θραχες Βενδειαν, Κρητες δε Διχτυνναν. Palæph. *de Incred.* Tab. XXXI. See also Diodor. Sic. lib. v. & Euripid. *Hippol.* v. 145.

in a certain fountain; [1] a miracle which I believe even modern legends cannot parallel.

In the vision of Ezekiel, God is described as descending upon the combined forms of the eagle, the bull, and the lion, [2] the emblems of the ætherial spirit, the creative and destructive powers, which were all united in the true God, though hypostatically divided in the Syrian trinity. Man was compounded with them, as representing the real image of God, according to the Jewish theology. The cherubim on the ark of the covenant, between which God dwelt, [3] were also compounded of the same forms, [4] so that the idea of them must have been present to the prophet's mind, previous to the apparition which furnished him with the description. Even those on the ark of the covenant, though made at the express command of God, do not appear to have been original; for a figure exactly answering to the description of them appears among those curious ruins existing at Chilminar, in Persia, which have been supposed to be those of the palace of Persepolis, burnt by Alexander; but for what reason, it is not easy to conjecture. They do not, certainly, answer to any ancient

[1] Pausan. lib. ii. c. 38.
[2] Ezek. ch. i. ver. 10, with Lowth's *Comm.*
[3] *Exod.* ch. xxv. ver. 22.
[4] Spencer *de Leg. Ritual Vet. Hebræor*, lib. iii. dissert. 5.

Fig.1.

Fig.2.

Fig.7.

Fig.4.

Fig.5.

Fig.6.

Fig.3.

PLATE XXI

BACCHUS AND MEDALS OF CAMARINA AND SYRACUSE

description extant of that celebrated palace; but, as far as we can judge of them in their present state, appear evidently to have been a temple.[1] But the Persians, as before observed, had no inclosed temples or statues, which they held in such abhorrence, that they tried every means possible to destroy those of the Egyptians; thinking it unworthy of the majesty of the deity to have his all-pervading presence limited to the boundary of an edifice, or likened to an image of stone or metal. Yet, among the ruins at Chilminar, we not only find many statues, which are evidently of ideal beings,[2] but also that remarkable emblem of the deity, which distinguishes almost all the Egyptian temples now extant.[3] The portals are also of the same form as those at Thebes and Philæ; and, except the hieroglyphics which distinguish the latter, are finished and ornamented nearly in the same manner. Unless, therefore, we suppose the Persians to have been so inconsistent as to erect temples in direct contradiction to the first principles of their own religion, and decorate them with sym-

[1] See Le Bruyn, *Voyage en Perse*, Planche cxxiii.

[2] See Le Bruyn and Niebuhr.

[3] See Plate xviii. Fig. 1 from the Isiac Table, and Plate xix. Fig 5 from Niebuhr's prints of Chilminar. See also Plate xviii. Fig. 2 and Plate xix. Fig. i from the Isiac Tables and the Egyptian Portals published by Norden and Pococke, on every one of which this singular emblem occurs.

bols and images, which they held to be impious and abominable, we cannot suppose them to be the authors of these buildings. Neither can we suppose the Parthians, or later Persians, to have been the builders of them; for both the style of workmanship in the figures, and the forms of the letters in the inscriptions, denote a much higher antiquity, as will appear evidently to any one who will take the trouble of comparing the drawings published by Le Bruyn and Niebuhr with the coins of the Arsacidæ and Sassanidæ. Almost all the symbolical figures are to be found repeated upon different Phœnician coins; but the letters of the Phœnicians, which are said to have come to them from the Assyrians, are much less simple, and evidently belong to an alphabet much further advanced in improvement. Some of the figures are also observable upon the Greek coins, particularly the bull and lion fighting, and the mystic flower, which is the constant device of the Rhodians. The style of workmanship is also exactly the same as that of the very ancient Greek coins of Acanthus, Celendaris, and Lesbos; the lines being very strongly marked, and the hair expressed by round knobs. The wings likewise of the figure, which resembles the Jewish cherubim, are the same as those upon several Greek sculptures now extant; such as the little images of Priapus attached to the ancient bracelets,

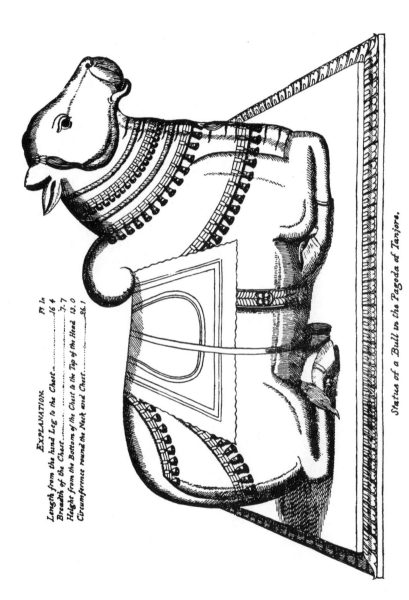

EXPLANATION

	Ft In
Length from the hind Leg to the Chest	16 4
Breadth of the Chest	7. 7
Height from the Bottom of the Chest to the Top of the Head	13. 0
Circumference round the Neck and Chest	26. 1

Statue of a Bull in the Pagoda of Tanjore.

PLATE XXII

the compound figures of the goat and lion upon the frieze of the Temple of Apollo Didymæus, &c. &c.[1] They are likewise joined to the human figure on the medals of Melita and Camarina,[2] as well as upon many ancient sculptures in relief found in Persia.[3] The feathers in these wings are turned upwards like those of an ostrich,[4] to which however they have no resemblance in form, but seem rather like those of a fowl brooding, though more distorted than any I ever observed in nature. Whether this distortion was meant to express lust or incubation, I cannot determine; but the compositions, to which the wings are added, leave little doubt, that it was meant for the one or the other. I am inclined to believe that it was for the latter, as we find on the medals of Melita a figure with four of these wings, who seems by his attitude to be brooding over something.[5] On his head is the cap of liberty, whilst in his right hand he holds the hook or attractor, and in his left the winnow or separator; so that he probably represents the Εϱως, or generative spirit brooding over matter, and giving

[1] See Le Bruyn, Planche cxxiii. *Ionian Antiquities*, vol. 1. c. 3. Plate ix., and Plate ii. Fig. 2.

[2] See Plate xx. Fig. 2, from one of Melita, belonging to me.

[3] See Le Bruyn, Planche cxxi.

[4] As those on Figures described by Ezekiel were. See c. 1. v. ii.

[5] See Plate xx. Fig. 2, engraved from one belonging to me.

liberty to its productive powers by the exertion of his own attributes, attraction and separation. On a very ancient Phœnician medal brought from Asia by Mr. Pullinger, and published very incorrectly by Mr. Swinton in the Philosophical Transactions of 1760, is a disc or ring surrounded by wings of different forms, of which some of the feathers are distorted in the same manner.[1] The same disc, surrounded by the same kind of wings, incloses the asterisc of the sun over the bull Apis, or Mnevis, on the Isiac Table,[2] where it also appears with many of the other Egyptian symbols, particularly over the heads of Isis and Osiris.[3] It is also placed over the entrances of most of the Egyptian temples described by Pococke and Norden as well as on that represented on the Isiac Table,[4] though with several variations, and without the asterisc. We find it equally without the asterisc, but with little or no variation, on the ruins at Chilmenar, and other supposed Persian antiquities in that neighbourhood:[5] but upon some of the Greek medals the asterisc alone is placed over the bull with

[1] See Plate IX. Fig. 9, engraved from the original medal, now belonging to me.

[2] See Plate XIX, Fig. 1, from Pignorius.

[3] See Plate XVIII. Fig. 2, from Pignorius.

[4] See Plate XVIII. Fig. 1, from Pignorius.

[5] See Niebuhr and Le Bruyn, and Plate XIX. Fig. 2, from the former.

the human face,[1] who is then the same as the Apis or Mnevis of the Egyptians; that is, the image of the generative power of the sun, which is signified by the asterisc on the Greek medals, and by the kneph, or winged disc, on the Oriental monuments. The Greeks however sometimes employed this latter symbol, but contrived, according to their usual practice, to join it to the human figure, as may be seen on a medal of Camarina, published by Prince Torremmuzzi.[2] On other medals of this city the same idea is expressed, without the disc or asterisc, by a winged figure, which appears hovering over a swan, the emblem of the waters, to show the generative power of the sun fructifying that element, or adding the *active* to the *passive* powers of production.[3] On the medals of Naples, a winged figure of the same kind is represented crowning the Taurine Bacchus with a wreath of laurel.[4] This antiquarians have called a Victory crowning the Minotaur; but the fabulous monster called the Minotaur was never said to have been victorious, even by the poets who invented it; and whenever the sculptors and painters represented

[1] See Plate IV. Fig. 2, and Plate XIX. Fig. 4, from a medal of Cales, belonging to me.

[2] See Plate XXI. Fig. 2, copied from it.

[3] See Plate XXI. Fig. 3, from one belonging to me.

[4] See Plate XIX. Fig. 5. The coins are common in all collections.

179

it, they joined the head of a bull to a human body, as may be seen in the celebrated picture of Theseus, published among the antiquities of Herculaneum, and on the medals of Athens, struck about the time of Severus, when the style of art was totally changed, and the mystic theology extinct. The winged figure, which has been called a Victory, appears mounting in the chariot of the sun, on the medals of queen Philistis,[1] and, on some of those of Syracuse, flying before it in the place where the asterisc appears on others of the same city.[2] I am therefore persuaded, that these are only different modes of representing one idea, and that the winged figure means the same, when placed over the Taurine Bacchus of the Greeks, as the winged disc over the Apis or Mnevis of the Egyptians. The Ægis, or snaky breastplate, and the Medusa's head, are also, as Dr. Stukeley justly observed,[3] Greek modes of representing this winged disc joined with the serpents, as it frequently is, both in the Egyptian sculptures, and those of Chilmenar in Persia. The expressions of rage and violence, which usually characterise the countenance of Medusa, signify the destroying attribute joined with the generative, as both were equally under the direction of

[1] See Plate xxi. Fig. 4, from one belonging to me.
[2] See Plate xxi. Fig. 5 and 6, from coins belonging to me.
[3] Abury, p. 93.

Minerva, or divine wisdom. I am inclined to believe, that the large rings, to which the little figures of Priapus are attached,[1] had also the same meaning as the disc; for, if intended merely to suspend them by, they are of an extravagant magnitude, and would not answer their purpose so well as a common loop.

On the Phœnician coin above mentioned, this symbol, the winged disc, is placed over a figure sitting, who holds in his hands an arrow, whilst a bow, ready bent, of the ancient Scythian form, lies by him.[2] On his head is a large loose cap, tied under his chin, which I take to be the lion's skin, worn in the same manner as on the heads of Hercules, upon the medals of Alexander; but the work is so small, though executed with extreme nicety and precision, and perfectly preserved, that it is difficult to decide with certainty what it represents, in parts of such minuteness. The bow and arrows, we know, were the ancient arms of Hercules;[3] and continued so, until the Greek poets thought proper to give him the club.[4] He was particularly worshipped at Tyre, the metropolis of Phœnicia;[5] and his head appears in the

[1] See Plate ɪɪ. Fig. 1, and Plate ɪɪɪ. Fig. 2.
[2] See Plate ɪx. Fig. 10 *b*.
[3] Homer's *Odyss.* Λ, ver. 606.
[4] Strabo, lib. xiv.
[5] Macrob. *Sat.* lib. i. c. 20.

usual form, on many of the coins of that people. We may hence conclude that he is the person here represented, notwithstanding the difference in the style and composition of the figure, which may be accounted for by the difference of art. The Greeks, animated by the spirit of their ancient poets, and the glowing melody of their language, were grand and poetical in all their compositions; whilst the Phœnicians, who spoke a harsh and untuneable dialect, were unacquainted with fine poetry, and consequently with poetical ideas; for words being the types of ideas, and the signs or marks by which men not only communicate them to each other, but arrange and regulate them in their own minds, the genius of a language goes a great way towards forming the character of the people who use it. Poverty of expression will produce poverty of conception; for men will never be able to form sublime ideas, when the language in which they *think* (for men always think as well as speak in some language) is incapable of expressing them. This may be one reason why the Phœnicians never rivalled the Greeks in the perfection of art, although they attained a degree of excellence long before them; for Homer, whenever he has occasion to speak of any fine piece of art, takes care to inform us that it was the work of Sidonians. He also mentions the Phœnician merchants bringing toys and ornaments of dress to sell to the Greeks, and practicing those frauds which merchants and factors are apt to practice upon ignorant people.[1] It is probable that their progress in the fine arts, like that of the Dutch (who are the Phœnicians of modern history), never went beyond a strict imitation of nature; which, compared to the more elevated graces of ideal composition, is like a newspaper narrative compared with one of Homer's battles. A figure of Hercules, therefore, executed by a Phœnician artist, if compared to one by Phidias or Lysippus, would be like a picture of Moses or David, painted by Teniers, or Gerard Dow, compared to one of the same, painted by Raphael or Annibal Caracci. This is exactly the difference between the figures on the medal now under consideration, and those on the coins of Gelo or Alexander. Of all the personages of the ancient mythology, Hercules is perhaps the most difficult to explain; for physical allegory and fabulous history are so entangled in the accounts we have of him, that it is scarcely possible to separate them. He appears however, like all the other gods, to have been originally a personified attribute of the sun. The eleventh of the Orphic Hymns [2] is addressed to

[1] Homer. *Odyss. 0*, ver. 414.
[2] *Ed. Gesner.*

him as the strength and power of the sun; and Macrobius says that he was thought to be the strength and virtue of the gods, by which they destroyed the giants; and that, according to Varro, the Mars and Hercules of the Romans were the same deity, and worshipped with the same rites.[1] According to Varro then, whose authority is perhaps the greatest that can be cited, Hercules was the destroying attribute represented in a human form, instead of that of a lion, tiger, or hippopotamus. Hence the terrible picture drawn of him by Homer, which always appeared to me to have been taken from some symbolical statue, which the poet not understanding, supposed to be of the Theban hero, who had assumed the title of the deity, and whose fabulous history he was well acquainted with. The description however applies in every particular to the allegorical personage. His attitude, ever fixed in the act of letting fly his arrow,[2] with the figures of lions and bears, battles and murders, which adorn his belt, all unite in representing him as the destructive attribute personified. But how happens it then that he is so frequently represented strangling the lion, the natural emblem of this power? Is this an historical fable belonging to the

[1] *Sat.* lib. i. c. 20.

[2] Αιει Βαλεοντι ἐοικως. *Odyss.* λ, ver. 607.

Theban hero, or a physical allegory of the destructive power destroying its own force by its own exertions? Or is the single attribute personified taken for the whole power of the deity in this, as in other instances already mentioned? The Orphic Hymn above cited seems to favour this last conjecture; for he is there addressed both as the devourer and generator of all (Παμφαγε, παγγενετωζ). However this may be, we may safely conclude that the Hercules armed with the bow and arrow, as he appears on the present medal, is like the Apollo, the destroying power of the diurnal sun.

On the other side of the medal [1] is a figure, somewhat like the Jupiter on the medals of Alexander and Antiochus, sitting with a beaded sceptre in his right hand, which he rests upon the head of a bull, that projects from the side of the chair. Above, on his right shoulder, is a bird, probably a dove, the symbol of the Holy Spirit, descending from the sun, but, as this part of the medal is less perfect than the rest, the species cannot be clearly discovered. In his left hand he holds a short staff, from the upper side of which springs an ear of corn, and from the lower a bunch of grapes, which being the two most esteemed productions of the earth, were the natural emblems

[1] See Plate ix. Fig. 10 *a.*

of general fertilization. This figure is therefore the generator, as that on the other side is the destroyer, whilst the sun, of whose attributes both are personifications, is placed between them. The letters on the side of the generator are quite entire, and, according to the Phœnician alphabet published by Mr. Dutens, are equivalent to the Roman ones which compose the words *Baal Thrz,* of which Mr. Swinton makes *Baal Tarz,* and translates *Jupiter of Tarsus;* whence he concludes that this coin was struck at that city. But the first letter of the last word is not a *Teth,* but a *Thau,* or aspirated T; and, as the Phœnicians had a vowel answering to the Roman A, it is probable they would have inserted it, had they intended it to be sounded: but we have no reason to believe that they had any to express the U or Y, which must therefore be comprehended in the preceding consonant whenever the sound is expressed. Hence I conclude that the word here meant is *Thyrz* or *Thurz,* the *Thor* or *Thur* of the Celtes and Sarmatians, the *Thurra* of the Assyrians, the *Turan* of the Tyrrhenians or Etruscans, the *Taurine Bacchus* of the Greeks, and the deity whom the Germans carried with them in the shape of a bull, when they invaded Italy; from whom the city of Tyre, as well as Tyrrhenia, or Tuscany, probably took its name. His symbol the bull, to which the name alludes, is represented on the chair or throne in which he sits; and his sceptre, the emblem of his authority, rests upon it. The other word, *Baal,* was merely a title in the Phœnician language, signifying *God, or Lord;* [1] and used as an epithet of the sun, as we learn from the name Baal-bec (*the city of Baal*), which the Greeks rendered Heliopolis (*the city of the sun*).

Thus does this singular medal show the fundamental principles of the ancient Phœnician religion to be the same as those which appear to have prevailed through all the other nations of the northern hemisphere. Fragments of the same system every where occur, variously expressed as they were variously understood, and oftentimes merely preserved without being understood at all; the ancient reverence being continued to the symbols, when their meaning was wholly forgotten. The *hypostatical* division and *essential* unity of the deity is one of the most remarkable parts of this system, and the farthest removed from common sense and reason; and yet this is perfectly reasonable and consistent, if considered together with the rest of it: for the emanations and personifications were only figurative abstractions of particular modes of action and existence, of which the primary cause and original essence still continued one and the same

[1] *Cleric. Comm. in* 2 *Reg.* c. i. ver. 2.

The three hypostases being thus only one being, each hypostasis is occasionally taken for all; as is the case in the passage of Apuleius before cited, where Isis describes herself as the universal deity. In this character she is represented by a small basaltine figure, of Egyptian sculpture, at Strawberry Hill, which is covered over with symbols of various kinds from top to bottom.[1] That of the bull is placed lowest, to show that the strength or power of the creator is the foundation and support of every other attribute. On her head are towers, to denote the earth; and round her neck is hung a crab-fish, which, from its power of spontaneously detaching from its body, and naturally reproducing, any limbs that are hurt or mutilated, became the symbol of the productive power of the waters; in which sense it appears on great numbers of ancient medals of various cities.[2] The nutritive power is signified by her many breasts, and the destructive by the lions which she bears on her arms. Other attributes are expressed by various

[1] A print of one exactly the same is published by Montfaucon, *Antiq. expliq.* vol. i. Plate xciii. Fig. i.

[2] See those of Agrigentum, Himera, and Cyrene. On a small one of the first-mentioned city, belonging to me, a cross, the abbreviated symbol of the male powers of generation, approaches the mouth of the crab, while the cornucopia issues from it (see Plate xx. Fig. 3): the one represents the cause, and the other the effect of fertilization.

other animal symbols, the precise meaning of which I have not sagacity sufficient to discover.

This universality of the goddess was more concisely represented in other figures of her, by the mystic instrument called a *Systrum*, which she carried in her hand. Plutarch has given an explanation of it,[1] which may serve to show that the mode here adopted of explaining the ancient symbols is not founded merely upon conjecture and analogy, but also upon the authority of one of the most grave and learned of the Greeks. The curved top, he says, represented the lunar orbit, within which the creative attributes of the deity were exerted, in giving motion to the four elements, signified by the four rattles below.[2] On the centre of the curve was a cat, the emblem of the moon; who, from her influence on the constitutions of women, was supposed to preside particularly over the passive powers of generation;[3] and below, upon the base, a head of Isis or Nepthus; instead of which, upon that which I have had engraved, as well as upon many others now extant, are the male organs of generation, representing the active powers of the creator, attributed to Isis with the

---

[1] *De Is. & Os.*

[2] See Plate x. Fig. 4, engraved from one in the collection of R. Wilbraham, Esq.

[3] Cic. *de Nat. Deor.* lib. ii. c. 46.

passive. The clattering noise, and various motions of the rattles being adopted as the symbols of the movement and mixture of the elements from which all things are produced; the sound of metals in general became an emblem of the same kind. Hence, the ringing of bells, and clattering of plates of metal, were used in all lustrations, sacrifices, &c.[1] The title Priapus, applied to the characteristic attribute of the creator, and sometimes to the Creator himself, is probably a corruption of Βριαπυοε (clamorous or loud); for the B and Π being both labials, the change of the one for the other is common in the Greek language. We still find many ancient images of this symbol, with bells attached to them,[2] as they were to the sacred robe of the high priest of the Jews, in which he administered to the Creator.[3] The bells in both were of a pyramidal form,[4] to shew the ætherial igneous essence of the god. This form is still retained in those used in our churches, as well as in the little ones rung by the Catholic priests at the elevation of the host. The use of them was early adopted by the Christians, in the same sense as they were employed

---

[1] Clem. Alex. Προτζ. p. 9. *Schol in Theocrit.* Idyll. ||. ver. 36.

[2] *Bronzi dell' Hercol. Tom.* vi. Plate xcviii.

[3] *Exod.* ch. xxviii.

[4] Bronzi dell' Hercol. Tom. vi. Plate xcviii. Maimonides in Patrick's *Commentary on Exodus*, ch. xxviii.

by the later heathens; that is, as, a charm against evil dæmons; [1] for, being symbols of the active exertions of the creative attributes, they were properly opposed to the emanations of the destructive. The Lacedemonians used to beat a pan or kettle-drum at the death of their king,[2] to assist in the emancipation of his soul at the dissolution of the body. We have a similar custom of tolling a bell on such occasions, which is very generally practised, though the meaning of it has been long forgotten. This emancipation of the soul was supposed to be finally performed by fire; which, being the visible image and active essence of both the creative and destructive powers, was very naturally thought to be the medium through which men passed from the present to a future life. The Greeks, and all the Celtic nations, accordingly, burned the bodies of the dead, as the Gentoos do at this day; while the Egyptians, among whom fuel was extremely scarce, placed them in pyramidal monuments, which were the symbols of fire; hence come those prodigious structures which still adorn that country. The soul which was to be emancipated was the divine emanation, the vital spark of heavenly flame, the principle of reason and perception, which

[1] Ovid. *Fast.* lib. v. ver. 441. *Schol. in* Theocrit Idyll. ii. ver. 36.

[2] *Schol. in* Theocrit. Idyll. ii. ver. 36.

was personified into the familiar dæmon, or genius,
supposed to have the direction of each individual,
and to dispose him to good or evil, wisdom or folly,
and all their consequences of prosperity and adver-
sity.[1]   Hence proceeded the doctrines, so uniformly
inculcated by Homer and Pindar,[2] of all human actions depending immediately upon the gods; which
were adopted, with scarcely any variations, by some
of the Christian divines of the apostolic age.   In the
Pastor of Hermas, and Recognitions of Clemens, we
find the angels of justice, penitence, and sorrow, instead of the genii, or dæmons, which the ancients
supposed to direct men's minds and inspire them
with those particular sentiments.   St. Paul adopted
the still more comfortable doctrine of grace, which
served full as well to emancipate the consciences of
the faithful from the shackles of practical morality.
The familiar dæmons, or divine emanations, were
supposed to reside in the blood; which was thought
to contain the principles of vital heat, and was therefore forbidden by Moses.[3]   Homer, who seems to have

[1] Pindar. *Pyth.* v. ver. 164.   Sophocl. *Trachin.* ver. 922.   Hor.
lib. ii. epist. ii. ver. 187.

[2] Εκ Θεων μαχαναι ηγσαι Βροτεαις αρεταις, και σοφοι, και
χερσι Βιαται, περιγλωσσοι τ' εφ Ιν. Pindar *Pyth.* i. ver. 79
Passages to the same purpose occur in almost every page of the
Iliad and *Odyssey.*

[3] *Levit.* ch. xvii. ver. 11 & 14.

collected little fragments of the ancient theology, and introduced them here and there, amidst the wild profusion of his poetical fables, represents the shades of the deceased as void of perception, until they had tasted of the blood of the victims offered by Ulysses; [1] by which their faculties were renewed by a reunion with the divine emanation, from which they had been separated. The soul of Tiresias is said to be entire in hell, and to possess alone the power of perception, because with him this divine emanation still remained. The shade of Hercules is described among the other ghosts, though he himself, as the poet says, was then in heaven; that is, the active principle of thought and perception returned to its native heaven, whilst the passive, or merely sensitive, remained on earth, from whence it sprung.[2] The final separation of these two did not take place till the body was consumed by fire, as appears from the ghost of Elpenor, whose body being still entire, he retained both, and knew Ulysses before he had tasted of the blood. It was from producing this separation, that the universal Bacchus, or double Apollo, the creator and destroyer, whose essence was fire, was

[1] *Odyss.* ζ, ver. 152.
[2] Those who wish to see the difference between sensation and perception clearly and fully explained, may be satisfied by reading the *Essai analytique sur l'Ame*, by Mr. Bonnet.

also called Λιχνιτης, the purifier,[1] by a metaphor taken from the winnow, which purified the corn from the dust and chaff, as fire purified the soul from its terrestrial pollutions. Hence this instrument is called by Virgil the mystic winnow of Bacchus.[2] The Ammonian Platonics and Gnostic Christians thought that this separation, or purification, might be effected in a degree even before death. It was for this purpose that they practised such rigid temperance, and gave themselves up to such intense study; for, by subduing and extenuating the terrestrial principle, they hoped to give liberty and vigour to the celestial, so that it might be enabled to ascend directly to the intellectual world, pure and unincumbered.[3] The clergy afterwards introduced Purgatory, instead of abstract meditation and study; which was the ancient mode of separation by fire, removed into an unknown country, where it was saleable to all such of the inhabitants of this world as had sufficient wealth and credulity.

It was the celestial or ætherial principle of the human mind, which the ancient artists represented under the symbol of the butterfly, which may be

[1] *Orph. Hymn.* 45.

[2] *Mystica vannus Iacchi.* Georg. i. ver. 166.

[3] Plotin. *Ennead.* vi. lib. iv. ch. 16. Mosheim, *Not y in* Cudw. *Syst. Intell.* ch. v. sect. 20.

considered as one of the most elegant allegories of their elegant religion. This insect, when hatched from the egg, appears in the shape of a grub, crawling upon the earth, and feeding upon the leaves of plants. In this state, it was aptly made the emblem of man, in his earthly form, in which the ætherial vigour and activity of the celestial soul, the *divine particula mentis,* was supposed to be clogged and incumbered with the material body. When the grub was changed to a chrysalis, its stillness, torpor, and insensibility seemed to present a natural image of death, or the intermediate state between the cessation of the vital functions of the body and the final releasement of the soul by the fire, in which the body was consumed. The butterfly breaking from the torpid chrysalis, and mounting in the air, was no less natural an image of the celestial soul bursting from the restraints of matter, and mixing again with its native æther. The Greek artists, always studious of elegance, changed this, as well as other animal symbols, into a human form, retaining the wings as the characteristic members, by which the meaning might be known. The human body, which they added to them, is that of a beautiful girl, sometimes in the age of infancy, and sometimes of approaching maturity. So beautiful an allegory as this would naturally be a favourite subject of art among a people whose taste had attained the utmost pitch of refinement. We accordingly find that it has been more frequently and more variously repeated than any other which the system of emanations, so favourable to art, could afford.

Although all men were supposed to partake of the divine emanation in a degree, it was not supposed that they all partook of it in an equal degree. Those who showed superior abilities, and distinguished themselves by their splendid actions, were supposed to have a larger share of the divine essence, and were therefore adored as gods, and honoured with divine titles, expressive of that particular attribute of the deity with which they seemed to be most favoured. New personages were thus enrolled among the allegorical deities; and the personified attributes of the sun were confounded with a Cretan and Thessalian king, an Asiatic conqueror, and a Theban robber. Hence Pindar, who appears to have been a very orthodox heathen, says, that the race of men and gods is one, that both breathe from one mother, and only differ in power.[1] This confusion of epithets and titles contributed, as much as any thing, to raise that vast and extravagant fabric of poetical mythology, which, in a manner, overwhelmed the ancient the-

[1] *Nem.* v. ver. i.

ology, which was too pure and philosophical to continue long a popular religion. The grand and exalted system of a general first cause, universally expanded, did not suit the gross conceptions of the multitude; who had no other way of conceiving the idea of an omnipotent god, but by forming an exaggerated image of their own despot, and supposing his power to consist in an unlimited gratification of his passions and appetites. Hence the universal Jupiter, the aweful and venerable, the general principle of life and motion, was transformed into the god who thundered from Mount Ida, and was lulled to sleep in the embraces of his wife; and hence the god whose spirit moved [1] upon the face of the waters, and impregnated them with the powers of generation, became a great king above all gods, who led forth his people to smite the ungodly, and rooted out their enemies from before them.

Another great means of corrupting the ancient theology, and establishing the poetical mythology, was the practice of the artists in representing the various attributes of the creator under human forms of various character and expression. These figures, being

[1] So the translators have rendered the expression of the original, which literally means brooding as a fowl on its eggs, and alludes to the symbols of the ancient theology, which I have before observed upon. See Patrick's *Commentary*.

distinguished by the titles of the deity which they were meant to represent, became in time to be considered as distinct personages, and worshipped as separate subordinate deities. Hence the many-shaped god, the πολυμορφος and μυριομορφος of the ancient theologists, became divided into many gods and goddesses, often described by the poets as at variance with each other and wrangling about the little intrigues and passions of men. Hence too, as the symbols were multiplied, particular ones lost their dignity; and that venerable one which is the subject of this discourse, became degraded from the representative of the god of nature to a subordinate rural deity, a supposed son of the Asiatic conqueror Bacchus, standing among the nymphs by a fountain,[1] and expressing the fertility of a garden, instead of the general creative power of the great active principle of the universe. His degradation did not stop even here; for we find him, in times still more prophane and corrupt, made a subject of raillery and insult, as answering no better purpose than holding up his rubicund snout to frighten the birds and thieves.[2] His talents were also perverted from their natural ends, and employed in base and abortive efforts in con-

[1] Theocrit. Idyll. i. ver. 21.
[2] Horat. lib. i. Sat. viii. Virg. *Georg.* iv.

formity to the taste of the times; for men naturally attribute their own passions and inclinations to the objects of their adoration; and as God made man in his own image, so man returns the favour, and makes God in his. Hence we find the highest attribute of the all-pervading spirit and first-begotten love foully prostituted to promiscuous vice, and calling out, *Hæc cunnum, caput hic, præbeat ille nates.*[1]

He continued however still to have his temple, priestess and sacred geese,[2] and offerings of the most exquisite kind were made to him:

> Crissabitque tibi excussis pulcherrima lumbis
> Hoc anno primum experta puella virum.

Sometimes, however, they were not so scrupulous in the selection of their victims, but suffered frugality to restrain their devotion:

> Cum sacrum fieret Deo salaci
> Conducta est pretio puella parvo.[3]

The bride was usually placed upon him immediately before marriage; not, as Lactantius says, *ut ejus pudicitiam prior Deus prælibasse videatur,* but that she might be rendered fruitful by her communion with the divine nature, and capable of fulfilling the

[1] Priap. Carm. 21.
[2] Petron. *Satyric.*
[3] Priap. Carm. 34.

duties of her station. In an ancient poem [1] we find a lady of the name of Lalage presenting the pictures of the "Elephantis" to him, and gravely requesting that she might enjoy the pleasures over which he particularly presided, in all the attitudes described in that celebrated treatise.[2] Whether or not she succeeded, the poet has not informed us; but we may safely conclude that she did not trust wholly to faith and prayer, but, contrary to the usual practice of modern devotees, accompanied her devotion with such good works as were likely to contribute to the end proposed by it.

When a lady had served as the victim in a sacrifice to this god, she expressed her gratitude for the benefits received, by offering upon his altar certain small images representing his characteristic attribute, the number of which was equal to the number of men who had acted as priests upon the occasion.[3] On an antique gem, in the collection of Mr. Townley, is one of these fair victims, who appears just returned from a sacrifice of this kind, and devoutly returning her thanks by offering upon an altar some of these images, from the number of which one may observe

[1] Priap. Carm. 3.

[2] The *Elephantis* was written by one Philænis, and seems to have been of the same kind with the *Puttana errante* of Aretin.

[3] Priap. Carm. 34. *Ed. Scioppii.*

that she has not been neglected.[1] This offering of thanks had also its mystic and allegorical meaning; for fire being the energetic principle and essential force of the Creator, and the symbol above mentioned the visible image of his characteristic attribute, the uniting them was uniting the material with the essential cause, from whose joint operation all things were supposed to proceed.

These sacrifices, as well as all those to the deities presiding over generation, were performed by night: hence Hippolytus, in Euripides, says, to express his love of chastity, that he likes none of the gods revered by night.[2] These acts of devotion were indeed attended with such rites as must naturally shock the prejudices of a chaste and temperate mind, not liable to be warmed by that ecstatic enthusiasm which is peculiar to devout persons when their attention is absorbed in the contemplation of the beneficent powers of the Creator, and all their faculties directed to imitate him in the exertion of his great characteristic attribute. To heighten this enthusiasm, the male and female saints of antiquity used to lie promiscuously together in the temples, and honour God by a liberal display and general communication of his bounties.[3]

[1] See Plate III. Fig. 3.
[2] Ver. 613.
[3] Herodot. lib. ii.

Herodotus, indeed, excepts the Greeks and Egyptians, and Dionysius of Halicarnassus, the Romans, from this general custom of other nations; but to the testimony of the former we may oppose the thousand sacred prostitutes kept at each of the temples of Corinth and Eryx; [1] and to that of the latter the express words of Juvenal, who, though he lived an age, later, lived when the same religion, and nearly the same manners, prevailed.[2]   Diodorus Siculus also tells us, that when the Roman prætors visited Eryx, they laid aside their magisterial severity, and honoured the goddess by mixing with her votaries, and indulging themselves in the pleasures over which she presided.[3]   It appears, too, that the act of generation was a sort of sacrament in the island of Lesbos; for the device on its medals (which in the Greek republics had always some relation to religion) is as explicit as forms can make it.[4]   The figures appear indeed to be mystic and allegorical, the male having evidently a mixture of the goat in his beard and features, and therefore probably represents Pan, the generative power of the universe incorporated in universal matter. The female has all that breadth and

[1] Strab. lib. viii.
[2] *Sat.* ix. ver. 24.
[3] Lib. iv. *Ed. Wessel.*
[4] See Plate ix. Fig. 8, from one belonging to me.

fulness which characterise the personification of the passive power, known by the titles of Rhea, Juno, Ceres, &c.

When there were such seminaries for female education as those of Eryx and Corinth, we need not wonder that the ladies of antiquity should be extremely well instructed in all the practical duties of their religion. The stories told of Julia and Messalina show us that the Roman ladies were no ways deficient; and yet they were as remarkable for their gravity and decency as the Corinthians were for their skill and dexterity in adapting themselves to all the modes and attitudes which the luxuriant imaginations of experienced votaries have contrived for performing the rites of their tutelar goddess.[1]

The reason why these rites were always performed by night was the peculiar sanctity attributed to it by the ancients, because dreams were then supposed to descend from heaven to instruct and forewarn men. The nights, says Hesiod, belong to the blessed gods; [2] and the Orphic poet calls night the source of all things (παντων γενεσις) to denote that productive power, which, as I have been told, it really possesses; it being observed that plants and animals grow more

[1] Philodemi *Epigr. Brunk. Analect.* vol. ii. p. 85.
[2] Εργ· ver. 730.

by night than by day. The ancients extended this power much further, and supposed that not only the productions of the earth, but the luminaries of heaven, were nourished and sustained by the benign influence of the night. Hence that beautiful apostrophe in the "Electra" of Euripides, Ω νὺξ μέλαινα, χυσεων αστρων τροφε, &c.

Not only the sacrifices to the generative deities, but in general all the religious rites of the Greeks, were of the festive kind. To imitate the gods, was, in their opinion, to feast and rejoice, and to cultivate the useful and elegant arts, by which we are made partakers of their felicity.[1] This was the case with almost all the nations of antiquity, except the [2] Egyptians and their reformed imitators the Jews,[3] who being governed by a hierarchy, endeavoured to make it awful and venerable to the people by an appearance of rigour and austerity. The people, however, sometimes broke through this restraint, and indulged themselves in the more pleasing worship of their neighbours, as when they danced and feasted before the golden calf which Aaron erected,[4] and devoted themselves to the worship of obscene idols, generally

[1] Strabo, lib. x.
[2] Herodot. lib. ii.
[3] See Spencer de Leg. Rit. Vet. Hebræor.
[4] Exod. ch. xxxii.

supposed to be of Priapus, under the reign of Abijam.[1]

The Christian religion, being a reformation of the Jewish, rather increased than diminished the austerity of its original. On particular occasions however it equally abated its rigour, and gave way to festivity and mirth, though always with an air of sanctity and solemnity. Such were originally the feasts of the Eucharist, which, as the word expresses, were meetings of joy and gratulation; though, as divines tell us, all of the spiritual kind: but the particular manner in which St. Augustine commands the ladies who attended them to wear clean linen,[2] seems to infer, that personal as well as spiritual matters were thought worthy of attention. To those who administer the sacrament in the modern way, it may appear of little consequence whether the women received it in clean linen or not; but to the good bishop, who was to administer the *holy kiss,* it certainly was of some importance. The *holy kiss* was not only applied as a part of the ceremonial of the Eucharist, but also of prayer, at the conclusion of which they welcomed each other with this natural sign of love and benevolence.[3] It was upon these occasions that

[1] *Reg.* c. xv. ver. 13 *Ed. Cleric.*
[2] Aug. *Serm.* clii.
[3] Justin Martyr. *Apolog.*

they worked themselves up to those fits of rapture and enthusiasm, which made them eagerly rush upon destruction in the fury of their zeal to obtain the crown of martyrdom.[1] Enthusiasm on one subject naturally produces enthusiasm on another; for the human passions, like the strings of an instrument, vibrate to the motions of each other: hence paroxysms of love and devotion have oftentimes so exactly accorded, as not to have been distinguished by the very persons whom they agitated.[2] This was too often the case in these meetings of the primitive Christians. The feasts of gratulation and love, the αγαπαι and nocturnal vigils, gave too flattering opportunities to the passions and appetites of men, to continue long, what we are told they were at first, pure exercises of devotion. The spiritual raptures and divine ecstasies encouraged on these occasions, were often ecstasies of a very different kind, concealed under the garb of devotion; whence the greatest irregularities ensued; and it became necessary for the reputation of the church, that they should be suppressed, as they afterwards were by the decrees of several councils. Their suppression may be considered as the final subversion of that part of the ancient re-

---

[1] Martini Kempii *de Osculis Dissert.* viii.

[2] See *Procès de la Cadiere.*

ligion which I have here undertaken to examine; for so long as those nocturnal meetings were preserved, it certainly existed, though under other names, and in a more solemn dress. The small remain of it preserved at Isernia, of which an account has here been given, can scarcely be deemed an exception; for its meaning was unknown to those who celebrated it; and the obscurity of the place, added to the venerable names of S. Cosimo and Damiano, was all that prevented it from being suppressed long ago, as it has been lately, to the great dismay of the chaste matrons and pious monks of Isernia. Traces and memorials of it seem however to have been preserved, in many parts of Christendom, long after the actual celebration of its rites ceased. Hence the obscene figures observable upon many of our Gothic Cathedrals, and particularly upon the ancient brass doors of St. Peter's at Rome, where there are some groups which rival the devices on the Lesbian medals.

It is curious, in looking back through the annals of superstition, so degrading to the pride of man, to trace the progress of the human mind in different ages, climates, and circumstances, uniformly acting upon the same principles, and to the same ends. The sketch here given of the corruptions of the religion of Greece, is an exact counterpart of the history of the corruptions of Christianity, which began in the pure theism of the eclectic Jews,[1] and by the help of inspirations, emanations, and canonizations, expanded itself, by degrees, to the vast and unwieldly system which now fills the creed of what is commonly called the Catholic Church. In the ancient religion, however, the emanations assumed the appearance of moral virtues and physical attributes, instead of ministering spirits and guardian angels; and the canonizations or deifications were bestowed upon heroes, legislators, and monarchs, instead of priests, monks, and martyrs. There is also this further difference, that among the moderns philosophy has improved, as religion has been corrupted; whereas, among the ancients, religion and philosophy declined together. The true solar system was taught in the Orphic school, and adopted by the Pythagoreans, the next regularly-established sect. The Stoics corrupted it a little, by placing the earth in the centre of the universe, though they still allowed the sun its superior magnitude.[2] At length arose the Epicureans, who confounded it entirely, maintaining that the sun was only a small globe of fire, a few inches in di-

[1] Compare the doctrines of Philo with those taught in the Gospel of St. John, and Epistles of St. Paul.

[2] Brucker, *Hist. Crit. Philos.* p. ii. lib. ii. c. 9. s. 1.

PLATE XXIII
TIGER AT THE BREAST OF A NYMPH

ameter, and the stars little transitory lights, whirled about in the atmosphere of the earth.[1]

How ill soever adapted the ancient system of emanations was to procure eternal happiness, it was certainly extremely well calculated to produce temporal good; for, by the endless multiplication of subordinate deities, it effectually excluded two of the greatest curses that ever afflicted the human race, dogmatical theology, and its consequent religious persecution. Far from supposing that the gods known in their own country were the only ones existing, the Greeks thought that innumerable emanations of the divine mind were diffused through every part of the universe; so that new objects of devotion presented themselves wherever they went. Every mountain, spring, and river, had its tutelary deity, besides the numbers of immortal spirits that were supposed to wander in the air, scattering dreams and visions, and superintending the affairs of men.

Τρις γαζ μυριοι εισιν επι χθονι πουλϋβοτειρη
Αθανατοι Ζηνος, φυλακες θνητων ανθρωπων.[2]

An adequate knowledge of these they never presumed to think attainable, but modestly contented

[1] Lucret. lib. v. 565, & seq.

[2] Hesiod. Εργα και 'Ημερ. ver. 252, μυριοι, &c., are always used as the ancient Greek poets.

themselves with revering and invoking them whenever they felt or wanted their assistance. When a
shipwrecked mariner was cast upon an unknown
coast, he immediately offered up his prayers to the
gods of the country, whoever they were; and joined
the inhabitants in whatever rites they thought proper
to propitiate them with.[1] Impious or prophane rites
he never imagined could exist, concluding that all
expressions of gratitude and submission must be
pleasing to the gods. Atheism was, indeed, punished
at Athens, as the obscene ceremonies of the Baccha-
nalians were at Rome; but both as civil crimes
against the state; the one tending to weaken the
bands of society by destroying the sanctity of oaths,
and the other to subvert that decency and gravity of
manners, upon which the Romans so much prided
themselves. The introduction of strange gods, without permission from the magistrate, was also pro-
hibited in both cities; but the restriction extended no
farther than the walls, there being no other parts of
the Roman empire, except Judea, in which any kind
of impiety or extravagance might not have been maintained with impunity, provided it was maintained
merely as a speculative opinion, and not employed as

[1] See Homer. *Odyss.* ε, ver. 445, & seq. The Greeks seem to
have adopted by degrees into their own ritual all the rites practised in the neighbouring countries.

an engine of faction, ambition, or oppression. The Romans even carried their condescension so far as to enforce the observance of a dogmatical religion, where they found it before established; as appears from the conduct of their magistrates in Judea, relative to Christ and his apostles; and from what Josephus has related, of a Roman soldier's being punished with death by his commander for insulting the Books of Moses. Upon what principle then did they act, when they afterwards persecuted the Christians with so much rancour and cruelty? Perhaps it may surprise persons not used to the study of ecclesiastical antiquities, to be told (what is nevertheless indisputably true) that the Christians were never persecuted on account of the speculative opinions of individuals, but either for civil crimes laid to their charge, or for withdrawing their allegiance from the state, and joining in a federative union dangerous by its constitution, and rendered still more dangerous by the intolerant principles of its members, who often tumultuously interrupted the public worship, and continually railed against the national religion (with which both the civil government and military discipline of the Romans were inseparably connected), as the certain means of eternal damnation. To break this union, was the great object of Roman policy during a long course of years; but the violent means employed only tended to cement it closer. Some of the Christians themselves indeed, who were addicted to Platonism, took a safer method to dissolve it; but they were too few in number to succeed. This was by trying to moderate the furious zeal which gave life and vigour to the confederacy, and to blend and soften the unyielding temper of religion with the mild spirit of philosophy. "We all," said they, "agree in worshipping one supreme God, the Father and Preserver of all. While we approach him with purity of mind, sincerity of heart, and innocence of manners, forms and ceremonies of worship are indifferent; and not less worthy of his greatness, for being varied and diversified according to the various customs and opinions of men. Had it been his will that all should have worshipped him in the same mode, he would have given to all the same inclinations and conceptions: but he has wisely ordered it otherwise, that piety and virtue might increase by an honest emulation of religions, as industry in trade, or activity in a race, from the mutual emulation of the candidates for wealth and honour."[1] This was too liberal and extensive a plan, to meet the approbation of a greedy and ambitious clergy, whose object was to establish a hierarchy for themselves,

[1] Symmach. *Ep.* 10 & 61.   Themist. *Orat ad Imperat.*

rather than to procure happiness for others. It was accordingly condemned with vehemence and success by Ambrosius, Prudentius, and other orthodox leaders of the age.

It was from the ancient system of emanations, that the general hospitality which characterised the manners of the heroic ages, and which is so beautifully represented in the *Odyssey* of Homer, in a great measure arose. The poor, and the stranger who wandered in the street and begged at the door, were supposed to be animated by a portion of the same divine spirit which sustained the great and powerful. *They are all from Jupiter,* says Homer, *and a small gift is acceptable.*[1] This benevolent sentiment has been compared by the English commentators to that of the Jewish moralist, who says, *that he who giveth to the poor lendeth to the Lord, who will repay him tenfold.*[2] But it is scarcely possible for anything to be more different: Homer promises no other reward for charity than the benevolence of the action itself; but the Israelite holds out that which has always been the great motive for charity among his countrymen— the prospect of being repaid ten-fold. They are always ready to show their bounty upon such incen-

[1] *Odyss.* ζ, ver. 207.
[2] See Pope's *Odyssey.*

tives, if they can be persuaded that they are founded upon good security. It was the opinion, however, of many of the most learned among the ancients, that the principles of the Jewish religion were originally the same as those of the Greek, and that their God was no other than the creator and generator Bacchus,[1] who, being viewed through the gloomy medium of the hierarchy, appeared to them a jealous and irascible God; and so gave a more austere and unsociable form to their devotion. The golden vine preserved in the temple at Jerusalem,[2] and the taurine forms of the cherubs, between which the Deity was supposed to reside, were symbols so exactly similar to their own, that they naturally concluded them meant to express the same ideas; especially as there was nothing in the avowed principles of the Jewish worship to which they could be applied. The ineffable name also, which, according to the Massorethic punctuation, is pronounced *Jehovah,* was anciently pronounced *Jaho,* Ιαω, or Ιευω,[3] which was a title of Bacchus, the nocturnal sun;[4] as was

[1] Tacit. *Histor.* lib. v.

[2] The vine and goblet of Bacchus are also the usual devices upon the Jewish and Samaritan coins, which were struck under the Asmonean kings.

[3] Hieron. *Comm. in Psalm.* viii. Dioidor. Sic. lib. i. Philo-Bybl. *ap. Euseb. Prep. Evang.* lib. i. c. ix.

[4] Macrob. *Sat.* lib. i. c. xviii.

also *Sabazius*, or *Sabadius*,[1] which is the same word as *Sabbaoth,* one of the scriptural titles of the true God, only adapted to the pronunciation of a more polished language. The Latin name for the Supreme God belongs aiso to the same root; Ιυ-πατηρ, Jupiter, signifying Father Ιευ, though written after the ancient manner, without the dipthong, which was not in use for many ages after the Greek colonies settled in Latium, and introduced the Arcadian alphabet. We find St. Paul likewise acknowledging, that the Jupiter of the poet Aratus was the God whom he adored;[2] and Clemens of Alexandria explains St. Peter's prohibition of worshipping after the manner of the Greeks, not to mean a prohibition of worshipping the same God, but merely of the corrupt mode in which he was then worshipped.[3]

[1] Macrob. *Sat.* lib. i. c. xviii.
[2] *Act. Apost.* c. xvii. ver. 28.
[3] Stramat. lib. v.

THE WORSHIP OF THE
GENERATIVE POWERS

DURING THE MIDDLE AGES
OF WESTERN EUROPE

BY

THOMAS WRIGHT

WITH PLATES

VOLUME II

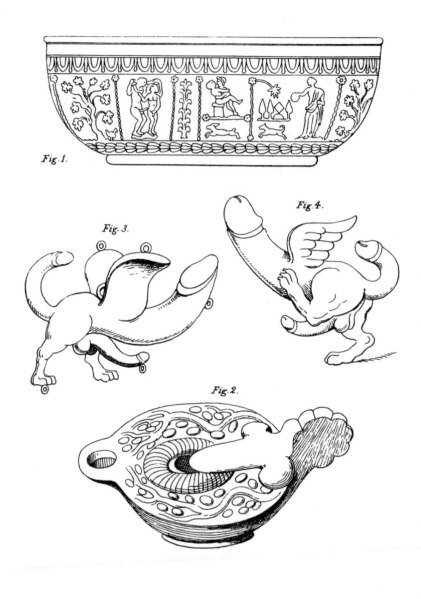

Fig. 1.

Fig. 3.

Fig. 4.

Fig. 2.

PLATE I

EX VOTI OF WAX, FROM ISERNIA

THE WORSHIP OF THE GENERATIVE
POWERS DURING THE MIDDLE AGES
OF WESTERN EUROPE

RICHARD PAYNE KNIGHT has written with great learning on the origin and history of the worship of Priapus among the ancients. This worship, which was but a part of that of the generative powers, appears to have been the most ancient of the superstitions of the human race,[1] has prevailed more or less among all known peoples before the introduction of Christianity, and, singularly enough, so deeply it seems to have been implanted in human nature, that even the promulgation of the Gospel did not abolish it, for it continued to exist, accepted and often encouraged by the mediæval clergy. The occasion of Payne Knight's work was the discovery that

---

[1] There appears to be a chance of this worship being claimed for a very early period in the history of the human race. It has been recently stated in the " Moniteur," that, in the province of Venice, in Italy, excavations in a bone-cave have brought to light, beneath ten feet of stalagmite, bones of animals, mostly postertiary, of the usual description found in such places, flint implements, with a needle of bone having an eye and point, and a plate of an argillaceous compound, on which was scratched a rude drawing of a phallus.—*Moniteur*, Jan. 1865.

---

this worship continued to prevail in his time, in a very remarkable form, at Isernia in the kingdom of Naples, a full description of which will be found in his work. The town of Isernia was destroyed, with a great portion of its inhabitants, in the terrible earthquake which so fearfully devastated the kingdom of Naples on the 26th of July, 1805, nineteen years after the appearance of the book alluded to. Perhaps with it perished the last trace of the worship of Priapus in this particular form; but Payne Knight was not acquainted with the fact that this superstition, in a variety of forms, prevailed throughout Southern and Western Europe largely during the Middle Ages, and that in some parts it is hardly extinct at the present day; and, as its effects were felt to a more considerable extent than people in general suppose in the most intimate and important relations of society, whatever we can do to throw light upon its mediæval existence, though not an agreeable subject, cannot but form an important and valuable contribution to the better knowledge of mediæval history. Many interesting facts relating to this subject were brought together in a volume published in Paris by Monsieur J. A. Dulaure, under the title, *Des Divinités Génératices chez les Anciens et les Modernes,* forming part of an *Histoire Abrégée des dif-*

férens Cultes, by the same author.[1] This book, however, is still very imperfect; and it is the design of the
following pages to give, with the most interesting of
the facts already collected by Dulaure, other facts
and a description and explanation of monuments,
which tend to throw a greater and more general light
on this curious subject.

The mediæval worship of the generative powers,
represented by the generative organs, was derived
from two distinct sources. In the first place, Rome
invariably carried into the provinces she had conquered her own institutions and forms of worship,
and established them permanently. In exploring the
antiquities of these provinces, we are astonished at
the abundant monuments of the worship of Priapus
in all the shapes and with all the attributes and ac-
companiments, with which we are already so well
acquainted in Rome and Italy. Among the remains
of Roman civilization in Gaul, we find statues or
statuettes of Priapus, altars dedicated to him, the
gardens and fields entrusted to his care, and the
phallus, or male member, figured in a variety of
shapes as a protecting power against evil influences
of various kinds. With this idea the well-known
figure was sculptured on the walls of public build-

---

[1] The second edition of this work, published in 1825, is by
much the best, and is considerably enlarged from the first.

ings, placed in conspicuous places in the interior of the house, worn as an ornament by women, and suspended as an amulet to the necks of children. Erotic scenes of the most extravagant description covered vessels of metal, earthenware, and glass, intended, on doubt, for festivals and usages more or less connected with the worship of the principle of fecundity.

At Aix in Provence there was found, on or near the site of the ancient baths, to which it had no doubt some relation, an enormous phallus, encircled with garlands, sculptured in white marble. At Le Chatelet, in Champagne, on the site of a Roman town, a colossal phallus was also found. Similar objects in bronze, and of smaller dimensions, are so common, that explorations are seldom carried on upon a Roman site in which they are not found, and examples of such objects abound in the museums, public or private, of Roman antiquities. The phallic worship appears to have flourished especially at Nemausus, now represented by the city of Nîmes in the south of France, where the symbol of this worship appeared in sculpture on the walls of its amphitheatre and on other buildings, in forms some of which we can hardly help regarding as fanciful, or even playful. Some of the more remarkable of these are figured in our plates, ii and iii.

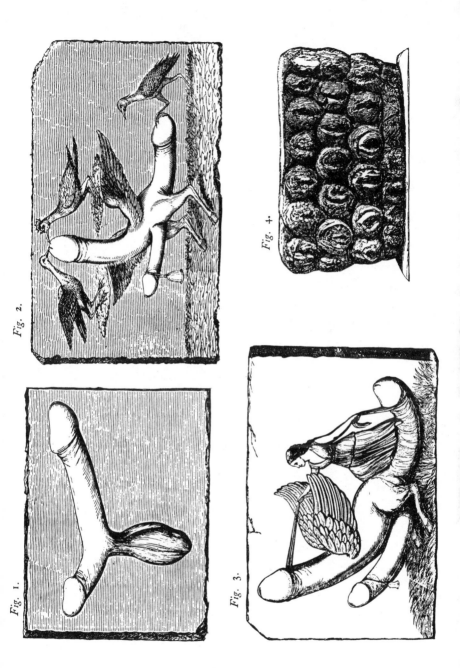

PLATE II
ROMAN SCULPTURES FROM NIMES

The first of these,[1] is the figure of a double phallus. It is sculptured on the lintel of one of the vomitories, or issues, of the second range of seats of the Roman amphitheatre, near the entrance-gate which looks to the south. The double and the triple phallus are very common among the small Roman bronzes, which appear to have served as amulets and for other similar purposes. In the latter, one phallus usually serves as the body, and is furnished with legs, generally those of the goat; a second occupies the usual place of this organ; and a third appears in that of a tail. On a pilaster of the amphitheatre of Nîmes we see a triple phallus of this description,[2] with goat's legs and feet. A small bell is suspended to the smaller phallus in front; and the larger organ which forms the body is furnished with wings. The picture is completed by the introduction of three birds, two of which are pecking the unveiled head of the principal phallus, while the third is holding down the tail with its foot.

Several examples of these triple phalli occur in the *Musée Secret* of the antiquities of Herculaneum and Pompeii. In the examples figured in that work, the hind part of the main phallus assumes clearly

---

[1] Plate II, Fig. 1.
[2] See our Plate II, Fig. 2.

the form of a dog; [1] and to most of them are attached small bells, the explanation of which appears as yet to be very unsatisfactory. The wings also are common attributes of the phallus in these monuments. Plutarch is quoted as an authority for the explanation of the triple phallus as intended to signify multiplication of its productive faculty. [2]

On the top of another pilaster of the amphitheatre at Nîmes, to the right of the principal western entrance, was a bas-relief, also representing a triple phallus, with legs of dog, and winged, but with a further accompaniment. [3] A female, dressed in the Roman stola, stands upon the phallus forming the tail, and holds both it and the one forming the body with a bridle. [4] This bas-relief was taken down in 1829, and is now preserved in the museum of Nîmes.

A still more remarkable monument of this class was found in the course of excavations made at

---

[1] The writer of the text to the *Musée Secret* supposes that this circumstance has some reference to the double meaning given to the Greek word κύων, which was used for the generative organ.

[2] See Auguste Pelet, *Catalogue du Musée de Nîmes.*

[3] Plate II, Fig. 3.

[4] A French antiquary has given an emblematical interpretation of this figure. " Perhaps," he says, " it signifies the empire of woman extending over the three ages of man; on youth, characterized by the bell; on the age of vigour, the ardour of which she restrains; and on old age, which she sustains." This is perhaps more ingenious than convincing.

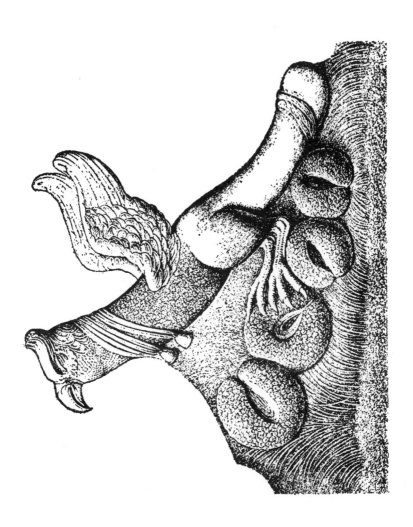

PLATE III

MONUMENT FOUND AT NIMES IN 1825

Nîmes in 1825. It is engraved in our plate xxvi, and represents a bird, apparently intended for a vulture, with spread wings and phallic tail, sitting on four eggs, each of which is designed, no doubt, to represent the female organ. The local antiquarians give to this, as to the other similar objects, an emblematical signification; but it may perhaps be more rightly regarded as a playful conception of the imagination. A similar design, with some modifications, occurs not unfrequently among Gallo-Roman antiquities. We have engraved a figure of the triple phallus governed, or guided, by the female,[1] from a small bronze plate, on which it appears in bas-relief; it is now preserved in a private collection in London, with a duplicate, which appears to have been cast from the same mould, though the plate is cut through, and they were evidently intended for suspension from the neck. Both came from the collection of M. Baudot of Dijon. The lady here bridles only the principal phallus; the legs are, as in the monument last described, those of a bird, and it is standing upon three eggs, apple-formed, and representing the organ of the other sex.

In regard to this last-mentioned object, another very remarkable monument of what appears at Nîmes to have been by no means a secret worship,

---

[1] See our Plate iii, Fig. 3.

was found there during some excavations on the site
of the Roman baths. It is a squared mass of stone,
the four sides of which, like the one represented in
our engraving, are covered with similar figures of
the sexual characteristics of the female, arranged in
rows.[1] It has evidently served as a base, probably to
a statue, or possibly to an altar. This curious monument is now preserved in the museum at Nîmes.

As Nîmes was evidently a centre of this Priapic
worship in the south of Gaul, so there appear to have
been, perhaps lesser, centres in other parts, and we
may trace it to the northern extremities of the Roman
province, even to the other side of the Rhine. On the
site of Roman settlements near Xanten, in lower
Hesse, a large quantity of pottery and other objects
have been found, of a character to leave no doubt as
to the prevalence of this worship in that quarter.[2]
But the Roman settlement which occupied the site of
the modern city of Antwerp appears to have been
one of the most remarkable seats of the worship of

---

[1] See Plate II, Fig. 4.

[2] Two Roman towns, Castra Vetera and Colonia Trajana, stood
within no great distance of Xanten, and Ph. Houben, a "no-
tarius" of this town, formed a private museum of antiquities
found there, and in 1839, published engravings of them, with a
text by Dr. Franz Fiedler. The erotic objects form a separate
work under the title, *Antike erotische Bildwerke in Houbens
Antiquarium zu Xanten.*

Priapus in the north of Gaul, and it continued to exist there till a comparatively modern period.

When we cross over to Britain we find this worship established no less firmly and extensively in that island. Statuettes of Priapus, phallic bronzes, pottery covered with obscene pictures, are found wherever there are any extensive remains of Roman occupation, as our antiquaries know well. The numerous phallic figures in bronze, found in England, are perfectly identical in character with those which occur in France and Italy. In illustration of this fact, we give two examples of the triple phallus, which appears to have been, perhaps in accordance with the explanation given by Plutarch, an amulet in great favour. The first was found in London in 1842.[1] As in the examples found on the continent, a principal phallus forms the body, having the hinder parts of apparently a dog, with wings of a peculiar form, perhaps intended for those of a dragon. Several small rings are attached, no doubt for the purpose of suspending bells. Our second example [2] was found at York in 1844. It displays a peculiarity of action which, in this case at least, leaves no doubt that the hinder parts were intended to be those of a dog. All antiquaries of any experience know the great num-

[1] See Plate I, Fig. 3.
[2] Plate I, Fig. 4.

19

ber of obscene subjects which are met with among the fine red pottery which is termed Samian ware, found so abundantly in all Roman sites in our island. They represent erotic scenes in every sense of the word, promiscuous intercourse between the sexes, even vices contrary to nature, with figures of Priapus, and phallic emblems. We give as an example one of the *less* exceptional scenes of this description, copied from a Samian bowl found in Cannon Street, London, in 1828.[1] The lamps, chiefly of earthenware, form another class of objects on which such scenes are frequently portrayed, and to which broadly phallic forms are sometimes given. One of these phallic lamps is here represented, on the same plate with the bowl of Samian ware just described.[2] It is hardly necessary to explain the subject represented by this lamp, which was found in London a few years ago.

All this obscene pottery must be regarded, no doubt, as a proof of a great amount of dissoluteness in the morals of Roman society in Britain, but it is evidence of something more. It is hardly likely that such objects could be in common use at the family table; and we are led to suppose that they were employed on special occasions, festivals, perhaps, connected with the licentious worship of which we are

[1] Plate I, Fig. 1.
[2] Plate I, Fig. 2.

speaking, and such as those described in such strong terms in the satires of Juvenal. But monuments are found in this island which bear still more direct evidence to the existence of the worship of Priapus during the Roman period.

In the parish of Adel, in Yorkshire, are considerable traces of a Roman station, which appears to have been a place of some importance, and which certainly possessed temples. On the site of these were found altars, and other stones with inscriptions, which, after being long preserved in an outhouse of the rectory at Adel, are now deposited in the museum of the Philosophical Society at Leeds. One of the most curious of these, which we have here engraved for the first time,[1] apears to be a votive offering to Priapus, who seems to be addressed under the name of Mentula. It is a rough, unsquared stone, which has been selected for possessing a tolerably flat and smooth surface; and the figure and letters were made with a rude implement, and by an unskilled workman, who was evidently unable to cut a continuous smooth line. The middle of the stone is occupied by the figure of a phallus, and round it we read very distinctly the words:—

PRIMINVS MENTLA.

1 Plate IV, Fig. 1.

The author of the inscription may have been an ignorant Latinist as well as unskilful sculptor, and perhaps mistook the ligulated letters, overlooking the limb which would make the L stand for VL, and giving A for AE. It would then read *Priminus Mentulæ*, Priminus to Mentula (the object personified), and it may have been a votive offering from some individual named Priminus, who was in want of an heir, or laboured under some sexual infirmity, to Priapus, whose assistance he sought. Another interpretation has been suggested, on the supposition that Mentla, or perhaps (the L being designed for IL ligulated) Mentila or Mentilla, might be the name of a female joined with her husband in this offering for their common good. The former of these interpretations seems, however, to be the most probable. This monument belongs probably to rather a late date in the Roman period. Another *ex voto* of the same class was found at Westerwood Fort in Scotland, one of the Roman fortresses on the wall of Antoninus. This monument [1] consisted of a square slab of stone, in the middle of which was a phallus, and under it the words EX : VOTO. Above were the let-

---

[1] See Plate IV, Fig. 2. Horseley, who engraved this monument in his *Brittania Romana*, Scotland, fig. xix. has inserted a fig-leaf in place of the phallus, but with slight indications of the form of the object it was intended to conceal. We are not aware if this monument is still in existence.

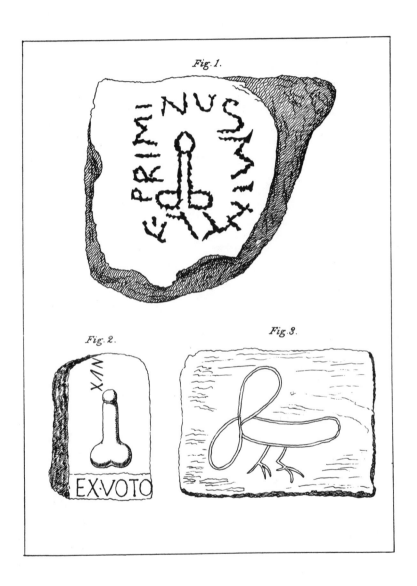

Fig. 1.

Fig. 2.

Fig. 3.

PLATE IV

PHALLIC MONUMENTS FOUND IN SCOTLAND

ters XAN, meaning, perhaps, that the offerer had laboured *ten years* under the grievance of which he sought redress from Priapus. We may point also to a phallic monument of another kind, which reminds us in some degree of the finer sculptures at Nîmes. At Housesteads, in Northumberland, are seen the extensive and imposing remains of one of the Roman stations on the Wall of Hadrian named Borcovicus. The walls of the entrance gateways are especially well preserved, and on that of the guard-house attached to one of them, is a slab of stone presenting the figure given in our plate IV, fig. 3. It is a rude delineation of a phallus with the legs of a fowl, and reminds us of some of the monuments in France and Italy previously described. These phallic images were no doubt exposed in such situations because they were supposed to exercise a protective influence over the locality, or over the building, and the individual who looked upon the figure believed himself safe, during that day at least, from evil influences of various descriptions. They are found, we believe, in some other Roman stations, in a similar position to that of the phallus at Housesteads.

Although the worship of which we are treating prevailed so extensively among the Romans and throughout the Roman provinces, it was far from being peculiar to them, for the same superstition formed part of the religion of the Teutonic race, and was carried with that race wherever it settled. The Teutonic god, who answered to the Roman Priapus, was called, in Anglo-Saxon, Fréa, in Old Norse, Freyr, and, in Old German, Fro. Among the Swedes, the principal seat of his worship was at Upsala, and Adam of Bremen, who lived in the eleventh century, when paganism still retained its hold on the north, in describing the forms under which the gods were there represented, tells us that " the third of the gods at Upsala was Fricco [another form of the name], who bestowed on mortals peace and pleasure, and who was represented *with an immense priapus;* " and he adds that, at the celebration of marriages, they offered sacrifice to Fricco. This god, indeed, like the Priapus of the Romans, presided over generation and fertility, either of animal life or of the produce of the earth, and was invoked accordingly. Ihre, in his *Glossarium Sueco-Gothicum,* mentions objects of antiquity dug up in the north of Europe, which clearly prove the prevalence of phallic rites. To this deity, or to his female representative of the same name, the Teutonic Venus, Friga, the fifth day of the week was dedicated, and on that account received its name, in Anglo-Saxon, Frige-dæg, and in modern English, Friday. Frigedæg appears to have been a name sometimes given in Anglo-Saxon to Frea himself; in

a charter of the date of 959, printed in Kemble's
Codex Diplomaticus, one of the marks on a boun-
dary-line of land is Frigedæges-Tréow, meaning apparently Frea's tree, which was probably a tree
dedicated to that god, and the scene of Priapic rites.
There is a place called Fridaythorpe in Yorkshire,
and Friston, a name which occurs in several parts
of England, means, probably, the stone of Frea or
of Friga; and we seem justified in supposing that
this and other names commencing with the syllable
Fri or Fry, are so many monuments of the existence
of the phallic worship among our Anglo-Saxon forefathers. Two customs cherished among our old English popular superstitions are believed to have been
derived from this worship, the need-fires, and the
procession of the boar's head at the Christmas festivities. The former were fires kindled at the period
of the summer solstice, and were certainly in their
origin religious observances. The boar was intimately connected with the worship of Frea.[1]

From our want of a more intimate knowledge of
this part of Teutonic paganism, we are unable to decide whether some of the superstitious practices of
the middle ages were derived from the Romans or
from the peoples who established themselves in the

---

[1] See Grimm's Deutsche Mythologie, p. 139, first edition.

provinces after the overthrow of the western empire; but in Italy and in Gaul (the southern parts especially), where the Roman institutions and sentiments continued with more persistence to hold their influence, it was the phallic worship of the Romans which, gradually modified in its forms, was thus preserved, and, though the records of such a worship are naturally accidental and imperfect, yet we can distinctly trace its existence to a very late period. Thus, we have clear evidence that the phallus, in its simple form, was worshipped by the mediæval Christians, and that the forms of Christian prayer and invocation were actually addressed to it. One name of the male organ among the Romans was *fascinum;* it was under this name that it was suspended round the necks of women and children, and under this name especially it was supposed to possess magical influences which not only acted upon others, but defended those who were under its protection from magical or other evil influences from without. Hence are derived the words to *fascinate* and *fascination*. The word is used by Horace, and especially in the epigrams of the *Priapeia,* which may be considered in some degree as the exponents of the popular creed in these matters. Thus we have in one of these epigrams the lines,—

" Placet, Priape ? qui sub arboris coma
Soles, sacrum revincte pampino caput,
Ruber sedere cum rebente *fascino*."
Priap. Carm. lxxxiv.

It seems probable that this had become the popular,
or vulgar, word for the phallus, at least taken in this
point of view, at the close of the Roman power, for
the first very distinct traces of its worship which we
find afterwards introduce it under this name, which
subsequently took in French the form *fesne.* The
mediæval worship of the *fascinum* is first spoken of
in the eighth century. An ecclesiastical tract entitled
Judicia Sacerdotalia de Criminibus, which is ascribed
to the end of that century, directs that " if any one
has performed incantation to the *fascinum,* or any
incantation whatever, except any one who chaunts
the Creed or the Lord's Prayer, let him do penance
on bread and water during three lents." An act of the
council of Châlons, held in the ninth century, pro-
hibits the same practice almost in the same words;
and Burchardus repeats it again in the twelfth century,[1] a proof of the continued existence of this worship. That it was in full force long after this is
proved by the statutes of the synod of Mans, held in
1247, which enjoin similarly the punishment for him
" who has sinned to the fascinum, or has performed

[1] D. Burchardi *Decretorum libri*, lib. x, c 49.

any incantations, except the creed, the pater noster, or other canonical prayer." This same provision was adopted and renewed in the statutes of the synod of Tours, held in 1396, in which, as they were published in French, the Latin *fascinum* is represented by the French *fesne*. The *fascinum* to which such worship was directed must have been something more than a small amulet.

This brings us to the close of the fourteenth century, and shows us how long the outward worship of the generative powers, represented by their organs, continued to exist in Western Europe to such a point as to engage the attention of ecclesiastical synods. During the previous century facts occurred in our own island illustrating still more curiously the continuous existence of the worship of Priapus, and that under circumstances which remind us altogether of the details of the phallic worship under the Romans. It will be remembered that one great object of this worship was to obtain fertility either in animals or in the ground, for Priapus was the god of the horticulturist and the agriculturist. St. Augustine, declaiming against the open obscenities of the Roman festival of the Liberalia, informs us that an enormous phallus was carried in a magnificent chariot into the middle of the public place of the town with great ceremony, where the most respectable matron advanced and placed a garland of flowers "on this obscene figure;" and this, he says,' was done to appease the god, and "to obtain an abundant harvest, and remove enchantments from the land."[1] We learn from the Chronicle of Lanercost that, in the year 1268, a pestilence prevailed in the Scottish district of Lothian, which was very fatal to the cattle, to counteract which some of the clergy—*bestiales, habitu claustrales, non animo*—taught the peasantry to make a fire by the rubbing together of wood (this was the need-fire), and to raise up the image of Priapus, as a means of saving their cattle. "When a lay member of the Cistercian order at Fenton had done this before the door of the hall, and had sprinkled the cattle with a dog's testicles dipped in holy water, and complaint had been made of this crime of idolatry against the lord of the manor, the latter pleaded in his defence that all this was done without his knowledge and in his absence, but added, 'while until the present month of June other people's cattle fell ill and died, mine were always found, but now every day two or three of mine die, so that I have few left for the labours of the field.'" Fourteen years after this, in 1282, an event of the same kind occurred at Inverkeithing, in the present county of Fife in Scot-

[1] S. Augustini *De Civit. Dei*, lib. vii, c. 21.

31

land. The cause of the following proceedings is not stated, but it was probably the same as that for which the cistercian of Lothian had recourse to the worship of Priapus. In the Easter week of the year just stated (March 29—April 5), a parish priest of Inverkeithing, named John, performed the rites of Priapus, by collecting the young girls of the town, and making them dance round the figure of this god; without any regard for the sex of these worshippers, he carried a wooden image of the male members of generation before them in the dance, and himself dancing with them, he accompanied their songs with movements in accordance, and urged them to licentious actions by his no less licentious language. The more modest part of those who were present felt scandalized with the priest, but he treated their words with contempt, and only gave utterance to coarser obscenities. He was cited before his bishop, defended himself upon the common usage of the country, and was allowed to retain his benefice; but he must have been rather a worldly priest, after the style of the middle ages, for a year afterwards he was killed in a vulgar brawl.

The practice of placing the figure of a phallus on the walls of buildings, derived, as we have seen, from the Romans, prevailed also in the middle ages, and the buildings especially placed under the influence of this symbol were churches. It was believed to be

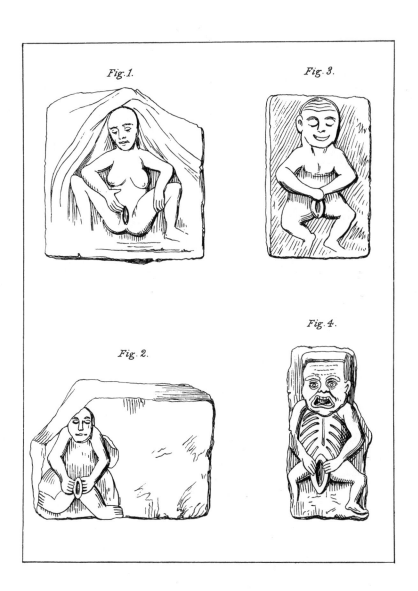

Fig. 1.

Fig. 3.

Fig. 2.

Fig. 4.

PLATE V

SHELAH-NA-GIG MONUMENTS

a protection against enchantments of all kinds, of which the people of those times lived in constant terror, and this protection extended over the place and over those who frequented it, provided they cast a confiding look upon the image. Such images were seen, usually upon the portals, on the cathedral church of Toulouse, on more than one church in Bourdeaux, and on various other churches in France, but, at the time of the revolution, they were often destroyed as marks only of the depravity of the clergy. Dulaure tells us that an artist, whom he knew, but whose name he has not given, had made drawings of a number of these figures which he had met with in such situations. A Christian saint exercised some of the qualities thus deputed to Priapus; the image of St. Nicholas was usually painted in a conspicuous position in the church, for it was believed that whoever had looked upon it was protected against enchantments, and especially against that great object of popular terror, the evil eye, during the rest of the day.

It is a singular fact that in Ireland it was the female organ which was shown in this position of protector upon the churches, and the elaborate though rude manner in which these figures were sculptured, show that they were considered as objects of great importance. They represented a female exposing herself to view in the most unequivocal manner, and are carved on a block which appears to have served as the key-stone to the arch of the door-way of the church, where they were presented to the gaze of all who entered. They appear to have been found principally in the very old churches, and have been mostly taken down, so that they are only found among the ruins. People have given them the name of *Shelah-na-Gig,* which, we are told, means in Irish Julian the Giddy, and is simply a term for an immodest woman; but it is well understood that they were intended as protecting charms against the fascination of the evil eye. We have given copies of all the examples yet known in our plates v and vi. The first of these [1] was found in an old church at Rochestown, in the county of Tipperary, where it had long been known among the people of the neighbourhood by the name given above. It was placed in the arch over the doorway, but has since been taken away. Our second example of the Shelah-na-Gig [2] was taken from an old church lately pulled down in the county Cavan, and is now preserved in the museum of the Society of Antiquaries of Dublin. The third [3] was found at Ballinahend Castle, also in

[1] Plate v, Fig. 1.
[2] Plate v, Fig. 2.
[3] Plate v, Fig. 3.

the county of Tipperary; and the fourth [1] is preserved in the museum at Dublin, but we are not informed from whence it was obtained. The next,[2] which is also now preserved in the Dublin Museum, was taken from the old church on the White Island, in Lough Erne, county Fermanagh. This church is supposed by the Irish antiquaries to be a structure of very great antiquity, for some of them would carry its date as far back as the seventh century, but this is probably an exaggeration. The one which follows [3] was furnished by an old church pulled down by order of the ecclesiastical commissioners, and it was presented to the museum at Dublin, by the late Dean Dawson. Our last example [4] was formerly in the possession of Sir Benjamin Chapman, Bart., of Killoa Castle, Westmeath, and is now in a private collection in London. It was found in 1859 at Chloran, in a field on Sir Benjamin's estate known by the name of the " Old Town," from whence stones had been removed at previous periods, though there are now very small remains of building. This stone was found at a depth of about five feet from the surface, which shows that the building, a church no doubt,

[1] Plate v, Fig. 4.

[2] Plate vi, Fig. 1.

[3] Plate vi, Fig. 2.

[4] Plate vi, Fig. 3.

must have fallen into ruin a long time ago. Contiguous to this field, and at a distance of about two hundred yards from the spot where the Shelah-na-Gig was found, there is an abandoned churchyard, separated from the Old Town field only by a loose stone wall.

The belief in the salutary power of this image appears to be a superstition of great antiquity, and to exist still among all peoples who have not reached a certain degree of civilization. The universality of this superstition leads us to think that Herodotus may have erred in the explanation he has given of certain rather remarkable monuments of a remote antiquity. He tells us that Sesostris, king of Egypt, raised columns in some of the countries he conquered, on which he caused to be figured the female organ of generation as a mark of contempt for those who had submitted easily.[1] May not these columns have been intended, if we knew the truth, as protections for the people of the district in which they stood, and placed in the position where they could most conveniently been seen? This superstitious sentiment may also offer the true explanation of an incident which is

---

[1] Herodotus, Euterpe, cap. 102. Diodorus Siculus adds to the account given by Herodotus, that Sesostris also erected columns bearing the male generative organ as a compliment to the peoples who had defended themselves bravely.

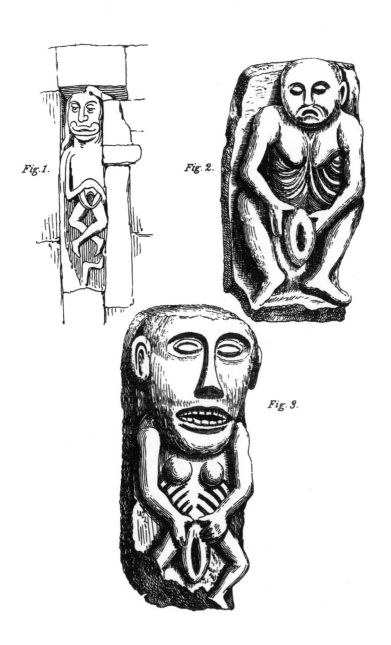

Fig. 1.

Fig. 2.

Fig. 3.

PLATE VI

SHELAH-NA-GIG MONUMENTS

said to have been represented in the mysteries of Eleusis. Ceres, wandering over the earth in search of her daughter Proserpine, and overcome with grief for her loss, arrived at the hut of an Athenian peasant woman named Baubo, who received her hospitably, and offered her to drink the refreshing mixture which the Greeks call Cyceon (κυκεων). The goddess rejected the offered kindness, and refused all consolation. Baubo, in her distress, bethought her of another expedient to allay the grief of her guest. She relieved her sexual organs of that outward sign which is the evidence of puberty, and then presented them to the view of Ceres, who, at the sight, laughed, forgot her sorrows, and drank the cyceon.[1] The prevailing belief in the beneficial influence of this sight, rather than a mere pleasantry, seems to afford the best explanation of this story.

This superstition which, as shown by the Shelah-na-Gigs of the Irish churches, prevailed largely in the middle ages, explains another class of antiquities which are not uncommon. These are small figures of nude females exposing themselves in exactly the same

---

[1] This story is told by the two Christian Fathers, Arnobius, *Adversus Gentes*, lib. v. c. 5, and Clemens Alexandrinus *Protrepticus*, p. 17, ed. Oxon. 1715. The latter writer merely states that Baubo exposed her parts to the view of the goddess, without the incident of preparation mentioned by Arnobius.

manner as in the sculptures on the churches in Ireland just alluded to. Such figures are found not only among Roman, Greek, and Egyptian antiquities, but among every people who had any knowledge of art, from the aborigines of America to the far more civilized natives of Japan; and it would be easy to give examples from almost every country we know, but we confine ourselves to our more special part of the subject. In the last century, a number of small statuettes in metal, in a rude but very peculiar style of art, were found in the duchy of Mecklenburg-Strelitz, in a part of Germany formerly occupied by the Vandals, and by the tribe of the Obotrites, considered as a division of the Vendes. They appeared to be intended to represent some of the deities worshipped by the people who made them; and some of them bore inscriptions, one of which was in Runic characters. From this circumstance we should presume that they belonged to a period not much, if any, older than the fall of the Western Empire. Some time afterwards, a few statuettes in metal were found in the island of Sardinia, so exactly similar to those just mentioned, that D'Hancarville, who published an account of them with engravings, considered himself justified in ascribing them to the Vandals, who occupied that island, as well as the tract of Germany alluded to.[1] One of these images, which D'Hancarville considers to be the Venus of the Vandal mythology, represents a female in a reclining position, with the wings and claws of a bird, holding to view a pomegranate, open, which, as D'Hancarville remarks, was considered as a sign representing the female sexual organ. In fact, it was a form and idea more unequivocally represented in the Roman figures which we have already described,[2] but which continued through the middle ages, and was preserved in a popular name for that organ, *abricot*, or expressed more energetically, *abricot fendu*, used by Rabelais, and we believe still preserved in France. This curious image is represented, after D'Hancarville, in three different points of view in our plate.[3] Several figures of a similar description, but representing the subject in a more matter-of-fact shape, were brought from Egypt by a Frenchman who held an official situation in that country, and three of them are now in a private collection in London. We have engraved one of these small bronzes,[4] which, as will be seen, presents an exact counterpart of the Shelah-na-Gig.

[1] D'Hancarville, *Antiquities Etrusques, Grecques, et Romaines*, Paris, 1785, tom. v. p. 61.

[2] See our Plates ii, Fig. 4, vii, and Plate xii, Fig. 3.

[3] Plate vii, Figs. 1, 2, 3.

[4] Plate vii, Fig. 4.

These Egyptian images belonged no doubt to the Roman period. Another similar figure,[1] made of lead, and apparently mediæval, was found at Avignon, and is preserved in the same private collection just alluded to; and a third,[2] was dug up, about ten years ago, at Kingston-on-Thames. The form of these statuettes seems to show that they were intended as portable images, for the same purpose as the Shelahs, which people might have ready at hand to look upon for protection whenever they were under fear of the influence of the evil eye, or of any other sort of enchantment.

We have not as yet any clear evidence of the existence of the Shelah-na-Gig in churches out of Ireland. We have been informed that an example has been found in one of the little churches on the coast of Devon; and there are curious sculptures, which appear to be of the same character, among the architectural ornamentation of the very early church of San Fedele at Como in Italy. Three of these are engraved in our plate VIII. On the top of the right hand jamb of the door [3] is a naked male figure, and in the same position on the other side a female,[4]

---

[1] Plate VII, Fig. 5.

[2] Plate XII, Fig. 4.

[3] Plate VIII, Fig. 1.

[4] Plate VIII, Fig. 2.

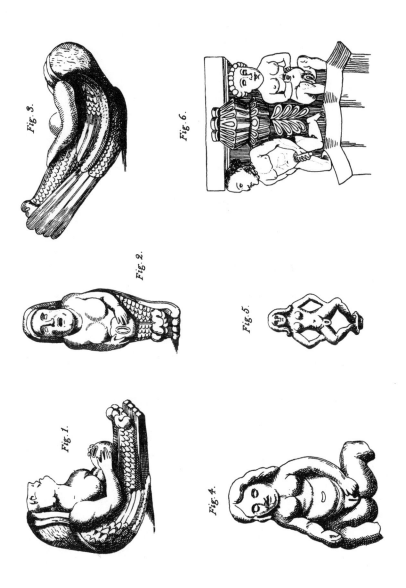

Fig. 3.

Fig. 6.

Fig. 2.

Fig. 5.

Fig. 1.

Fig. 4.

PLATE VII

VENUS OF THE VANDALS, BRONZE AND LEAD IMAGES, AND
CAPITAL OF A COLUMN

which are described to us as representing Adam and
Eve, and our informant, to whom we owe the drawings describes that at the apex [1] merely as "the
figure of a woman holding her legs apart." We understand that the surface of the stone in these sculptures is so much worn that it is quite uncertain
whether the sexual parts were ever distinctly marked,
but from the postures and positions of the hands, and
the situation in which these figures are placed, they
seem to resemble closely, except in their superior
style of art, the Shelah-na-Gigs of Ireland. There
can be little doubt that the superstition to which these
objects belonged gave rise to much of the indecent
sculpture which is so often found upon mediæval
ecclesiastical buildings. The late Baron von Hammer-
Pürgstall published a very learned paper upon monuments of various kinds which he considered as
illustrating the secret history of the order of the
Templars, from which we learn that there was in
his time a series of most extraordinary obscene sculptures in the church of Schoengraber in Austria, of
which he intended to give engravings, but the drawings had not arrived in time for his book; [2] but he
has engraved the capital of a column in the church of

---

[1] Plate VIII, Fig. 3.

[2] See Von Hammer-Pürgstall, *Fundgruben des Orients*, vol. vi,
p. 26.

Egra, a town of Bohemia, of which we give a copy,[1] in which the two sexes are displaying to view the members, which were believed to be so efficatious against the power of fascination.

The figure of the female organ, as well as the male, appears to have been employed during the middle ages of Western Europe far more generally than we might suppose, placed upon buildings as a talisman against evil influences, and especially against witchcraft and the evil eye, and it was used for this purpose in many other parts of the world. It was the universal practice among the Arabs of Northern Africa to stick up over the door of the house or tent, or put up nailed on a board in some other way, the generative organ of a cow, mare, or female camel, as a talisman to avert the influence of the evil eye. It is evident that the figure of this member was far more liable to degradation in form than that of the male, because it was much less easy, in the hands of rude draughtsmen, to delineate in an intelligible form, and hence it soon assumed shapes which though intended to represent it, we might rather call symbolical of it, though no symbolism was intended. Thus the figure of the female organ easily assumed the rude form of a horseshoe, and as the original

[1] Von Hammer-Pürgstall, *Fundgruben des Orients*, vol. vi, p. 35, and Plate iv, Fig. 31—See our Plate vii, Fig. 6.

meaning was forgotten, would be readily taken for that object, and a real horseshoe nailed up for the same purpose. In this way originated, apparently, from the popular worship of the generative powers, the vulgar practice of nailing a horseshoe upon buildings to protect them and all they contain against the power of witchcraft, a practice which continues to exist among the peasantry in some parts of England at the present day. Other marks are found, sometimes among the architectural ornaments, such as certain triangles and triple loops, which are perhaps typical forms of the same object. We have been informed that there is an old church in Ireland where the male organ is drawn on one side of the door, and the Shelah-na-Gig on the other, and that, though perhaps comparatively modern, their import as protective charms are well understood. We can easily imagine men, under the influence of these superstitions, when they were obliged to halt for a moment by the side of a building, drawing upon it such a figure, with the design that it should be a protection to themselves, and thus probably we derive from superstitious feelings the common propensity to draw phallic figures on the sides of vacant walls and in other places.

Antiquity had made Priapus a god, the middle ages raised him into a saint, and that under several names.

In the south of France, Provence, Languedoc, and the Lyonnais, he was worshipped under the title of St. Foutin.[1] This name is said to be a mere corruption of Fotinus or Photinus, the first bishop of Lyons, to whom, perhaps through giving a vulgar interpretation to the name, people had transferred the distinguishing attribute of Priapus. This was a large phallus of wood, which was an object of reverence to the women, especially to those who were barren, who scraped the wooden member, and, having steeped the scrapings in water, they drank the latter as a remedy against their barrenness, or administered it to their husbands in the belief that it would make them vigorous. The worship of this saint, as it was practiced in various places in France at the commencement of the seventeenth century, is described in that singular book, the *Confession de Sancy*.[2] We there learn that at Varailles in Provence, waxen images of the members of both sexes were offered to St. Foutin, and suspended to the ceiling of his chapel, and the writer remarks that, as the ceiling was covered with them, when the wind blew them about, it

---

[1] Our material for the account of these phallic saints is taken mostly from the work of M. Dulaure.

[2] La Confession de Sancy forms the fifth volume of the *Journal d'Henri III*, by Pierre de L'Estoile, ed. Duchat. See pp. 383, 391, of that volume.

produced an effect which was calculated to disturb very much the devotions of the worshippers. We hardly need remark that this is just the same kind of worship which existed at Isernia, in the kingdom of Naples, where it was presented in the same shape. At Embrun, in the department of the Upper Alps, the phallus of St. Foutin was worshipped in a different form; the women poured a libation of wine upon the head of the phallus, which was collected in a vessel, in which it was left till it became sour; it was then called the "sainte vinaigre," and the women employed it for a purpose which is only obscurely hinted at. When the Protestants took Embrun in 1585, they found this phallus laid up carefully among the relics in the principal church, its head red with the wine which had been poured upon it. A much larger phallus of wood, covered with leather, was an object of worship in the church of St. Eutropius at Orange, but it was seized by the Protestants and burnt publicly in 1562. St. Foutin was similarly an object of worship at Porigny, at Cives in the diocese of Viviers, at Vendre in the Bourbonnais, at Auxerre, at Puy-en-Velay, in the convent of Girouet near Sampigny, and in other places. At a distance of about four leagues from Clermont in Auvergne, there is (or was) an isolated rock, which presents the form of an immense phallus, and which is popularly called

St. Foutin. Similar phallic saints were worshipped under the names of St. Guerlichon, or Greluchon, at Bourg-Dieu in the diocese of Bourges, of St. Gilles in the Cotentin in Britany, of St. René in Anjou, of St. Regnaud in Burgundy, of St. Arnaud, and above all of St. Guignolé near Brest and at the village of La Chatelette in Berri. Many of these were still in existence and their worship in full practice in the last century; in some of them, the wooden phallus is described as being much worn down by the continual process of scraping, while in others the loss sustained by scraping was always restored by a miracle. This miracle, however, was a very clumsy one, for the phallus consisted of a long staff of wood passed through a hole in the middle of the body, and as the phallic end in front became shortened, a blow of a mallet from behind thrust it forward, so that it was restored to its original length.

It appears that it was also the practice to worship these saints in another manner, which also was derived from the forms of the worship of Priapus among the ancients, with whom it was the custom, in the nuptial ceremonies, for the bride to offer up her virginity to Priapus, and this was done by placing her sexual parts against the end of the phallus, and sometimes introducing the latter, and even completing the sacrifice. This ceremony is represented in a bas-relief in marble, an engraving of which is given in the *Musée Secret* of the antiquities of Herculaneum and Pompeii; its object was to conciliate the favour of the god, and to avert sterility. It is described by the early Christian writers, such as Lactantius and Arnobius, as a very common practice among the Romans; and it still prevails to a great extent over most part of the East, from India to Japan and the islands of the Pacific. In a public square in Batavia, there is a cannon taken from the natives and placed there as a trophy by the Dutch government. It presents the peculiarity that the touch-hole is made on a phallic hand, the thumb placed in the position which is called the " fig," and which we shall have to describe a little further on. It is always the same idea of reverence to the fertilizing powers of nature, of which the garland or the bunch of flowers was an appropriate emblem. There are traces of the existence of this practice in the middle ages. In the case of some of the priapic saints mentioned above, women sought a remedy for barrenness by kissing the end of the phallus; sometimes they appear to have placed a part of their body naked against the image of the saint, or to have sat upon it. This latter trait was perhaps too bold an adoption of the indecencies of pagan worship to last long, or to be praticed openly; but it appears to have been more innocently represented by lying upon the body of the saint, or sitting upon a stone, understood to represent him without the presence of the energetic member. In a corner in the church of the village of St. Fiacre, near Mouceaux in France, there is a stone called the chair of St. Fiacre, which confers fecundity upon women who sit upon it; but it is necessary that nothing should intervene between their bare skin and the stone. In the church of Orcival in Auvergne, there was a pillar which barren women kissed for the same purpose, and which had perhaps replaced some less equivocal object.[1] Traditions, at least, of similar practices were connected with St. Foutin, for it appears to have been the custom for girls on the point of marriage to offer their last maiden robe to that saint. This superstition prevailed to such an extent that it became proverbial. A story is told of a young bride who, on the wedding night, sought to deceive her husband on the question of her previous chastity, although, as the writer expresses it, " she had long ago deposited the robe of her virginity on the altar of St. Foutin." From this form of superstition is said to have arisen a vice which is understood to prevail especially in

---

[1] Dulaure relates that one day a villager's wife entering this church, and finding only a burly canon in it, asked him earnestly, " Where is the pillar which makes women fruitful ? " " I," said the canon, " I am the pillar."

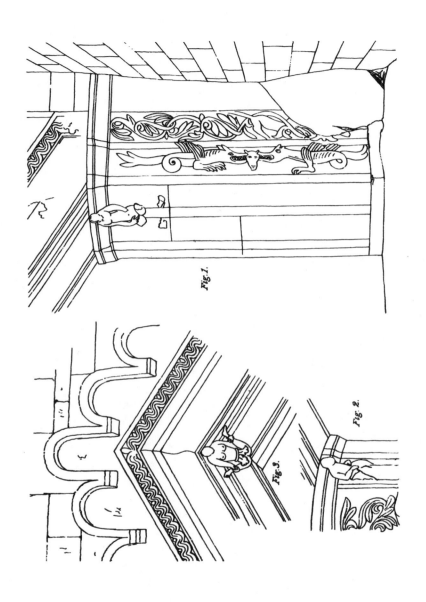

Fig. 1.

Fig. 2.

Fig. 3.

PLATE VIII

CAPITAL OF A COLUMN

nunneries—the use by women of artificial phalli, which appears in its origin to have been a religious ceremony. It certainly existed at a very remote period, for it is distinctly alluded to in the Scriptures,[1] where it is evidently considered as a part of pagan worship. It is found at an early period of the middle ages, described in the Ecclesiastical Penitentials, with its appropriate amount of penitence. One of these penitential canons of the eighth century speaks of " a woman who, by herself or with the help of another woman, commits uncleanness," for which she was to do penance for three years, one on bread and water; and if this uncleanness was committed with a nun, the penance was increased to seven years, two only on bread and water. Another Penitential of an early date provides for the case in which both the women who participated in this act should be nuns; and Burchardus, bishop of Worms, one of the most celebrated authorities on such subjects, describes the instrument and use of it in greater detail. The practice had evidently lost its religious character and degenerated into a mere indulgence of the passions.

---

[1] Ezekiel, xvi, 17. Within a few years there has been a considerable manufacture of these objects in Paris, and it was understood that they were chiefly exported to Italy, where they were sold in the nunneries.

Antwerp has been described as the Lampsacus of Belgium, and Priapus was, down to a comparatively modern period, its patron saint, under the name of Ters, a word the deriviation of which appears to be unknown, but which was identical in meaning with the Greek *phallus* and the Latin *fascinum*. John Goropius Becan, who published a learned treatise on the antiquities of Antwerp in the middle of the sixteenth century, informs us how much this Ters was reverenced in his time by the Antwerpians, especially by the women, who invoked it on every occasion when they were taken by surprise or sudden fear.[1] He states that " if they let fall by accident a vessel of earthenware, or stumbled, or if any unexpected accident caused them vexation, even the most respectable women called aloud for the protection of Priapus under this obscene name." Goropius Becanus adds that there was in his time, over the door of a house adjoining the prison, a statue which had been furnished with a large phallus, then worn away or broken off. Among other writers who mention this statue is Abraham Golnitz, who published an account of his travels in France and Belgium, in 1631,[2] and he informs us that it was a carving in stone, about a foot

---

[1] Johannis Goropii Becani *Origines Antwerpianae*, 1569, lib. i, pp. 26, 101.

[2] Golnitzii *Itinerarium Belgico-Gallicum*, p. 52.

high, with its arms raised up, and its legs spread out, and that the phallus had been entirely worn out by the women, who had been in the habit of scraping it and making a potion of the dust which they drank as a preservative against barrenness. Golnitz further tells us that a figure of Priapus was placed over the entrance gate to the enclosure of the temple of St. Walburgis at Antwerp, which some antiquaries imagined to have been built on the site of a temple dedicated to that deity. It appears from these writers that, at certain times, the women of Antwerp decorated the phalli of these figures with garlands.

The use of priapic figures as amulets, to be carried on the person as preservatives against the evil eye and other noxious influences, which we have spoken of as so common among the Romans, was certainly continued through the middle ages, and, as we shall see presently, has not entirely disappeared. It was natural enough to believe that if this figure were salutary when merely looked upon, it must be much more so when carried constantly on the person. The Romans gave the name *fascinum*, in old French *fesne*, to the phallic amulet, as well as to the same figure under other circumstances. It is an object of which we could hardly expect to find direct mention in mediæval writers, but we meet with examples of the object itself, usually made of lead (a proof of its popular character), and ranging in date perhaps from the fourteenth to the earlier part of the sixteenth century. As we owe our knowledge of these phallic amulets almost entirely to one collector, M. Forgeais of Paris, who obtained them chiefly from one source—the river Seine, our present acquaintance with them may be considered as very limited, and we have every reason for believing that they had been in use during the earlier period. We can only illustrate this part of the subject by describing a few of these mediæval phallic amulets, which are preserved in some private collections; and we will first call attention to a series of objects, the real purpose of which appears to be very obscure. They are small leaden tokens or medalets, bearing on the obverse the figure of the male or female organ, and on the reverse a cross, a curious intimation of the adoption of the worship of the generative powers among Christians. These leaden tokens, found in the river Seine, were first collected and made known to antiquaries by M. Forgeais, who published examples of them in his work on the leaden figures found in that river.[1] We give five examples of the medals of each sex, obverse and reverse.[2] It will be seen that the phalli on

---

[1] Notice sur des Plombs Historiés trouvés dans la Seine, et recueillis par Arthur Forgeais. 8vo. Paris, 1858.

[2] See our Plate IX.

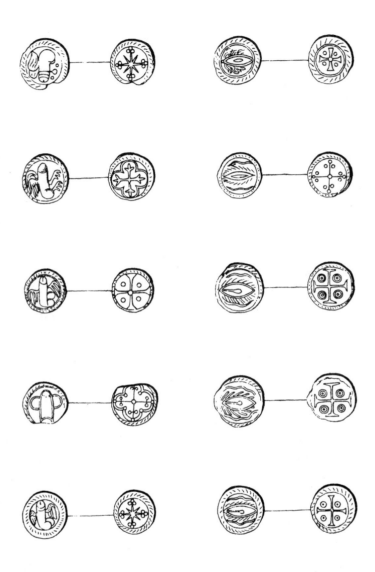

PLATE IX

ORNAMENTS FROM THE CHURCH OF SAN FEDELE

these tokens are nearly all furnished with wings; one
has a bird's legs and claws; and on another there is
an evident intention to represent a bell suspended
to the neck . These characteristics show either a very
distinct tradition of the forms of the Roman phallic
ornament, or an imitation of examples of Roman
phalli then existing—possibly the latter. But this is
not necessary, for the bells borne by two examples,
given in our next plate, and also taken from the collection of M. Forgeais are mediæval, and not Roman
bells, though these also represent well-known ancient forms of treating the subject. In the first,[1] a
female is riding upon the phallus, which has men's
legs, and is held by a bridle. This figure was evidently intended to be attached to the dress as a
brooch, for the pin which fixed it still remains on
the back. Two other examples [2] present figures of
winged phalli, one with a bell, and the other with the
ring remaining from which the bell has no doubt
been broken. One of these has the dog's legs. A
fourth example [3] represents an enormous phallus attached to the middle of a small man. In another,[4]
which was evidently intended for suspension, prob-

[1] Plate x, Fig. 1.

[2] Plate x, Figs. 2 and 3.

[3] Plate x, Fig. 4.

[4] Plate x, Fig. 5.

ably at the neck, the organs of the two sexes are joined together. Three other leaden figures,[1] apparently amulets, which were in the Forgeais collection, offer a very peculiar variety of form, representing a figure, which we might suppose to be a male by its attributes, though it has a very feminine look, and wears the robe and hood of a woman. Its peculiarity consists in having a phallus before and behind. We have on the same plate[2] a still more remarkable example of the combination of the cross with the emblems of the worship of which we are treating, in an object found at San Agati di Goti, near Naples, which was formerly in the Beresford Fletcher collection, and is now in that of Ambrose Ruschenberger, Esq., of Boston, U. S. It is a *crux ansata*, formed by four phalli, with a circle of female organs round the centre; and appears by the loop to have been intended for suspension. As this cross is of gold, it had no doubt been made for some personage of rank, possibly an ecclesiastic; and we can hardly help suspecting that it had some connection with priapic ceremonies or festivities. The last figure on the same plate is also taken from the collection of M. Forgeais.[3] From the monkish cowl and the cord

---

[1] Plate xi, Figs. 1, 2, and 3.

[2] Plate xi, Fig. 4.

[3] Plate xi, Fig. 5.

round the body, we may perhaps take it for a satire upon the friars, some of whom wore no breeches, and they were all charged with being great corruptors of female morals.

In Italy we can trace the continuous use of these phallic amulets down to the present time much more distinctly than in our more Western countries. There they are still in very common use, and we give two examples [1] of bronze amulets of this description, which are commonly sold in Naples at the present day for a carlo, equivalent to fourpence in English money, each. One of them, it will be seen, is encircled by a serpent. So important are these amulets considered for the personal safety of those who possess them, that there is hardly a peasant who is without one, which he usually carries in his waistcoat pocket.

There was another, and less openly apparent, form of the phallus, which has lasted as an amulet during almost innumerable ages. The ancients had two forms of what antiquaries have named the phallic hand, one in which the middle finger was extended at length, and the thumb and other fingers doubled up, while in the other the whole hand was closed, but the thumb was passed between the first and middle

---

[1] Plate XII, Figs. 1 and 2.

fingers. The first of these forms appears to have been the more ancient, and is understood to have been intended to represent, by the extended middle finger, the *membrum virile*, and by the bent fingers on each side the testicles. Hence the middle finger of the hand was called by the Romans, *digitus impudicus*, or *infamis*. It was called by the Greeks καταπύγων, which had somewhat the same meaning as the Latin word, except that it had reference especially to degrading practices, which were then less concealed than in modern times. To show the hand in this form was expressed in Greek by the word πχιμαλἶζειν, and was considered as a most contemptuous insult, because it was understood to intimate that the person to whom it was addressed was addicted to unnatural vice. This was the meaning also given to it by the Romans, as we learn from the first lines of an epigram of Martial:—

> " Rideto, multum, qui te, Sextille, cinædum
> Dixerit, et *digitum* porrigito *medium*."
> Martial, *Ep.* ii, 28.

Nevertheless, this gesture of the hand was looked upon at an early period as an amulet against magical influences, and, formed of different materials, it was carried on the person in the same manner as the phallus. It is not an uncommon object among Roman

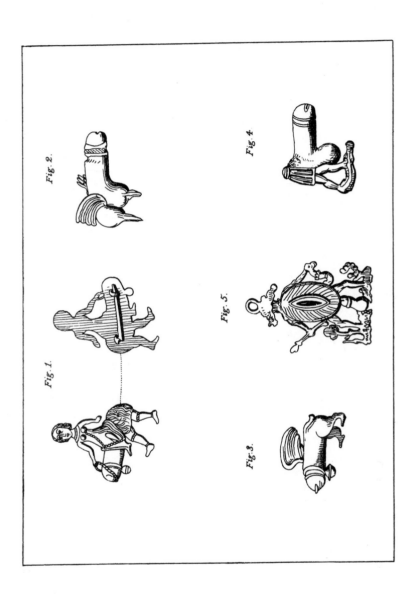

PLATE X

PHALLIC LEADEN TOKENS FROM THE SEINE

antiquities, and was adopted by the Gnostics as one of their symbolical images. The second of these forms of the phallic hand, the intention of which is easily seen (the thumb forming the phallus), was also well known among the Romans, and is found made of various material, such as bronze, coral, lapis lazuli, and chrystal, of a size which was evidently intended to be suspended to the neck or to some other part of the person. In the *Musée Secret* at Naples, there are examples of such amulets, in the shape of two arms joined at the elbow, one terminating in the head of a phallus, the other having a hand arranged in the form just described, which seem to have been intended for pendents to ladies' ears. This gesture of the hand appears to have been called at a later period of Latin, though we have no knowledge of the date at which this use of the word began, *ficus,* a fig. *Ficus* being a word in the feminine gender, appears to have fallen in the popular language into the more common form of feminine nouns, *fica,* out of which arose the Italian *fica* (now replaced by *fico*), the Spanish *higa,* and the French *figue.* Florio, who gives the word *fica,* a fig, says that it was also used in the sense of " a woman's quaint," so that it may perhaps be classed with one or two other fruits, such as the pomegranate and the apricot, to which a similar erotic meaning was given.[1] The form, under this name, was preserved through the middle ages, especially in the South of Europe, where Roman traditions were strongest, both as an amulet and as an insulting gesture. The Italian called this gesture *fare la fica,* to make or do the fig to any one; the Spaniard, *dar una higa,* to give a fig; and the Frenchman, like the Italian, *faire la figue.* We can trace this phrase back to the thirteenth century at least. In the judicial proceedings against the Templars in Paris in 1309, one of the brethren of the Order was asked, jokingly, in his examination, because he was rather loose and flippant in his replies, " if he had been ordered by the said receptor (the officer of the Templars who admitted the new candidate) to make with his fingers the fig at the crucifix." Here the word used is the correct Latin *ficus;* and it is the same in the plural, in a document of the year 1449, in which an individual is said to have *made figs* with both hands at another. This phrase appears to have been introduced into the English language in the time of Elizabeth and to have been taken from the Spaniards, with whom our relations were then intimate. This we

---

[1] See before, page 43. Among the Romans, the fig was considered as a fruit consecrated to Priapus, on account, it is said, of its productiveness.

---

assume from the circumstance that the English phrase was " to give the fig " (*dar la higa*),[1] and that the writers of the Elizabethan age call it " the fig of Spain." Thus, " ancient " Pistol, in Shakespeare:—

> —— " A figo for thy friendship! —
> The fig of Spain." *Henry V*, iii. 6.

The phrase has been preserved in all these countries down to modern times and we still say in English, " a fig for anybody," or " for anything," not meaning that we estimate them at no more than the value of a fig, but that we throw at them that contempt which was intimated by showing them the phallic hand, and which the Greeks, as stated above, called σκιμαλίζειν. The form of showing contempt which was called the fig is still well known among the lower classes of society in England, and it is preserved in most of the countries of Western Europe. In Baretti's Spanish Dictionary, which belongs to the commencement of the present century, we find the word *higa* interpreted as "A manner of scoffing at people, which consists in showing the thumb between the first and second finger, closing the first, and pointing at the person to whom we want to give this hateful mark of contempt." Baretti also gives as still in use the original meaning of the word, "*Higa*, a little hand

---

[1] " Behold next I see contempt, *giving me the fico*." *Wit's Misery*, quoted in Nares, v. *Fico*.

made of jet, which they hang about children to keep them from evil eyes; a superstitious custom." The use of this amulet is still common in Italy, and especially in Naples and Sicily; it has an advantage over the mere form of the phallus, that when the artificial *fica* is not present, an individual, who finds or believes himself in sudden danger, can make the amulet with his own fingers. So profound is the belief of its efficacy in Italy, that it is commonly believed and reported there that, at the battle of Solferino, the king of Italy held his hand in his pocket with this arrangement of the fingers as a protection against the shots of the enemy.

There were personages connected with the worship of Priapus who appear to have been common to the Romans under and before the empire, and to the foreign races who settled upon its ruins. The Teutonic race believed in a spiritual being who inhabited the woods, and who was called in old German *scrat.* His character was more general than that of a mere habitant of the woods, for it answered to the English hobgoblin, or to the Irish cluricaune. The scrat was the spirit of the woods, under which character he was sometimes called a *waltscrat,* and of the fields, and also of the household, the domestic spirit, the ghost haunting the house. His image was probably looked upon as an amulet, a protection to the house,

Fig. 1.   Fig. 2.   Fig. 3.

Fig. 4.   Fig. 5.

PLATE XI

LEADEN ORNAMENTS FROM THE SEINE

as an old German vocabulary of the year 1482, explains *schrætlin*, little scrats,' by the Latin word *penates*. The lascivious character of this spirit, if it wanted more direct evidence, is implied by the fact that *fcritta*, in Anglo-Saxon, and *scrat*, in old English, meant a hermaphrodite. Accordingly, the mediæval vocabularies explain *scrat* by Latin equivalents, which all indicate companions or emanations of Priapus, and in fact, Priapus himself. Isidore gives the name of *Pilosi*, or hairy men, and tells us that they were called in Greek, Panitæ (apparently an error for Ephialtæ), and in Latin, Incubi and Inibi, the latter word derived from the verb *inire*, and applied to them on account of their intercourse with animals. They were in fact the fauns and satyrs of antiquity, haunted like them the wild woods, and were characterized by the same petulance towards the other sex. Woe to the modesty of maiden or woman who ventured incautiously into their haunts. As Incubi, they visited the house by night, and violated the persons of the females, and some of the most celebrated heroes of early mediæval romances, such as Merlin, were thus the children of incubi. They were known at an early period in Gaul by the name of Dusii, from which, as the church taught that all these mythic personages were devils, we derive our modern word *Deuce*, used in such

phrases as " the Deuce take you! " The term *ficarii*
was also applied to them in mediæval Latin, either
from the meaning of the word *ficus*, mentioned before,[1] or because they were fond of figs. Most of these
Latin synonyms are given in the Anglo-Saxon vocabulary of Alfric, and are interpreted as meaning " evil
men, spirits of the woods, evil beings." One of the
old commentators on the Scriptures describes these
spirits of the woods as " monsters in the semblance
of men, whose form begins with the human shape
and ends in the extremity of a beast." They were,
in fact, half man, half goat, and were identical with
a class of hobgoblins, who at a rather later period
were well known in England by the popular name of
Robin Goodfellows, whose Priapic character is sufficiently proved by the pictures of them attached to
some of our early printed ballads, of which we give
facsimiles. The first [2] is a figure of Robin Goodfellow, which forms the illustration to a very popular
ballad of the earlier part of the seventeenth century, entitled " The mad merry Pranks of Robin
Goodfellow; " he is represented party-coloured, and
with the priapic attribute. The next [3] is a second il-

---

[1] See before, p. 70.

[2] See Plate XII, Fig. 5. From a copy of the black-letter
ballad in the library of the British Museum.

[3] Plate XII, Fig. 2. From the same ballad.

lustration of the same ballad, in which Robin Good-fellow is represented as Priapus, goat-shaped, with his attributes still more strongly pronounced, and surrounded by a circle of his worshippers dancing about him. He appears here in the character assumed by the demon at the sabbath of the witches, of which we shall have to speak a little further on. The Romish Church created great confusion in all these popular superstitions by considering the mythic persons with whom they were connected as so many devils; and one of these Priapic demons is figured in a cut which seems to have been a favorite one, and is often repeated as an illustration of the broadside ballads of the age of James I. and Charles I.[1] It is Priapus reduced to his lowest step of degradation.

Besides the invocations addressed principally to Priapus, or to the generative powers, the ancients had established great festivals in their honour, which were remarkable for their licentious gaiety, and in which the image of the phallus was carried openly and in triumph. These festivities were especially celebrated among the rural population, and they were held chiefly during the summer months. The preparatory labours of the agriculturist were over,

---

[1] Plate XIII, Fig. 1. From two black-letter ballads in the British Museum, one entitled, " A warning for all Lewd Livers," the other, " A strange and true News from Westmoreland."

and people had leisure to welcome with joyfulness the activity of nature's reproductive powers, which was in due time to bring their fruits. Among the most celebrated of these festivals were the Liberalia, which were held on the 17th of March. A monstrous phallus was carried in procession in a car, and its worshippers indulged loudly and openly in obscene songs, conversation, and attitudes, and when it halted, the most respectable of the matrons ceremoniously crowned the head of the phallus with a garland. The Bacchanalia, representing the Dionysia of the Greeks, were celebrated in the latter part of October, when the harvest was completed, and were attended with much the same ceremonies as the Liberalia. The phallus was similarly carried in procesion, and crowned, and, as in the Liberalia, the festivities being carried on into the night, as the celebrators became heated with wine, they degenerated into the extreme of licentiousness, in which people indulged without a blush in the most infamous vices. The festival of Venus was celebrated towards the beginning of April, and in it the phallus was again carried in its car, and led in procession by the Roman ladies to the temple of Venus outside the Colline gate, and there presented by them to the sexual parts of the goddess. This part of the scene is represented in a well-known intaglio, which has

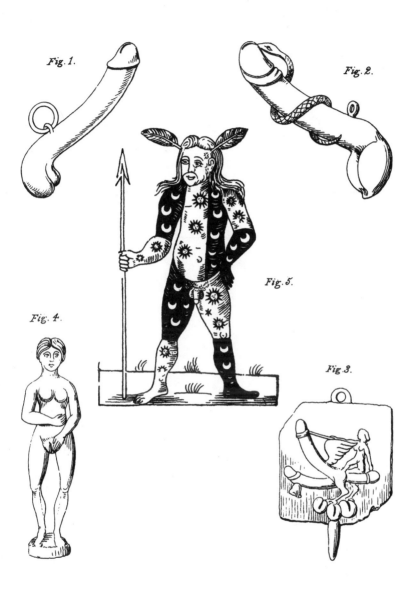

Fig. 1.

Fig. 2.

Fig. 5.

Fig. 4.

Fig. 3.

PLATE XII

AMULETS OF GOLD AND LEAD

been published in several works on antiquities. At the close of the month last mentioned came the Floralia, which, if possible, excelled all the others in licence. Ausonius, in whose time (the latter half of the fourth century) the Floralia were still in full force, speaks of their lasciviousness—

> Nec non lascivi Floralia læta theatri,
> Quæ spectare volunt qui voluisse negant.
> Ausonii *Eclog. de Feriis Romanis.*

The loose women of the town and its neighbourhood, called together by the sounding of horns, mixed with the multitude in perfect nakedness, and excited their passions with obscene motions and language, until the festival ended in a scene of mad revelry, in which all restraint was laid aside. Juvenal describes a Roman dame of very depraved manners as—

> . . . . Dignissima prorsus
> Florali matrona tuba.
> Juvenalis *Sat.* vi, 1. 249.

These scenes of unbounded licence and depravity, deeply rooted in people's minds by long established customs, caused so little public scandal, that it is related of Cato the younger that, when he was present at the celebration of the Floralia, instead of showing any disapproval of them, he retired, that his well-known gravity might be no restraint upon them, because the multitude manifested some hesitation in stripping the women naked in the presence of a man so celebrated for his modesty. The festivals more specially dedicated to Priapus, the Priapeia, were attended with similar ceremonies and similarly licentious orgies. Their forms and characteristics are better known, because they are so frequently represented to us as the subjects of works of Roman art. The Romans had other festivals of similar character, but of less importance, some of which were of a more private character, and some were celebrated in strict privacy. Such were the rites of the Bona Dea, established among the Roman matrons in the time of the republic, the disorders of which are described in such glowing language by the satirist Juvenal, in his enumeration of the vices of the Roman women:—

> Nota Bonæ secreta Deæ, quum tibia lumbos
> Incitat, et cornu pariter vinoque feruntur
> Attonitæ, crinemque rotant, ululantque Priapi
> Mænades. O quantus tunc illis mentibus ardor
> Concubitus! quæ vox saltante libidine! quantus
> Ille meri veteris per crura madentia torrens!
> Lenonum ancillas posita Saufeia corona
> Provocat, et tollit pendentis præmia coxæ.
> Ipsa Medullinæ fluctum crissantis adorat.
> Palmam inter dominas virtus natalibus æquat.
> Nil ibi per ludum simulabitur: omnia fient
> Ad verum, quibus incendi jam frigidus ævo
> Laomedontiades et Nestoris hernia possit.
> Tunc prurigo moræ impatiens, tunc femina simplex,
> Et toto pariter repetitus clamor ab antro:
> Jam fas est: admitte viros! —Juvenalis *Sat.* vi, l. 314.

Among the Teutonic, as well as among most other peoples, similar festivals appear to have been celebrated during the summer months; and, as they arose out of the same feelings, they no doubt presented the same general forms. The principal popular festivals of the summer during the middle ages occurred in the months of April, May, and June, and comprised Easter, May-day, and the feast of the summer solstice. All these appear to have been originally accompanied with the same phallic worship which formed the principal characteristic of the great Roman festivals; and, in fact, these are exactly those popular institutions and traits of popular manners which were most likely to outlive, also without any material change, the overthrow of the Roman empire by the barbarians. Although, at the time when we become intimately acquainted with these festivals, most of the prominent marks of their phallic character had been abandoned and forgotten, yet we meet during the interval with scattered indications which leave no room to doubt of their former existence. It will be interesting to examine into some of these points, and to show the influence they exerted on mediæval society.

The first of the three great festivals just mentioned was purely Anglo-Saxon and Teutonic; but it appears in the first place to have been identified with the

Roman Liberalia, and it was further transformed by the Catholic church into one of the great Christian religious feasts. In the primitive Teutonic mythology there was a female deity named, in Old German, *Ostara*, and, in Anglo-Saxon, *Eastre*, or *Eostre*, but all we know of her is the simple statement of our father of history, Bede, that her festival was celebrated by the ancient Saxons in the month of April, from which circumstance, that month was named by the Anglo-Saxons *Easter-monath*, or *Eoster-monath*, and that the name of the goddess had been subsequently given to the Paschal time, with which it was identical. The name of this goddess was given to the same month by the old Germans and by the Franks, so that she must have been one of the most highly honoured of the Teutonic deities, and her festival must have been a very important one, and deeply implanted in the popular feelings, or the church would not have sought to identify it with one of the greatest Christian festivals of the year. It is understood that the Romans considered this month as dedicated to Venus, no doubt because it was that in which the productive power of nature began to be visibly developed. When the Pagan festival was adopted by the church, it became a moveable feast instead of being fixed to the month of April. Among other objects offered to the goddess at this time were

Fig. 1.

Fig. 2.

PLATE XIII
ROBIN GOODFELLOW AND PHALLIC ORNAMENTS

cakes, made no doubt of fine flour, but of their form we are ignorant. The Christians, when they seized upon the Easter festival, gave them the form of a bun, which, indeed, was at that time the ordinary form of bread; and to protect themselves, and those who eat them, from any enchantment, or other evil influences which might arise from their former heathen character, they marked them with the Christian symbol—the cross. Hence were derived the cakes we still eat at Easter under the name of hot-cross-buns, and the superstitious feelings attached to them, for multitudes of people still believe that if they failed to eat a hot-cross-bun on Good-Friday they would be unlucky all the rest of the year. But there is some reason for believing that, at least in some parts, the Easter-cakes had originally a different form—that of the phallus. Such at least appears to have been the case in France, where the custom still exists. In Saintonge, in the neighbourhood of La Rochelle, small cakes, baked in the form of a phallus, are made as offerings at Easter, and are carried and presented from house to house; and we have been informed that similar practices exist in some other places. When Dulaure wrote, the festival of Palm Sunday, in the town of Saintes, was called the *fête des pinnes, pinne* being a popular and vulgar word for the *membrum virile*. At this *fête* the women and children carried in the procession, at the end of their palm branches, a phallus made of bread, which they called undisguisedly a *pinne,* and which, having been blest by the priest, the women carefully preserved during the following year as an amulet. A similar practice existed at St. Jean-d'Angély, where small cakes, made in the form of the phallus, and named *fateux,* were carried in the procession of the Fête-Dieu, or Corpus Christi.[1] Shortly before the time when Dulaure wrote, this practice was suppressed by a new sous-préfet, M. Maillard. The custom of making cakes in the form of the sexual members, male and female, dates from a remote antiquity and was common among the Romans. Martial made a phallus of bread (*Priapus siligineus*) the subject of an epigram of two lines:—

> Si vis esse satur, nostrum potes esse priapum:
> Ipse licet rodas inguina, purus eris.
>
> Martial, lib. xiv, ep. 69.

The same writer speaks of the image of a female organ made of the same material in another of his epigrams, to explain which, it is only necessary to state that these images were composed of the finest wheaten flour (*siligo*):—

---

[1] Dulaure, *Histoire Abrégée des Différent Cultes,* vol. ii, p. 285. Second Edition. It was printed in 1825.

Pauper amicitiæ cum sis, Lupe, non es amicæ;
Et queritur de te mentula sola nihil.
Illa siligineis pinguescit adultera cunnis;
Convivam pascit nigra farina tuum.

Martial, lib. ix, ep. 3.

This custom appears to have been preserved from
the Romans through the middle ages, and may be
traced distinctly as far back as the fourteenth or
fifteenth century. We are informed that in some of
the earlier inedited French books on cookery, re-
ceipts are given for making cakes in these obscene
forms, which are named without any concealment;
and the writer on this subject, who wrote in the sixteenth century, Johannes Bruerinus Campegius, describing the different forms in which cakes were
then made, enumerates those of the secret members
of both sexes, a proof, he says of " the degeneracy
of manners, when Christians themselves can delight
in obscenities and immodest things even among their
articles of food." He adds that some of these were
commonly spoken of by a gross name, *des cons
sucrés*. When Dulaure wrote, that is just forty years
ago, cakes of these forms continued to be made in
various parts of France, and he informs us that those
representing the male organ were made in the Lower
Limousin, and especially at Brives, while similar
images of the female organ were made at Clermont

in Auvergne, and in other places. They were popularly called *miches*.[1]

There is another custom attached to Easter, which has probably some relation to the worship of which we are treating, and which seems once to have prevailed throughout England, though we believe it is now confined to Shropshire and Cheshire. In the former county it is called *heaving*, in the latter *lifting*. On Easter Monday the men go about with chairs, seize the women they meet, and, placing them in the chairs, raise them up, turn them round two or three times, and then claim the right of kissing them. On Easter Tuesday, the same thing is done by the women to the men. This, of course, is only practiced now among the lower classes, except sometimes as a frolic among intimate friends. The chair appears to have been a comparatively modern addition, since such articles have become more abundant. In the last century four or five of the one sex took the victim of the other sex by the arms and legs, and lifted her or him in that manner, and the operation was attended, at all events on the part of the men, with much indecency. The women usually expect a small contribution of money from the men they have lifted. More anciently, in the time of Durandus, that is, in

---

[1] Dulaure, vol. ii, pp. 255-257.

the thirteenth century, a still more singular custom prevailed on these two days. He tells us that in many countries, on the Easter Monday, it was the rule for the wives to beat their husbands, and that on the Tuesday the husbands beat their wives. Brand, in his *Popular Antiquities*, tells us that in the city of Durham, in his time, it was the custom for the men, on the one day, to take off the women's shoes, which the latter were obliged to purchase back, and that on the other day the women did the same to the men.

In mediæval poetry and romance, the month of May was celebrated above all others as that consecrated to Love, which seemed to pervade all nature, and to invite mankind to partake in the general enjoyment. Hence, among nearly all peoples, its approach was celebrated with festivities, in which, under various forms, worship was paid to Nature's reproductiveness. The Romans welcomed the approach of May with their Floralia, a festival we have already described as remarkable for licentiousness; and there cannot be a doubt that our Teutonic forefathers had also their festival of the season long before they became acquainted with the Romans. Yet much of the mediæval celebration of May-day, especially in the South, appears to have been derived from the Floralia of the latter people. As in the Floralia, the arrival of the festival was announced by the sounding of horns during the preceding night, and no sooner had midnight arrived than the youth of both sexes proceeded in couples to the woods to gather branches and make garlands, with which they were to return just at sunrise for the purpose of decorating the doors of their houses. In England the grand feature of the day was the Maypole. This maypole was the stem of a tall young tree cut down for the occasion, painted of various colours, and carried in joyous procession, with minstrels playing before, until it reached the village green, or the open space in the middle of a town, where it was usually set up. It was there decked with garlands and flowers, the lads and girls danced round it, and people indulged in all sorts of riotous enjoyments. All this is well described by a Puritan writer of the reign of Queen Elizabeth—Philip Stubbes—who says that, " against Maie," " every parishe, towne, and village assemble themselves together, bothe men, women, and children, olde and yong, even all indifferently; and either goyng all together, or devidyng themselves into companies, they goe some to the woodes and groves, some to the hilles and mountaines, some to one place, some to another, where they spend all the night in pleasant pastymes, and in the mornyng thei returne, bryngyng with them birch bowes and braunches of trees to deck their assemblies withall, ... But their cheerest jewell thei bryng from thence is their Maie pole, whiche thei bryng home with greate veneration, as thus: Thei have twentie or fourtie yoke of oxen, every oxe havyng a sweete nosegaie of flowers placed on the tippe of his hornes, and these oxen drawe home this Maie poole (this stinckyng idoll rather), whiche is covered all over with flowers and hearbes, bound rounde about with strynges, from the top to the bottome, and sometyme painted with variable colours, with twoo or three hundred men, women, and children following it, with greate devotion. And thus beyng reared up, with handekerchiefes and flagges streamyng on the toppe, thei strawe the grounde aboute, binde greene boughes about it, sett up sommer haules, bowers, and arbours hard by it. And then fall thei to banquet and feast, to leape and daunce aboute it, as the heathen people did, at the dedication of their idolles, whereof this is a perfect patterne, or rather the thyng itself." [1]

The Puritans were deeply impressed with the belief that the maypole was a substantial relic of Paganism; and they were no doubt right. There appears to be reason sufficient for supposing that, at a period which cannot now be ascertained, the maypole had taken the place of the phallus. The ceremonies at-

[1] Stubbes, *Anatomie of Ahuses*, fol. 94, 8vo. London, 1583.

tending the elevation of the two objects were identical. The same joyous procession in the Roman festivals, described above, conducted the phallus into the midst of the town or village, where in the same manner it was decked with garlands, and the worship partook of the same character. We may add, too, that both festivals were attended with the same licentiousness. "I have heard it credibly reported," says the Puritan Stubbes, "and that *viva voce* by menne of greate gravitie and reputation, that of fourtie, three score, or a hundred maides goyng to the woode over night, there have scarcely the third part returned home again undefiled."

The day generally concluded with bonfires. These represented the need-fire, which was intimately connected with the ancient priapic rites. Fire itself was an object of worship, as the most powerful of the elements; but it was supposed to lose its purity and sacred character in being propagated from one material to another, and the worshippers sought on these solemn occasions to produce it in its primitive and purest form. This was done by the 1apid friction of two pieces of wood, attended with superstitious ceremonies; the pure element of fire was believed to exist in the wood, and to be thus forced out of it, and hence it was called need-fire (in Old German *not-feur*, and in Anglo-Sayon, *neod-fyr*), meaning literally a forced fire, or fire extracted by force. Before the process of thus extracting the fire from the wood, it was necessary that all the fires previously existing in the village should be extinguished, and they were afterwards revived from the bonfire which had been lit from the need-fire. The whole system of bonfires originated from this superstition; they had been adopted generally on occasions of popular rejoicing, and the bonfires commemorating the celebrated gunpowder plot are only particular applications of the general practice to an accidental case. The superstition of the need-fire belongs to a very remote antiquity in the Teutonic race, and existed equally in ancient Greece. It is proscribed in the early capitularies of the Frankish emperors of the Carlovingian dynasty. The universality of this superstition is proved by the circumstance that it still exists in the Highlands of Scotland, especially in Caithness, where it is adopted as a protection for the cattle when attacked by disease which the Highlanders attribute to witchcraft.[1] It was from the remotest ages the custom to cause cattle, and even children, to pass across the need-fire, as a protection to them for the rest of their lives. The need-fire was kindled at Easter, on May-day, and especially at the

---

[1] Logan, *The Scottish Gael*, vol. ii, p. 64, and Jamieson's *Scottish Dictionary*, Suppl. sub. v. *Neidfyre*.

---

summer solstice, on the eve of the feast of St. John
the Baptist, or of Midsummer-day.[1]

The eve of St. John was in popular superstition one
of the most important days of the mediæval year.
The need-fire—or the St. John's fire, as it was called—
was kindled just at midnight, the moment when the
solstice was supposed to take place, and the young
people of both sexes danced round it, and, above all
things, leaped over it, or rushed through it, which
was looked upon not only as a purification, but as a
protection against evil influences. It was the night
when ghosts and other beings of the spiritual world
were abroad, and when witches had most power. It
was believed, even, that during this night people's
souls left the body in sleep, and wandered over the
world, separated from it. It was a night of the great
meetings of the witches, and it was that in which they
mixed their most deadly poisons, and performed
their most effective charms. It was a night especially
favourable to divination in every form, and in which
maidens sought to know their future sweethearts and
husbands. It was during this night, also, that plants
possessed their greatest powers either for good or for
evil, and that they were dug up with all due ceremonies and cautions. The more hidden virtues of

[1] See Grimm, *Deutsche Mythologie*, pp. 341-349.

plants, indeed, depended much on the time at which, and the ceremonies with which, they were gathered, and these latter were extremely superstitious, no doubt derived from the remote ages of paganism. As usual, the clergy applied a half-remedy to the evil; they forebade any rites or incantations in the gathering of medicinal herbs except by repeating the creed and the Lord's prayer.

As already stated, the night of St. John's, or Mid-summer-eve, was that when ghosts and spirits of all descriptions were abroad, and when witches assembled, and their potions, for good or for evil, and charms were made with most effect. It was the night for popular divination, especially among the young maidens, who sought to know who were destined to be their husbands, what would be their characters, and what their future conduct. The medicinal virtues of many plants gathered on St. John's eve, and with the due ceremonies, were far more powerful than if gathered at other times. The most secret practices of the old popular superstitions are now mostly forgotten, but when, here and there, we meet with a few traces of them, they are of a character which leads us to believe that they belonged to a great extent to that same worship of the generative powers which prevailed so generally among all peoples. We remember that, we believe in one of the earlier editions of Mother Bunch, maidens who wished to know if their lovers were constant or not were directed to go out exactly at midnight on St. John's eve, to strip themselves entirely naked, and in that condition to proceed to a plant or shrub, the name of which was given, and round it they were to form a circle and dance, repeating at the same time certain words which they had been taught by their instructress. Having completed this ceremony, they were to gather leaves of the plant round which they had danced, which they were to carry home and place under their pillows, and what they wished to know would be revealed to them in their dreams. We have seen in some of the mediæval treatises on the virtue of plants directions for gathering some plants of especial importance, in which it was required that this should be performed by young girls in a similar state of complete nakedness.

Plants and flowers were, indeed, intimately connected with this worship. We have seen how constantly they are introduced in the form of garlands, and they were always among the offerings to Priapus. It was the universal practice, in dancing round the fire on St. John's eve, to conclude by throwing various kinds of flowers and plants into it, which were considered to be propitiatory, to avert certain evils to which people were liable during the following year. Among the plants they offered are mentioned mother-wort, vervain, and violets. It is perhaps to this connection of plants with the old priapic worship that we owe the popular tendency to give them names which were more or less obscene, most of which are now lost, or are so far modified as to present no longer the same idea. Thus the well-known arum of our hedge-bottoms received the names, no doubt suggested by its form, of cuckoo's pintle, or priest's pintle, or dog's pintle; and, in French, those of *vit de chien* and *vit de prestre;* in English it is now abbreviated into cuckoo-pint, or, sometimes, cuckoo-point. The whole family of the orchides was distinguished by a corresponding word, accompanied with various qualifications. We have in William Coles's *Adam in Eden,* (fol. 1659) the different names, for different varieties, of doggs-stones, fool-stones, fox-stones; in the older *Herbal* of Gerard (fol. 1597) triple ballockes, sweet ballockes, sweet cods, goat's-stones, hare's-stones, &c.; in French, *couillon de bouc* (the goat was especially connected with the priapic mysteries) and *couille,* or *couillon de chien.* In French, too, as we learn from Cotgrave and the herbals, " a kind of sallet hearbe " was called *couille à l' évêque;* the greater stone-crop was named *couille au loup;* and the spindle-tree was known by the name of *couillon de prêtre.* There are several plants which possess somewhat the appearance of a rough bush of hair. One of these, a species of *adiantum*, was known even in Roman times by the name of *Capillus Veneris*, and in more modern times it has been called maiden-hair, and our lady's hair. Another plant, the *asplenium trichomanes*, was and is also called popularly maiden-hair, or maiden's-hair; and we believe that the same name has been given to one or two other plants. There is reason for believing that the hair implied in these names was that of the pubes.[1] We might collect a number of other old popular names of plants of a similar character with these just enumerated.

In an old calendar of the Romish church, which is often quoted in Brand's *Popular Antiquities*, the seeking of plants for their hidden virtues and magical properties is especially noted as part of the practices on the eve of St. John (*herbæ diversi generis quæruntur*); and one plant is especially specified in terms too mysterious to be easily understood. Fern-seed, also, was a great object of search on this night; for, if found and properly gathered, it was believed to possess powerful magical properties, and especially

---

[1] Fumitory was another of these plants, and in a vocabulary of plants in a MS. of the middle of the thirteenth century, we find its names in Latin, French, and English given as follows, "*Fumus terrae, fumeterre, cunteboare.*" See Wright's *Volume of Vocabularies*, p. 17.

that of rendering invisible the individual who carried it upon his person. But the most remarkable of all the plants connected with these ancient priapic superstitions was the mandrake (*mandragora*), a plant which has been looked upon with a sort of feeling of reverential fear at all periods, and almost in all parts. Its Teutonic name, *alrun,* or, in its more modern form, *alraun,* speaks at once of the belief in its magical qualities among that race. People looked upon it as possessing some degree of animal life, and it was generally believed that, when it was drawn out of the earth, it uttered a cry, and that this cry carried certain death or madness to the person who extracted it. To escape this danger, the remedy was to tie a string round it, which was to be attached to a dog, and the latter, being driven away, dragged up the root in its attempt to run off, and experienced the fatal consequences. The root was the important part of the plant; it has somewhat the form of a forked radish, and was believed to represent exactly the human form below the waist, with, in the male and female plants, the human organs of generation distinctly developed. The mandrake, when it could be obtained, was used in the middle ages in the place of the phallic amulet, and was carefully carried on the person, or preserved in the house. It conferred fertility in more senses than one, for it was believed that as long as you kept it locked up with your money, the latter would become doubled in quantity every year; and it had at the same time all the protective qualities of the phallus. The Templars were accused of worshipping the mandrake, or *mandragora*, which became an object of great celebrity in France during the reigns of the weak monarchs Charles VI. and Charles VII. In 1429 one Friar Richard, of the order of the Cordeliers, preached a fierce sermon against the use of this amulet, the temporary effect of which was so great, that a certain number of his congregation delivered up their "mandragoires" to the preacher to be burnt.[1]

It appears that the people who dealt in these amulets helped nature to a rather considerable extent by the means of art, and that there was a regular process of cooking them up. They were necessarily aware that the roots themselves, in their natural state, presented, to say the least, very imperfectly the form which men's imagination had given to them, so they obtained the finest roots they could, which, when fresh from the ground, were plump and soft, and readily took any impression which might be given to them. They then stuck grains of millet or barley into the parts where they wished to have hair, and again

---

[1] *Journal a'un Bourgeois de Paris,* under the year 1429.

put it into a hole in the earth, until these grains had germinated and formed their roots. This process, it was said, was perfected within twenty days. They then took up the mandrake again, trimmed the fibrous roots of millet or barley which served for hair, retouched the parts themselves so as to give them their form more perfectly and more permanently, and then sold it.[1]

Besides these great and general priapic festivals, there were doubtless others of less importance, or more local in their character, which degenerated in aftertimes into mere local ceremonies and festivities. This would be the case especially in cities and corporate towns, where the guilds came in, to perpetuate the institution, and to give it gradually a modified form. Most towns in England had once festivals of this character, and at least three representatives of them are still kept up, the procession of Lady Godiva at Coventry, the Shrewsbury show, and the guild festival at Preston in Lancashire. In the first of these, the lady who is supposed to ride naked in the procession probably represents some feature in the ancient priapic celebration; and the story of the manner in which the Lady Godiva averted the anger of her husband from the townsmen, which is certainly a mere

---

[1] See the authorities for these statements in Dulaure, pp. 254—256.

fable, was no doubt invented to explain a feature of the celebration, the real meaning of which had in course of time been forgotten. The pageantry of the Shrewsbury show appears to be similarly the unmeaning reflection of forms belonging to older and forgotten practices and principles. On the Continent there were many such local festivals, such as the feast of fools, the feast of asses (the ass was an animal sacred to Priapus), and others, all which were adapted by the mediæval church exactly as the clergy had taken advantage of the profit to be derived from the phallic worship in other forms.

The leaden tokens, or medalets, which we have already described,[1] seem to point evidently to the existence in the middle ages of secret societies or clubs connected with this obscene worship, besides the public festivals. Of these it can hardly be expected that any description would survive, but, if not the fact, the belief in it is clearly established by the eagerness with which such obscene rites were laid to the charge of most of the mediæval secret societies, whether lay clubs or religious sects, and we know that secret societies abounded in the middle ages. However willing the Romish clergy were to make profit out of the popular phallic worship, they were

---

[1] See before, p. 60, and Plate ix.

equally ready to use the belief in it as a means of exciting prejudice against any sects which the church chose to regard as religious or political heretics.

It is very evident that, in the earlier ages of the church, the conversion of the Pagans to Christianity was in a vast number of cases less than a half-conversion, and that the preachers of the gospel were satisfied by people assuming the name of Christians, without inquiring too closely into the sincerity of their change, or into their practice. We can trace in the expressions of disapproval in the writings of some of the more zealous of the ecclesiastical writers, and in the canons of the earlier councils, the alarm created by the prevalence among Christians of the old popular festivals of paganism; and the revival of those particular canons and deprecatory remarks in the ecclesiastical councils and writings of a later period of the middle ages, shows that the existence of the evil had continued unabated. There was an African council in the year 381, from which Burchardus, who compiled his condensation of ecclesiastical decrees for the use of his own time, professes to derive his provisions against " the festivals which were held with Pagan ceremonies." We are there told that, even on the most sacred of the Christian commemoration days, these rites derived from the Pagans were introduced, and that dancing was practiced in the open street of so infamous a character, and accompanied with such lascivious language and gestures, that the modesty of respectable females was shocked to a degree that prevented their attendance at the service in the churches on those days. It is added that th se Pagan ceremonies were even carried into the churches, and that many of the clergy took part in them.

It is probable, too, that when Paganism itself had become an offence against the state, and those who continued attached to it were exposed to persecution, they embraced the name of Christians as a cover for the grossest superstitions, and formed sects who practised the rites of Paganism in their secret conventicles, but were placed by the church among the Christian heresies. In some of these, especially among those of an early date, the obscene rites and principles of the phallic worship seem to have entered largely, for, though their opponents probably exaggerated the actual vice carried on under their name, yet much of it must have had an existence in truth. It was a mixture of the licence of the vulgar Paganism of antiquity with the wild doctrines of the latter eastern philosophers. The older orthodox writers dwell on the details of these libidinous rites. Among the earliest in date were the Adamiani, or Adamites, who proscribed marriage, and held that the most per-

fect innocence was consistent only with the community of women. The chose *latibula,* or caverns,
for their conventicles, at which both sexes assembled
together in perfect nakedness. This sect perhaps
continued to exist under different forms, but it was
revived among the intellectual vagaries of the fifteenth century, and continued at least to be much
talked of till the seventeenth. The doctrine of the
munity of women. They chose *latibula,* or caverns,
ous sexual intercourse in their meetings, were ascribed by the early Christian controversialists to several sects, such as the followers of Florian, and of
Carpocratian, who were accused of putting out the
lamps in their churches at the end of the evening
service, and indulging in sexual intercourse indis-
criminately; the Nicolaitæ, who held their wives in
common; the Ebionei; and especially the Gnostics,
or followers of Basilides, and the Manichæans. The
Nicolaites held that the only way to salvation lay
through frequent intercourse between the sexes.[1]
Epiphanius speaks of a sect who sacrificed a child in
their secret rites by pricking it with brazen pins, and
then offering its blood.[2] The Gnostics were accused
of eating human flesh as well as of lasciviousness,
and they also are said to have held their women in

[1] Epiphanii *Panarium,* vol. I, p. 72.
[2] Epiphanius, vol. i, p. 416.

common, and taught that it was a duty to prostitute their wives to their guests.[1] Théy knew their fellow sectarians by a secret sign, which consisted in tickling the palm of the hand with the finger in a peculiar manner. The sign having been recognized, mutual confidence was established, and the stranger was invited to supper; after they had eaten their fill, the husband removed from the side of his wife, and said to her, " Go, exhibit charity to our guest," which was the signal for those further scenes of hospitality. This account is given us by St. Epiphanius, bishop of Constantia. We are told further of rites practiced by the Gnostics, which were still more disgusting, for they were said, after these libidinous scenes, to offer and administer the *semen virile* as their sacrament.[2] A similar practice is described as existing among women in the middle ages for the purpose of securing the love of their husbands, and was perhaps derived from the Gnostics and Manichæans, whose doctrines, brought from the East, appear to have spread themselves extensively into Western Europe.

Of these doctrines, however, we have no traces at

[1] On the secret worship and character of the Gnostics, see Epiphanii *Panarium*, vol. 1, pp. 84—102.

[2] See details on this subject in Epiphanii *Panarium*, ib. Conf. Prædestinati *Adversus Haeres.*, lib. 1, c. 46, where the same thing is said of the Manichæans.

least until the eleventh century, when a great intellectual agitation began in Western Europe, which brought to the surface of society a multitude of strange creeds and strange theories. The popular worship displayed in the great annual festivals, and the equally popular local *fêtes,* urban or rural, were hardly interfered with, or any secret societies belonging to the old worship; the mediæval church did not consider them as heresies, and let them alone. Thus, except now and then a provision of some ecclesiastical council expressed in general terms against superstitions, which was hardly heard at the time and not listened to, they are passed over in silence. But the moment anything under the name of heresy raised its head, the alarm was great. Gnosticism and Manichæism, which had indeed been identical, were the heresies most hated in the Eastern empire, and, as may be supposed, most persecuted; and this persecution was destined to drive them westward. In the seventh century they became modified into a sect which took the name of Paulicians, it is said, from an Armenian enthusiast named Paulus, and they seem to have still further provoked the hatred of the church by making themselves, in their own interests, the advocates of freedom of thought and of ecclesiastical reform. If history be to be believed, their Christian feelings cannot have been very strong, for, unable to resist persecution within the empire, they retired into the territory held by the Saracens, and united with the enemies of the Cross in making war upon the Christian Greeks. Others sought refuge in the country of the Bulgarians, who had very generally embraced their doctrines, which soon spread thence westward. In their progress through Germany to France they were known best as Bulgarians, from the name of the country whence they came; in their way through Italy they retained their name of Paulicians, corrupted in the Latin of that period of the middle ages into *Populicani, Poplicani, Publicani,* &c; and, in French, into *Popelican, Poblican, Policien,* and various other forms which it is unnecessary to enumerate. They began to cause alarm in France at the beginning of the eleventh century, in the reign of king Robert, when, under the name of Popelicans, they had established themselves in the diocese of Orleans, in which city a council was held against them in 1022, and thirteen individuals were condemned to be burnt. The name appears to have lasted into the thirteenth century, but the name of Bulgarians became more permanent, and, in its French form of *Bolgres, Bougres,* or *Bogres,* became the popular name for heretics in general. With these heresies, through the more sensual parts of Gnosticism and Manichæism, there appears to be left hardly room for doubt that the ancient phallic worship, probably somwhat modified, and under the shadow of secret rites, was imported into Western Europe; for, if we make allowance for the willing exaggerations of religious hatred, and consequent popular prejudice, the general conviction that these sectarians had rites and practices of a licentious character appears too strong to be entirely disregarded, nor does it present anything contrary to what we know of the state of mediæval society, or to the facts which have already been brought forward in the present essay. These early sects apear to have professed doctrines rather closely resembling modern communism, including, like those of their earlier sectarian predecessors, the community of women; and this community naturally implies the abolition of distinctive affinities. One of the writers against the mediæval heretics assures us that there were "many professed Christians, both men and women, who feared no more to go to their sister, or son or daughter, or brother, or nephew or niece, or kin or relation, than to their own wife or husband." They were accused, beyond this, of indulging in unnatural vices, and this charge was so generally believed, that the name of Bulgarus, or heretic, became equivalent with Sodomite, and hence came the modern French word *bougre*, and its English representatives.

In the course of the eleventh century the sectarians appeared in Italy under the name of Patarini, Paterini, or Patrini, which is said to have been taken from an old quarter of the city of Milan named Pataria, in which they first held their assemblies. A contemporary Englishman, Walter Mapes, gives us a singular account of the Paterini and their secret rites. Some apostates from this heresy, he tells us, had related that, at the first watch of night, they met in their synagogues, closed carefully the doors and windows, and waited in silence, until a black cat of extraordinary bigness descended among them by a rope, and that, as soon as they saw this strange animal, they put out the lights, and muttering through their teeth instead of singing their hymns, felt their way to this object of their worship, and kissed it, according to their feelings of humility or pride, some on the feet, some under the tail, and others on the genitals, after which each seized upon the nearest person of a different sex, and had carnal intercourse as long as he was able. Their leaders taught them that the most perfect degree of charity was " to do or suffer in this manner whatever a brother or sister might desire and ask," and hence, says Mapes, they were called Paterini, *a patiendo*. Other writers have suggested a different derivation, but the one first given appears to be that most generally accepted. The different sects or congregations in Italy and the south, indeed, appear generally to have taken their names from the towns in which they had their seats or head-quarters. Thus, those who were seated at Bagnols, in the department of the Gard, in the south of France, were called by the Latin writers Bagnolenses; the same writers give the name of Concordenses, or Concorezenses, to the heretics of Concordia in Lombardy; and the city of Albi, now the capital of the department of the Tarn, gave its name to the sect of the Albigenses, or Albigeois, the most extensive of them all, which spread over the whole of the south of France. A rich enthusiast of the city of Lyons, named Waldo, who had collected his wealth by mercantile pursuits, and who lived in the twelfth century, sold his property and distributed it among the poor, and he became the head of a sect which possessed poverty as one of its tenets, and received from the name of its founder that of Waldenses or Vaudois. From their posession of voluntary poverty they are sometimes spoken of by the name of *Pauperes de Lugduno,* the paupers of Lyons. Contemporaries speak of the Waldenses as being generally poor ignorant people; yet they spread widely over that part of France and into the valleys of Switzerland, and became so celebrated, that at last nearly all the mediæval heretics were usually classed under the head of Waldenses. Another sect, usually classed with the Waldenses, were called Cathari. The Novatians, a sect which sprang up in the church in the third century, assumed also the name of Cathari, as laying claim to extraordinary purity (καθαροι), but there is no reason for believing that the ancient sect was revived in the Cathari of the later period, or even that the two words are identical. The name of the latter sect is often spelt Gazari, Gazeri, Gaçari, and Chazari; and, as they were more especially a German sect, it is supposed to have been the origin of the German words *Ketzer* and *Ketzerie,* which became the common German terms for a heretic and heresy. It was suggested by Henschenius that this name was derived from the German *Katze* or *Ketze,* a cat, in allusion to the common report that they assembled at night like cats, or ghosts; or the cat may have been an allusion to the belief that in their secret meetings they worshipped that animal. This sect must have been very ignorant and superstitious if it be true which some old writers tell us, that they believed that the sun was a demon, and the moon a female called Heva, and that these two had sexual intercourse every month.[1] Like the other heretical sects, these Cathari were accused of indulging in unnatural vices,

[1] Bonacursus, *Vita Haereticornm,* in D'Achery, *Spicilegium,* tom. i, p. 209. This book is considered to have been written about the year 1190.

and the German words *Ketzerie* and *Ketzer* were eventually used to signify sodomy and a sodomite, as well as heresy and a heretic.

The Waldenses generally, taking all the sects which people class under this name, including also the older Bulgari and Publicani, were charged with holding secret meetings, at which the devil appeared to them in the shape, according to some, of a goat, whom they worshipped by offering the kiss *in ano,* after which they indulged in promiscuous sexual intercourse. Some believed that they were conveyed to these meetings by unearthly means. The English chronicler, Ralph de Coggeshall, tells a strange story of the means of locomotion possessed by these heretics. In the city of Rheims, in France, in the time of St. Louis, a handsome young woman was charged with heresy, and carried before the archbishop, in whose presence she avowed her opinions, and confessed that she had received them from a certain old woman of that city. The old woman was then arrested, convicted of being an obstinate heretic, and condemned to the stake. When they were preparing to carry her out to the fire, she suddenly turned to the judges and said, "Do you think that you are able to burn me in your fire? I care neither for it nor for you!" And taking a ball of thread, she threw it out at a large window by which she was standing, holding the end of the thread in her hands, and exclaiming, "Take it!" (*recipe*).

In an instant, in the sight of all who were there, the old woman was lifted from the ground, and, following the ball of thread, was carried into the air nobody knew where; and the archbishop's officers burnt the young woman in her place.[1] It was the belief of most of the old sects of this class, as well as of the more ancient Pagans from whom they were derived, that those who were fully initiated into their most secret mysteries became endowed with powers and faculties above those possessed by ordinary individuals. A list of the errors of the Waldenses, printed in the *Reliquiæ Antiquæ*, from an English manuscript, enumerates among them that they met to indulge in promiscuous sexual intercourse, and held perverse doctrines in accordance with it; that, in some parts, the devil appeared to them in the form of a cat, and that each kissed him under the tail; and that in other parts they rode to the place of meeting upon a staff anointed with a certain unguent, and were conveyed thither in a moment of time. The writer adds that,

---

[1] Radulphus Cogeshalenfis, in the *Amplissima Collectio* of Martene and Durand. On the offences with which the different sects comprised under the name of Waldenses were charged, see Gretser's *Scriptores contra Sectam Waldensium*, which will be found in the twelfth volume of his works, Bonacursus, *Vita Haereticorum*, in the first volume of D'Achery's *Spicilegium*, and the work of a Carthusian monk in Martene and Durand, *Amplissima Collectio*, vol. vi, col. 57 et seq.

in the parts where he lived, these practices had not been known to exist for a long time.[1]

Our old chroniclers exult over the small success which attended the efforts of these heretics from France and the South to introduce themselves into our island.[2] These sects, with secret and obscene rites, appear, indeed, to have found most favour among the peoples who spoke a dialect derived from the Latin, and this we might naturally be led to expect, for the fact of the preservation of the Latin tongue is itself a proof of the greater force of the Roman element in the society, that from which these secret rites appear to have been chiefly derived. It is a curious circumstance, in connection with this subject, that the popular oaths and exclamations among the people speaking the languages derived from the Romans are almost all composed of the names of the objects of this phallic worship, an entire contrast to the practice of the Teutonic tribes—the vulgar oaths of the people speaking Neo-Latin dialects are obscene, those of the German race are profane. We have seen how the women of Antwerp, who, though perhaps they did not speak the Roman dialect, appear to have been much influenced by Roman sentiments, made their

---

[1] Wright and Halliwell, *Reliquæ Antiquae*, vol. i, p. 247.

[2] See, for example, Guil, Neubrigensis, *De Rebus Anglicis*, lib. ii, c. 13, and Walter Mapes, *de Nugis Curialium*, p. 62.

appeal to their genius Ters. When a Spaniard is irritated or suddenly excited, he exclaims, *Carajo!* (the virile member) or *Cojones!* (the testicles). An Italian, under similar circumstances, uses the exclamation *Cazzo!* (the virile member). The Frenchman apostrophizes the act, *Foutre!* The female member, *coño* with the Spaniard, *conno* with the Italian, and *con* with the Frechman, was and is used more generally as an expression of contempt, which is also the case with the testicles, *couillons,* in French—those who have had experience in the old days of " diligence " travelling will remember how usual it was for the driver, when the horses would not go quick enough, to address the leader in such terms as, " *Va, donc, vieux con!* " We have no such words used in this manner in the Germanic languages, with the exception, perhaps, of the German *Potz!* and *Potztausend!* and the English equivalent, *Pox!* which last is gone quite out of use. There was an attempt among the fashionables of our Elizabethan age of literature, to introduce the Italian *cazzo* under the form of *catso,* and the French *foutre* under that of *foutra,* but these were mere affectations of a moment, and were so little in accord with our national sentiments that they soon disappeared.

The earliest accounts of a sect which held secret meetings for celebrating obscene rites is found in

France. It appears that, early in the eleventh century, there was in the city of Orleans a society consisting of members of both sexes, who assembled at certain times in a house there, for the purposes which are described rather fully in a document found in the cartulary of the abbey of St. Père at Chartres. As there stated, they went to the meeting, each carrying in the hand a lighted lamp, and they began by chaunting the names of demons in the manner of a litany, until a demon suddenly descended among them in the form of an animal. This was no sooner seen, than they all extinguished their lamps, and each man took the first female he put his hand upon, and had sexual intercourse with her, without regard if she were his mother, or his sister, or a consecrated nun; and this intercourse, we are told, was looked upon by them as an act of holiness and religion. The child which was the fruit of this intercourse was taken on the eighth day and purified by fire, " in the manner of the ancient Pagans,"—so says the contemporary writer of this document,—it was burnt to ashes in a large fire made for that purpose. The ashes were collected with great reverence, and preserved, to be administered to members of the society who were dying, just as good Christians received the viaticum. It is added that there was such a virtue in these ashes, that an individual who had once tasted them would hardly ever after be able to turn his mind from that heresy and take the path of truth.

Whatever degree of truth there may have been in this story, it must have been greatly exaggerated; but the conviction of the existence of secret societies of this character during the middle ages appears to have been so strong and so generally held, that we must hesitate in rejecting it. Perhaps we may take the leaden tokens already described, and represented in one of our plates,[1] as evidence of the existence of such societies, for these curious objects appear to admit of no other satisfactory explanation than that of having been in use in secret clubs of a very impure character.

It has been already remarked that people soon seized upon accusations of this kind as excuses for persecution, religious and political, and we meet with a curious example in the earlier half of the thirteenth century. The district of Steding, in the north of Germany, now known as Oldenburg, was at the beginning of the thirteenth century inhabited by a people who lived in sturdy independence, but the archbishops of Bremen seem to have claimed some sort of feudal superiority over them, which they resisted by force. The archbishop, in revenge, declared them

---

[1] See before, p. 60, and Plate IX.

heretics, and proclaimed a crusade against them. Crusades against heretics were then in fashion, for it was just at the time of the great war against the Albigeois. The Stedingers maintained their independence successfully for some years. In 1232 and 1233, the pope issued two bulls against the offending Stedingers, in both of which he charges them with various heathen and magical practices, but in the second he enters more fully into details. These Stedingers, the pope (Gregory IX.) tells us, performed the following ceremonies at the initiation of a new convert into their sect. When the novice was introduced, a toad presented itself, which all who were present kissed, some on the posteriors, and others on the mouth, when they drew its tongue and spittle into their own mouths. Sometimes this toad appeared of only the natural size, but sometimes it was as big as a goose or duck, and often its size was that of an oven. As the novice proceeded, he encountered a man who was extraordinarily pale, with large black eyes, and whose body was so wasted that his flesh seemed to be all gone, leaving nothing but the skin hanging on his bones. The novice kissed this personage, and found him as cold as ice; and after this kiss all traces of the Catholic faith vanished from his heart. Then they all sat down to a banquet; and when this was over, there stepped out of a statue, which stood in their place of meeting, a black cat, as large as a moderate sized dog, which advanced backwards to them, with its tail turned up. The novice first, then the master, and then all the others in their turns, kissed the cat under the tail, and then returned to their places, where they remained in silence, with their heads inclined towards the cat. Then the master suddenly pronounced the words "Spare us!" which he addressed to the next in order; and the third answered, "We know it, lord;" and a fourth added, "We ought to obey." At the close of this ceremony the lights were extinguished, and each man took the first woman who came to hand, and had carnal intercourse with her. When this was over, the candles were again lighted, and the performers resumed their places. Then out of a dark corner of the room came a man, the upper part of whom, above the loins, was bright and radiant as the sun, and illuminated the whole room, while his lower parts were rough and hairy like a cat. The master then tore off a bit of the garment of the novice, and said to the shining personage, "Master, this is given to me, and I give it again to thee." The master replied, "Thou hast served me well, and thou wilt serve me more and better; what thou hast given me I give unto thy keeping." When he had said this, the shining man vanished, and the meeting broke up.

Such were the secret ceremonies of the Stedingers, according to the deliberate statement of Pope Gregory IX, who also charges them with offering direct worship to Lucifer.[1]

But the most remarkable, and at the same time the most celebrated, affair in which these accusations of secret and obscene ceremonies were brought to bear, was that of the trial and dissolution of the order of the knights templars. The charges against the knights templars were not heard of for the first time at the period of their dissolution, but for many years it had been whispered abroad that they had secret opinions and practices of an objectionable character. At length the wealth of the order, which was very great in France, excited the cupidity of King Philippe IV, and it was resolved to proceed against them, and despoil them of their possessions. The grounds for these proceedings were furnished by two templars, one a Gascon, the other an Italian, who were evidently men of bad character, and who, having been imprisoned for some offence or offences, made a confession of the secret practices of their order, and upon these confessions certain articles of accusation were drawn up. These appear to have

---

[1] Baronius, *Annales Ecclesiastici*, tom. xxi, p. 89, where the two bulls are printed, and where the details of the history of the Stedingers will be found.

been enlarged afterwards. In 1307, Jacques de Molay, the grand master of the order, was treacherously allured to Paris by the king, and there seized and thrown into prison. Others, similarly committed to prison in all parts of the kingdom, were examined individually on the charges urged against them, and many confessed, while others obstinately denied the whole. Amongst these charges were the following: I. That on the admission of a new member of the order, after having taken the oath of obedience, he was obliged to deny Christ, and to spit, and sometimes also to trample, upon the cross; 2. That they then received the kiss of the templar, who officiated as receiver, on the mouth, and afterwards were obliged to kiss him *in ano*, on the navel, and sometimes on the generative member; 3. That, in despite of the Saviour, they sometimes worshipped a cat, which appeared amongst them in their secret conclave; 4. That they practised unnatural vice together; 5. That they had idols in their different provinces; in the form of a head, having sometimes three faces, sometimes two, or only one, and sometimes a bare skull, which they called their saviour, and believed its influence to be exerted in making them rich, and in making flowers grow and the earth germinate; and 6. That they always wore about their bodies a cord which had been rubbed against the head, and which served for their protection.[1]

The ceremonies attending the reception into the order were so universally acknowledged, and are described in terms which have so much the appearance of truthfulness, that we can hardly altogether disbelieve in them. The denial was to be repeated thrice, no doubt in imitation of St. Peter. It appears to have been considered as a trial of the strength of the obedience they had just sworn to the order, and they all pleaded that they had obeyed with reluctance, that they had denied with the mouth but not with the heart; and that they had intentionally spit beside the cross and not upon it. In one instance the cross was of silver, but it was more commonly of brass, and still more frequently of wood; on one occasion the cross painted in a missal was used, and the cross on the templar's mantle often served the purpose. When one Nicholas de Compiegne protested against these two acts, all the templars who were present told him that he must do them, for it was the custom of the order.[2] Baldwin de St. Just at first refused, but the receptor warned him that if he persisted in his refusal, it would be the worse for him *(aliter male accideret sibi)*, and then " he was so

[1] *Procès des Templiers*, edited by M. Michelet, vol. i, pp. 90-92.
[2] *Procès des Templiers*, ii, 418.

much alarmed that his hair stood on end." Jacques de Trecis said that he did it under fear, because his receptor stood by with a great naked sword in his hand.[1] Another, Geoffrey de Thatan, having similarly refused, his receptor told him that they were "points of the order," and that if he did not comply, "he should be put in such a place that he would never see his own feet." And another who refused to utter the words of denial was thrown into prison and kept there until vespers, and when he saw that he was in peril of death, he yielded, and did whatever the receptor required of him, but he adds that he was so troubled and frightened that he had forgotten whether he spat on the cross or not. Gui de la Roche, a presbyter of the diocese of Limoges, said that he uttered the denial with great weeping. Another, when he denied Christ, "was all stupified and troubled, and it seemed as if he were enchanted, not knowing what counsel to take, as they threatened him heavily if he did not do it." When Etienne de Dijon similarly refused to deny his Saviour, the preceptor told him that he must do it because he had sworn to obey his orders, and then "he denied with his mouth," he said, "but not with his heart; and he did this with great grief," and he adds that when it

---

[1] *Procès*, 1, 254.

was done, he was so conscience-struck that "he wished he had been outside at his liberty, even though it had been with the loss of one of his arms." When Odo de Dompierre, with great reluctance, at length spat on the cross, he said that he did it with such bitterness of heart that he would rather have had his two thighs broken. Michelet, in the account of the proceedings against the templars in his "History of France," offers an ingenious explanation of these ceremonies of initiation which gives them a typical meaning. He imagines that they were borrowed from the figurative mysteries and rites of the early Church, and supposes that, in this spirit, the candidate for admission into the order was first presented as a sinner and renegade, in which character, after the example of Peter, he was made to deny Christ. This denial, he suggests, was a sort of pantomime in which the novice expressed his reprobate state by spitting on the cross; after which he was stripped of his profane clothing, received, through the kiss of the order, into a higher state of faith, and clothed with the garb of its holiness. If this were the case, the true meaning of the performance must have been very soon forgotten.

This was especially the case with the kiss. According to the articles of accusation, one of the ceremonies of initiation required the novice to kiss the receiver on the mouth, on the *anus,* or the end of the spine, on the navel, and on the *virga virilis.* The last is not mentioned in the examinations, but the others are described by so many of the witnesses that we cannot doubt of their truth. From the depositions of many of the templars examined, it would appear that the usual order was to kiss the receptor first *in ano,* next on the navel, and then on the mouth.[1] The first of these was an act which would, of course, be repulsive to most people, and the practice arose gradually of only kissing the end of the spine, or, as it was called in mediæval Latin, *in anca.* Bertrand de Somorens, of the diocese of Amiens, describing a reception at which more than one new member was admitted, says that the receiver next told them that they must kiss him *in ano;* but, instead of kissing him there, they lifted up his clothes and kissed him on the spine. The receptor, it appears, had the power of remitting this kiss when he judged there was a sufficient reason. Etienne de Dijon, a presbyter of the diocese of Langres, said that, when he was admitted into the order, the preceptor told him that he ought, "according to the observances of the order," to kiss his receiver *in ano,* but that in consideration of his being a presbyter, he would spare him and remit this kiss. Pierre de Grumenil, also a

---

[1] See the *Procès,* ii. 286, 362, 364.

presbyter, when called upon to perform this act, refused, and was allowed to kiss his receiver on the navel only. A presbyter named Ado de Dompierre was excused for the same reason,[1] as well as many others. Another templar, named Pierre de Lanhiac, said that, at his reception into the order, his receptor told him that he must kiss him *in ano,* because that was one of the points of the order, but that, at the earnest supplication of his uncle, who was present, and must therefore have been a knight of the order, he obtained a remission of this kiss.

Another charge against the templars was still more disgusting. It was said that they proscribed all intercourse with women, and one of the men examined stated, which was also confessed by others, that his receptor told him that, from that hour, he was never to enter a house in which a woman lay in labour, nor to take part as godfather at the baptism of any child, but he added that he had broken his oath, for he had assisted at the baptism of several children while still in the order, which he had left about a year before the seizure of the templars, for the love of a woman of whom he had become enamoured. On the other hand, those who replied to the interrogatory of the king's officers in this process, were all but unanimous in the avowal that on entering the order

[1] *Procès,* i, 307.

they received the permission to commit sodomy amongst themselves. Two or three professed not to have understood this injunction in a bad sense, but to have supposed that it only meant that, when the brethren were short of beds, each was to be ready to lend half of his bed to his fellow. One of them, named Gillet de Encraye, said that he at first supposed it to be meant innocently, but that his receptor immediately undeceived him, by repeating it in less covert terms, at which he was himself so horrified that he wished himself far away from the chapel in which the ceremony took place. A great number of templars stated that, after the kisses of initiation, they were informed that if they felt moved by natural heat, they might call any one of the brethren to their relief, and that they ought to relieve their brethren when appealed to under the same circumstances. This appears to have been the most common form of the injunction. In one or two instances the receiver is described as adding that this was an act of contempt towards the other sex, which may perhaps be considered as showing that the ceremony was derived from some of the mysteries of the strange sects which appeared in the earlier ages of Christianity. Jean de St. Loup, who held the office of master of the house of templars at Soisiac, said that, on his reception into the order, he received the injunction not

to have intercourse with women, but, if he could not
persevere in continence, he might have the same intercourse with men; and others were told that it
would "be better to satisfy their lust among themselves, whereby the order would escape evil report,
than if they went to women." But although the almost unanimity of the confessions leave hardly room
for a doubt that such injunctions were given, yet on
the other hand they are equally unanimous in deny-
ing that these injunctions were carried into practice.
Almost every templar, as the questions were put to
him, after admitting that he was told that he might
indulge in such vice with the other brethren, asserted
that he had never done this, and that he had never
been asked to do so by any of them. Theobald de
Taverniac, whose name tells us that he came from
the south, denied indignantly the existence of such a
vice among their order but in terms which themselves told not very much in favour of the morality
of the templars in other respects. He said that, " as
to the crime of sodomy," he believed the charge to
be totally untrue, "because they could have very
handsome and elegant women when they liked, and
that they did have them frequently when they were
rich and powerful enough to afford it, and that on
this account he and other brothers of the order were
removed from their houses, as he said." We have

an implied acknowledgment that the templars did not entirely neglect the other sex in a statement quoted by Du Puy that, if a child were born from the intercourse between a templar and a virgin, they roasted it, and made an unguent of its fat, with which they anointed their idol. Those who confessed to the existence of the vice were so few, and their evidence so indefinite or indirect, that they are deserving of no consideration. One had heard that some brethren beyond the sea had committed unnatural vices.[1] Another, Hugh de Faure, had heard say that two brothers of the order, dwelling in the Chateau Pelerin, had been charged with sodomy; that, when this reached the ears of the master, he gave orders for their arrest, and that one had been killed in the attempt to escape, while the other was taken and imprisoned for life. Peter Brocart, a templar of Paris, declared that one of the order, one night, called him and committed sodomy with him; adding that he had not refused, because he considered himself bound to obedience by the rules of the order.[2] The evidence is decidedly strong against the prevalence of such a vice among the templars, and the alleged permission was perhaps a mere form of words, which concealed some occult meaning unknown to the mass of the

[1] *Procès*, ii, 213.
[2] *Procès*, ii, 294.

templars themselves. We are not inclined to reject altogether the theory of the baron von Hammer-Pürgstall, that the templars had adopted some of the mysterious tenets of the eastern Gnostics.

In regard to the secret idolatry with which the templars were charged, it is a subject involved in great obscurity. The cat is but little spoken of in the depositions. Some Italian knights confessed that they had been present at a secret chapter of twelve knights held at Brindisi, when a grey cat suddenly appeared amongst them, and they worshipped it. At Nismes, some templars declared that they had been present at a chapter at Montpellier, when the demon appeared to them in the form of a cat, and promised them worldly prosperity, but they appear to have been visionaries not to be trusted, for they stated that at the same time devils appeared in the shape of women. An English templar, examined in London, deposed that in England they did not adore the cat, or the idol, but that he had heard it positively stated that the cat and the idol were worshipped by the templars in parts beyond sea. A solitary Freshman, examined in Paris, Gillet de Encreyo, spoke of the cat, and said that he had heard, but had forgotten who were his informants, and did not believe them, that beyond sea a certain cat had appeared to the templars in their battles. The cat belongs to a lower class of popular superstitions, perhaps, than that of the templars.

This, however, was not the case with the idol, which was generally described as the figure of a human head, and appears only to have been shown in the more secret chapter meetings on particular occasions. Many of the templars examined before the commissioners, said that they had heard this idol head spoken of as existing in the order, and others deposed to having seen it. It was generally described as being about the natural size of a man's head, with a very fierce-looking face and a beard, the latter sometimes white. Different witnesses varied as to the material of which it was made, and, indeed, in various other particulars, which lead us to suppose that each house of the templars, where the idol existed, had its own head, and that they varied in form. They agreed generally that this head was an object of worship. One templar deposed that he was present at a chapter of the order in Paris, when the head was brought in, but he was unable to describe it at all, for, when he saw it, he was so struck with terror that he hardly knew where he was. Another, Ralph de Gysi, who held the office of receptor for the province of Champagne, said that he had seen the head in many chapters; that, when it was introduced, all present threw themselves on the ground and adored it: and when asked to describe it, he said, on his oath, that its countenance was so terrible, that it seemed to him to be the figure of a demon—using the French word *un maufé,* and that as often as he saw it, so great a fear took possession of him, that he could hardly look upon it without fear and trembling. Jean Taylafer said that, at his reception into the order, his attention was directed to a head upon the altar in the chapel, which he was told he must worship; he described it as of the natural size of a mans head, but could not describe it more particularly, except that he thought it was of a reddish colour.[1] Raynerus de Larchent saw the head twice in a chapter, especially once in Paris, where it had a beard, and they adored and kissed it, and called it their saviour. Guillermus de Herbaleyo saw the head with its beard, at two chapters. He thought it was of silver gilt, and wood inside. He " saw the brethren adore it, and he went through the form of adoring it himself, but he did it not in his heart." According to one witness, Deodatus Jaffet, a knight from the south of France who had been received at Pedenat, the receptor showed him a head, or idol, which appeared to have three faces, and said to him, " You must adore this as your saviour, and the saviour of the order of the temple," and he added that he was made to worship the idol,

---

[1] *Procès*, i, 190.

saying, "Blessed be he who shall save my soul!"
Another deponent gave a very similar account. Another knight of the order, Hugo de Paraudo, said
that, in a chapter at Montpellier, he had both seen,
held, and felt, the idol or head, and that he and the
other brothers adored it but he, like the others,
pleaded that he did not adore it in his heart. He
described it as supported on four feet, two before
and two behind.[1] Guillaume de Arrablay, the king's
almoner *(eleemosynarius regius)*, said that in the
chapter at which he was received, a head made of
silver was placed on the altar, and adored by those
who formed the chapter; he was told that it was the
head of one of the eleven thousand virgins, and had
always believed this to be the case, until after the arrest of the order, when, hearing all that was said on
the matter, he "suspected" that it was the idol; and
he adds in his deposition that it seemed to him to
have two faces, a terrible look, and a silver beard.
It does not appear very clear why he should have
taken a head with two faces, a fierce look, and a
beard, for one of the eleven thousand virgins, but
this is, perhaps, partly explained by the deposition
of another witness, Guillaume Pidoye, who had the
charge of the relics, &c., belonging to the Temple in
Paris, and who produced a head of silver gilt, hav-

---

[1] *Procès*, ii, 363.

ing a woman's face, and a small skull, resembling that of a woman, inside, which was said to be that of one of the eleven thousand virgins. At the same time another head was brought forward, having a beard, and supposed to be that of the idol.[1] Both these witnesses had no doubt confounded two things. Pierre Garald, of Mursac, another witness, said that after he had denied Christ and spitten on the cross, the receptor drew from his bosom a certain small image of brass or gold, which appeared to represent the figure of a woman, and told him that "he must believe in it, and have faith in it, and that it would be well for him." Here the idol appears in the form of a statuette. There was also another account of the idol, which perhaps refers to some further object of superstition among the templars. According to one deponent, it was an old skin embalmed, with bright carbuncles for eyes, which shone like the light of heaven. Others said that it was the skin of a man, but agreed with the others in regard to the carbuncles.[2] In England a minorite friar deposed that an English knight of the Temple had assured him that the templars had four principal idols in this country, one in the sacristy of the Temple in London, another at Bristelham, a third at Brueria (Bruern in

---

[1] *Procès*, ii, 218.
[2] Du Puy, *Hist. des Templ.*, pp. 22, 24.

Lincolnshire), and the fourth at some place beyond the Humber.[1]

Another piece of information relating to this "idol," which has been the subject of considerable discussion among modern writers, was elicited from the examination of some knights from the south. Gauserand de Montpesant, a knight of Provence, said that their superior showed him an idol made in the form of Baffomet; another, named Raymond Rubei, described it as a wooden head, on which the figure of Baphomet was painted, and adds, "that he worshipped it by kissing its feet, and exclaiming, 'Yalla,' which was," he says, "*verbum Saracenorum*," a word taken from the Saracens.[2] A templar of Florence declared that, in the secret chapters of the order, one brother said to the other, showing the idol, "Adore this head—this head is your god and your Mahomet." The word Mahomet was used commonly in the middle ages as a general term for an idol or false god; but some writers have suggested that Baphomet is itself a mere corruption of Mahomet, and suppose that the templars had secretly embraced Mahometanism. A much more remarkable explanation of this word has, however, been proposed, which is, at the least, worthy of very great consideration, especially

[1] Wilkins, *Concil.*, vol. ii, p. 363.

[2] Du Puy, *Hist. des Templiers*, p. 21.

as it comes from so distinguished an orientalist and scholar as the late baron Joseph von Hammer-Pürgstall. It arose partly from the comparison of a number of objects of art, ornamented with figures, and belonging apparently to the thirteenth century. These objects consist chiefly of small images, or statuettes, coffers, and cups.

Von Hammer has described, and given engravings of, twenty-four such images, which it must be acknowledged answer very well to the descriptions of their "idol" given by the templars in their examinations, except only that the templars usually speak of them as of the size of life, and as being merely heads. Most of them have beards, and tolerably fierce countenances. Among those given by Von Hammer are seven which present only a head, and two with two faces, backwards and forwards, as described in some of the depositions. These two appear to be intended for female heads. Altogether Von Hammer has described fifteen cups and goblets, but a much smaller number of coffers. Both cups and coffers are ornamented with extremely curious figures, representing a continuous scene, apparently religious ceremonies of some kind or other, but certainly of an obscene character, all the persons engaged in which are represented naked. It is not a part of our subject to enter into a detailed examination of these mysteries. The most interesting of the coffers described by Von Hammer, which was preserved in the private museum of the duc de Blacas, is of calcarous stone, nine inches long by seven broad, and four and a half deep, with a lid about two inches thick. It was found in Burgundy. On the lid is sculptured a figure, naked, with a head-dress resembling that given to Cybele in ancient monuments, holding up a chain with each hand, and surrounded with various symbols, the sun and moon above, the star and the pentacle below, and under the feet a human skull.[1] The chains are explained by Von Hammer as representing the chains of æons of the Gnostics. On the four sides of the coffer we see a series of figures engaged in the performance of various ceremonies, which are not easily explained, but which Von Hammer considers as belonging to the rites of the Gnostics and Ophians. The offering of a calf figures prominently among these rites, a worship which is said still to exist among the Nossarii, or Nessarenes, the Druses, and other sects in the East. In the middle of the scene on one side, a human skull is seen, raised upon a pole. On another side an androgynous figure is represented as the object of worship of two candidates for initiation, who wear masks apparently of a cat, and whose form of adoration reminds us of the kiss enacted at the initi-

---

[1] See our plate XIV.

PLATE XIV

PRIAPIC ILLUSTRATIONS FROM OLD BALLADS

ation of the templars.[1] This group reminds us, too, of the pictures of the orgies in the worship of Priapus, as represented on Roman monuments. The second of the coffers in the cabinet of the duc de Blacas was found in Tuscany, and is rather larger than the one just described, but made of the same material, though of a finer grain. The lid of this coffer is lost, but the sides are covered with sculpture of a similar character. A large goblet, or bowl, of marble, in the imperial museum at Vienna, is surrounded by a series of figures of similar character, which are engraved by Von Hammer, who sees in one group of men (who are furnished in the original with prominent phalli) and serpents, a direct allusion to Ophite rites. Next after these comes a group which we have reproduced in our plate,[2] representing a strange figure seated upon an eagle, and accompanied with two of the symbols represented on the coffer found in Burgundy, the sun and moon. The two symbols below are considered by Von Hammer to represent, according to the rude mediæval notions of its form, the womb, or matrix; the fecundating organ is penetrating the one, while the infant is emerging from the other. The last figure in this series, which we have also copied,[3]

[1] Plate xv, fig. 1.
[2] Plate xv, fig. 2.
[3] Plate xv, fig. 3.

is identical with that on the lid of the coffer found in Burgundy, but it is distinctly represented as androgynous. We have exactly the same figure on another coffer, in the Vienna museum,[1] with some of the same symbols, the star, pentacle, and human skull. Perhaps, in this last, the beard is intended to show that the figure must be taken as androgynous.

On an impartial comparison we can hardly doubt that these curious objects,—images, coffers, cups, and bowls,—have been intended for use in some secret and mysterious rites, and the arguments by which Von Hammer attempts to show that they belonged to the templars seem at least to be very plausible. Several of the objects represented upon them, even the skull, are alluded to in some of the confessions of the templars, and these evidently only confessed a part of what they knew, or otherwise they were very imperfectly acquainted with the secrets of their order. Perhaps the most secret doctrines and rites were only communicated fully to a small number. There is, however, another circumstance connected with these objects which appears to furnish an almost irresistible confirmation of Von Hammer's theory. Most of them bear inscriptions, written in Arabic, Greek, and Roman characters. The inscriptions on the images appear to be merely proper names, probably those of

[1] Plate xv, fig. 4.

their possessors. But with the coffers and bowls the case is different, for they contain a nearly uniform inscription in Arabic characters, which, according to the interpretation given by Von Hammer, contains a religious formula. The Arabic characters, he says, have been copied by a European, and not very skilful, carver, who did not understand them, from an Eastern original, and the inscriptions contain corruptions and errors which either arose from this circumstance, or, as Von Hammer suggests, may have been introduced designedly, for the purpose of concealing the meaning from the uninitiated. A good example of this inscription surrounds the lid of the coffer found in Burgundy, and is interpreted as follows by Von Hammer, who regards it as a sort of parody on the *Cantate laudes Domini*. In fact, the word under the feet of the figure, between them and the skull, is nothing more than the Latin *cantate* expressed in Arabic letters. The words with which this *Cantate* begins are written above the head of the figure, and are read by Von Hammer as *Fah la Sidna*, which is more correctly *Fella Sidna*, i. e. O God, our Lord! The formula itself, to which this is an introduction, commences on the right side, and the first part of it reads *Houvè Mete Zonar feseba* (or *sebaa*) *B. Mounkir teaala tiz.* There is no such word in Arabic as *mete*, and Von Hammer considers it to be simply the Greek word μῆτις, wisdom, a personification in what we may perhaps call the Gnostic mythology answering to the Sophia of the Ophianites. He considers that the name Baphomet is derived from the Greek words Βαφη μητοες, i. e. the baptism· of Metis, and that in its application it is equivalent with the name Mete itself. He has further shown, we think conclusively, that Baphomet, instead of being a corruption of Mahomet, was a name known among the Gnostic sects in the East. *Zonar* is not an Arabic word, and is perhaps only a corruption or error of the sculptor, but Von Hammer thought it meant a girdle, and that it alluded to the mysterious girdle of the templars, of which so much is said in their examinations. The letter *B* is supposed by Von Hammer to stand here for the name Baphomet, or for that of Barbalo, one of the most important personages in the Gnostic mythology. *Mounkir* is the Arabic word for a person who denies the orthodox faith. The rest of the formula is given on the other side of the figure, but as the inscription here presents several corruptions, we will give Von Hammer's translation (in Latin) of the more correct copy of the formula inscribed on the bowl or goblet preserved in the museum at Vienna. In the Vienna bowl, the formula of faith is written on a sort of large placard, which is held up to view by a figure apparently intended for

PLATE XV
"IDOL" OF THE KNIGHTS TEMPLARS

another representation of Mete or Baphomet. Von Hammer translates it:—

"Exaltetur Mete germinans, stirps nostra ego et septem fuere, *tu renegans reditus* ὥϱωϰτὸς fis."

This still is, it must be confessed, rather mysterious, and, in fact, most of these copies of the formula of faith are more or less defective, but, from a comparison of them, the general form and meaning of the whole is made perfectly clear. This may be translated, "Let Mete be exalted, who causes things to bud and blossom! he is our root; it (the root) is one and seven; abjure (the faith), and abandon thyself to all pleasures." The number seven is said to refer to the seven archons of the Gnostic creed.

There are certainly several points in this formula which present at least a singular coincidence with the statements made in the examinations of the templars. In the first place the invocation which precedes the formula, Yalla (Jah la), agrees exactly with the statement of Raymond Rubei, one of the Provencal templars that when the superior exhibited the idol, or figure of Baphomet, he kissed it and exclaimed "Yalla!" which he calls "a word of the Saracens," i. e. Arabic.[1] It is evident that, in this case, the witness not only knew the word, but that he knew to what language it belonged. Again, the epithet *germi-*

---

[1] Du Puy, *Hist. des Templiers*, p. 94.

nans, applied to Mete, or Baphomet, is in accord with the statement in the formal list of articles of accusation against the templars, that they worshipped their idol because " it made the trees to flourish and the earth to germinate." The abjuration of the formula on the monuments seems to be identical with the denial in the initiation of novices to the order of the Temple; and it may be added, that the closing words of the formula involve in the original an idea more obscene than is expressed in the translation, an allusion to the unnatural vice in which the templars are stated to have received permission to indulge. There is another curious statement in the examinations which seems to point directly to our images and coffers—one of the English witnesses under examination, named John de Donington, who had left the order and become a friar at Salisbury, said that an old templar had assured him that " some templars carried such idols in their coffers." They seem to have been treasured up for the same reason as the mandrake, for one article in the articles against the templars is that they worshipped their idol because " it could make them rich, and that it had brought all their great wealth to the order."

The two other classes of what the Baron Von Hammer supposed to be relics of the secret worship of the templars, appear to us to be much less satisfactorily explained. These are sculptures on old churches, and coins or medals. Such sculptures are found, according to Von Hammer, on the churches of Schöngraber, Waltendorf, and Bercktoldorf, in Austria; in that of Deutschaltenburg, and in the ruins of that of Postyén, in Hungary; and in those of Murau, Prague, and Egra, in Bohemia. To these examples we are to add the sculptures of the church of Montmorillon, in Poitou, some of which have been engraved by Montfaucon,[1] and those of the church of Ste. Croix, in Bordeaux. We have already[2] remarked the rather frequent prevalence of subjects more or less obscene in the sculptures which ornament early churches, and suggested that they may be explained in some degree by the tone given to society by the existence of this priapic worship; but we are not inclined to agree with Von Hammer's explanation of them, or to think that they have any connection with the templars. We can easily understand the existence of such direct allusions on coffers or other objects intended to be concealed, or at least kept in private; but it is hardly probable that men who held opinions and practised rites the very rumour of which was then so full of danger, would proclaim them publicly on the walls of their buildings, for the wall

---

[1] Montfaucon, *Antiquité Expliquée*, Suppl. tom. ii, plate 59.
[2] See before, p. 139.

of a church was then, perhaps, the most effectual medium of publication. The question of the supposed templar medals is very obscure. Von Hammer has engraved a certain number of these objects, which present various singular subjects on the obverse, sometimes with a cross on the reverse, and sometimes bracteate. Antiquaries have given the name of abbey tokens to a rather numerous class of such medals, the use of which is still very uncertain, although there appears to be little doubt of its being of a religious character. Some have supposed that they were distributed to those who attended at certain sacraments or rites of the Church, who could thus, when called up, prove by the number of their tokens, the greater or less regularity of their attendance. Whether this were the case or not, it is certain that the burlesque and other societies of the middle ages, such as the feast of fools, parodied these "tokens," and had burlesque medals, in lead and sometimes in other metals, which were perhaps used for a similar purpose. We have already spoken more than once of obscene medals, and have engraved specimens of them, which were perhaps used in secret societies derived from, or founded upon, the ancient phallic worship. It is not at all improbable that the templars may have employed similar medals, and that those would contain allusions to the rites in which they were employed. The medals published by Von Hammer are said to have been found chiefly on the sites of settlements of the order of the Temple. However, the comparison of facts stated in the confessions of many of the templars, as preserved in the official reports, with the images and sculptured cups and coffers given by Von Hammer-Pürgstall, lead to the conclusion that there is truth in the explanation he gives of the latter, and that the templars, or at least some of them, had secretly adopted a form of the rites of Gnosticism, which was itself founded upon the phallic worship of the ancients. An English templar, Stephen de Staplebridge, acknowledged that " there were two 'professions' in the order of the Temple, the first lawful and good, the second contrary to the faith." He had been admitted to the first of these when he first entered the order, eleven years before the time of his examination, but he was only initiated into the second or inner mysteries about a year afterwards; and he gives almost a picturesque description of this second initiation, which occurred in a chapter held at " Dineslee " in Herefordshire. Another English templar, Thomas de Tocci, said that the errors had been brought into England by a French knight of high position in the order.[1]

---

[1] Wilkins, *Concil.*, ii, 387.

We have thus seen in how many various forms the old phallic, or priapic, worship presented itself in the middle ages, and how pertinaciously it held its ground through all the changes and developments of society, until at length we find all the circumstances of the ancient priapic orgies, as well as the mediæval additions, combined in that great and extensive superstition—witchcraft. At all times the initiated were believed to have obtained thereby powers which were not possessed by the uninitiated, and they only were supposed to know the proper forms of invocation of the deities who were the objects of their worship, which deities the Christian teachers invariably transformed into devils. The vows which the people of antiquity addressed to Priapus, those of the middle ages addressed to Satan. The witches' " Sabbath " was simply the last form which the Priapeia and Liberalia assumed in Western Europe, and in its various details all the incidents of those great and licentious orgies of the Romans were reproduced. The Sabbath of the witches does not appear to have formed a part of the Teutonic mythology, but we can trace it from the South through the countries in which the Roman element of society predominated. The incidents of the Sabbath are distinctly traced in Italy as early as the beginning of the fifteenth century, and soon afterwards they are found in the south of France. Towards the middle of that century an individual named Robinet de Vaulx, who had lived the life of a hermit in Burgundy, was arrested, brought to a trial at Langres, and burnt. This man was a native of Artois; he stated that to his knowledge there were a great number of witches in that province, and he not only confessed that he had attended these nocturnal assemblies of the witches, but he gave the names of some inhabitants of Arras whom he had met there. At this time—it was in the year 1459—the chapter general of the Jacobins, or friars preachers, was held at Langres, and among those who attended it was a Jacobin friar named Pierre de Broussart, who held the office of inquisitor of the faith in the city of Arras, and who eagerly listened to the circumstances of Robinet's confession. Among the names mentioned by him as having been present at the witches' meetings, were those of a prostitute named Demiselle, then living at Douai, and a man named Jehan Levite, but who was better known by the nickname of *Abbé de peu de sens* (the abbot of little sense). On Broussart's return to Arras, he caused both these persons to be arrested and brought to that city, where they were thrown into prison. The latter, who was a painter, and a composer and singer of popular songs, had left Arras before Robinet de Vaulx had made his confession, but he was traced to Abbeville, in Ponthieu, and captured there. Confessions were extorted from these persons which compromised others, and a number of individuals were committed to prison in consequence. In the sequel a certain number of them were burnt, after they had been induced to unite in a statement to the following effect. At this time, in this part of France at least, the term Vauderie, or, as it was then written, Vaulderie, was applied to the practice or profession of witchcraft. They said that the place of meeting was commonly a fountain in the wood of Mofflaines, about a league distant from Arras, and that they sometimes went thither on foot. The more usual way of proceeding, however, according to their own account, was this—they took an ointment given to them by the devil, with which they annointed a wooden rod, at the same time rubbing the palms of their hands with it, and then, placing the rod between their legs, they were suddenly carried through the air to the place of assembly. They found there a multitude of people, of both sexes, and of all estates and ranks, even wealthy burghers and nobles—and one of the persons examined declared that he had seen there not only ordinary ecclesiastics, but bishops and even cardinals. They found tables already spread, covered with all sorts of meats, and abundance of wines. A devil presided, usually in the form of a goat, with the tail of an ape, and a human countenance. Each first did oblation and homage to him by offering him his or her soul, or, at least some part of their body, and then, as a mark of adoration, kissed him on the posteriors. All this time the worshippers held burning torches in their hands. The abbot of little sense, already mentioned, held the office of master of the ceremonies at these meetings, and it was his duty to see that the new-comers duly performed their homage. After this they trampled on the cross, and spit upon it, in despite of Jesus and of the Holy Trinity, and performed other profane acts. They then seated themselves at the tables, and after they had eaten and drunk sufficiently, they rose and joined in a scene of promiscuous intercourse between the sexes, in which the demon took part, assuming alternately the form of either sex, according to that of his temporary partner. Other wicked acts followed, and then the devil preached to them, and enjoined them especially not to go to church, or hear mass, or touch holy water, or perform any other of the duties of good Christians. After this sermon was ended, the meeting was dissolved, and they separated and returned to their several homes.[1]

[1] The account of the witch trials at Arras was published in the supplementary additions to Monstrelet; but the original records of the proceedings have since been found and printed.

The violence of these witch persecutions at Arras led to a reaction, which, however, was not lasting, and from this time to the end of the century, the fear of witchcraft spread over Italy, France, and Germany, and went on increasing in intensity. It was during this period that witchcraft, in the hands of the more zealous inquisitors, was gradually worked up into a great system, and books of considerable extent were compiled, containing accounts of the various practices of the witches, and directions for proceeding against them. One of the earliest of these writers was a Swiss friar, named John Nider, who held the office of inquisitor in Switzerland, and has devoted one book of his *Formicarium* to witchcraft as it existed in that country. He makes no allusion to the witches' Sabbath, which, therefore, appears then not to have been known among the Swiss. Early in 1489, Ulric Molitor published a treatise on the same subject, under the title of *De Pythonicis Mulieribus,* and in the same year, 1489, appeared the celebrated book, the *Malleus Maleficarum,* or Hammer of Witches, the work of the three inquisitors for Germany, the chief of whom was Jacob Sprenger. This work gives us a complete and very interesting account of witchcraft as it then existed as an article of belief in Germany. The authors discuss various questions connected with it, such as that of the mysterious transport of witches from one place to another, and they decide that this transport was real, and that they were carried bodily through the air. It is remarkable, however, that even the *Malleus Maleficarum* contains no direct allusion to the Sabbath, and we may conclude that even then this great priapic orgie did not form a part of the Germanic creed; it was no doubt brought in there amid the witchcraft mania of the sixteenth century. From the time of the publication of the *Malleus Maleficarum* until the beginning of the seventeenth century, through all parts of Western Europe, the number of books upon sorcery which issued from the press was immense; and we must not forget that a monarch of our own, King James I, shone among the writers on witchcraft.

Three quarters of a century nearly had passed since the time of the *Malleus,* when a Frenchman named Bodin, Latinised into Bodinus, published a rather bulky treatise which became from that time the text-book on witchcraft. The Sabbath is described in this book in all its completeness. It was usually held in a lonely place, and when possible on the summits of mountains or in the solitude of forests. When the witch prepared to attend it, she went to her bedroom, stripped herself naked, and anointed her body with an ointment made for that purpose. She next took a staff, which also in many cases she anointed, and placing it between her legs and uttering a charm, she was carried through the air, in an incredibly short space of time, to the place of meeting. Bodin discusses learnedly the question whether the witches were really carried through the air corporeally or not, he decides it in the affirmative. The Sabbath itself was a great assemblage of witches, of both sexes, and of demons. It was a point of emulation with the visitors to bring new converts with them, and on their arrival they presented these to the demon who presided, and to whom they offered their adoration by the unclean kiss upon his posteriors. They next rendered an account of all the mischief they had perpetrated since the previous meeting, and received reward or reproof according to its amount. The devil, who usually took the form of a goat, next distributed among them powders, unguents, and other articles to be employed in similar evil doings in future. The worshippers now made offerings to the devil, consisting of sheep, or other articles, or, in some cases, of a little bird only, or of a lock of the witches' hair, or of some other equally trifling object. They were then obliged to seal their denial of the Christian faith by trampling on the cross and blaspheming the saints. The devil then, or in the course of the meeting, had sexual intercourse with the new witch, placed his mark upon some concealed part of her body, very commonly in her sexual parts, and gave her a familiar or imp, who was to be at her bidding and assist in the perpetration of evil. All this was what may be called the business of the meeting, and when it was over, they all went to a great banquet, which was set out on tables, and which sometimes consisted of sumptuous viands, but more frequently of loathsome or unsubstantial food, so that the guests often left the meeting as hungry as though they had tasted nothing. After the feast they all rose from the table to dance, and a scene of wild and uproarious revelry followed. The usual dance on this occasion appears to have been the *carole* of the middle ages, which was no doubt the common dance of the peasantry; a party, alternately a male and a female, held each other's hands in a circle, with this peculiarity that, whereas in ordinary life the dancers turned their faces inward into the circle, here they turned them outwards, so that their backs were towards the interior of the circle. It was pretended that this arrangement was designed to prevent them from seeing and recognizing each other; but others supposed that it was a mere caprice of the evil one, who wished to do everything in a form contrary to that in which it was usually done by Christians. Other dances were introduced, of a more violent, and some of them of an obscene, character. The songs, too, which were sung in this orgie were either obscene or vulgarly ridiculous. The music was often drawn from burlesque instruments, such as a stick or a bone for a flute, a horse's skull for a lyre, the trunk of a tree for a drum, and a branch for a trumpet. As they became excited, they became more licentious, and at last they abandoned themselves to indiscriminate sexual intercourse, in which the demons played a very active part. The meeting separated in time to allow the witches, by the same expeditious conveyance which brought them, to reach their homes before the cock crowed.[1]

Such is the account of the Sabbath, as described by Bodin; but we have reviewed it briefly in order to describe this strange scene from the much fuller and more curious narrative of another Frenchman, Pierre de Lancre. This man was a conseiller du roi, or judge in the parliament of Bordeaux, and was joined in 1609 with one of his colleagues in a commission to proceed against persons accused of sorcery in Labourd, a district in the Basque provinces, then celebrated for its witches, and apparently for

---

[1] The first edition of the work of Bodin, *De la Démonomanie des Sorciers*, was published at Paris, in 4to, in 1580. It went through many editions, and was translated into Latin and other languages.

---

the low state of morality among its inhabitants. It is a wild, and, in many parts, desolate region, the inhabitants of which held to their ancient superstitions with great tenacity. De Lancre, after arguing learnedly on the nature and character of demons, discusses the question why there were so many of them in the country of Labourd, and why the inhabitants of that district were so much addicted to sorcery. The women of the country, he says, were naturally of a lascivious temperament, which was shown even in their manner of dressing, for he describes their headdress as being singularly indecent, and describes them as commonly exposing their person very immodestly. He adds, that the principal produce of this country consisted of apples, and argues thence, it is not very apparent why, that the women partook of the character of Eve, and yielded more easily to temptation than those of other countries. After having spent four months in dealing out rather severely what was then called "justice" to these ignorant people, the two commissioners returned to Bordeaux, and there De Lancre, deeply struck with what he had seen and heard, betook himself to the study of witchcraft, and in due time produced his great work on the subject, to which he gave the title of *Tableau de l' Inconstance des Mauvais Anges et*

Démons.[1] Pierre de Lancre writes honestly and conscientiously, and he evidently believes everything he has written. His book is valuable for the great amount of new information it contains, derived from the confessions of the witches, and given apparently in their own words. The second book is devoted entirely to the details of the Sabbath.

It was stated by the witches in their examinations that, in times back, they had appointed Monday to be the day, or rather night, of assembly, but that in their time they had two nights of meeting in the week, those of Wednesday and Friday. Although some stated that they had been carried to the place of meeting in the middle of the day, they mostly agreed in saying that the hour at which they were carried to the Sabbath was midnight. The place of assembly was usually chosen at a spot where roads crossed, but this was not always the case, for De Lancre tells us that they were accustomed to hold their Sabbath in some lonely and wild locality, as in the middle of a heath, which was selected especially for being far from the haunts or habitations of man. To this place, he says, they gave the name of Aquelarre, which he interprets as meaning *Lane de Bouc,* that is, the heath of the goat, meaning that it was the place where the

[1] 4to. Paris, 1612. A new and improved edition appeared in 1613.

goat, the usual form assumed by Satan, convoked his assemblies. And he goes on to express his opinion that these wild places were the original scenes of the Sabbath, though subsequently other places had been often adopted. "For we have heard more than fifty witnesses who assured us that they had been at the Goat's Heath to the Sabbath held on the mountain of La Rhune, sometimes on the open mountain, sometimes in the chapel of the St. Esprit, which is on the top of it, and sometimes in the church of Dordach, which is on the borders of Labourd. At times they held it in private houses, as when we held the trial, in the parish of St. Pé, the Sabbath was held one night in our hotel, called Barbare-nena, and in that of Master —— de Segure, assessor-criminal at Bayonne, who, at the same time when we were there, made a more ample inquisition against certain witches, by an authority of an arrest of the parliament of Bordeaux. Then they went the same night to hold it at the residence of the lord of the place, who is Sieur d'Amou, and in his castle of St. Pé. But we have not found in the whole country of Labourd any other parish but that of St. Pé where the devil held the Sabbath in private houses."

The devil is further described as seeking for his places of meeting, besides the heaths, old decayed houses, and ruins of old castles, especially when they were situated on the summits of mountains. An old cemetery was sometimes selected, where, as De Lancre quaintly observes, there were " no houses but the houses of the dead," especially if it were in a solitary situation, as when attached to solitary churches and chapels, in the middle of the heaths, or on the tops of cliffs on the sea shore, such as the chapel of the Portuguese at St. Jean de Luz, called St. Barbe, situated so high that it serves as a land-mark to the ships approaching the coast, or on a high mountain, as La Rhune in Labourd, and the Puy de Dome in Perigord, and other such places.

At these meetings, sometimes, but rarely, Satan was absent, in which case a little devil took his place. De Lancre enumerates the various forms which the devil usually assumed on these occasions, with the remark that these forms were as numerous as " his movements were inconstant, full of uncertainty, il-lusion, deception, and imposture." Some of the witches he examined, among whom was a girl of thirteen years of age, named Marie d'Aguerre, said that at these assemblies there appeared a great pitcher or jug in the middle of the Sabbath, and that out of it the devil issued in the form of a goat, which suddenly became so large that it was " frightful," and that at the end of the Sabbath he returned into the pitcher. Others described him as being like the great trunk of a tree, without arms or feet, seated in a chair, with the face of a great and frightful looking man. Others spoke of him as resembling a great goat, with two horns before and two behind, those before turned up in the semblance of a woman's perruque. According to the most common account, De Lancre says he had three horns, the one in the middle giving out a flame, with which he used at the Sabbath to give both light and fire to the witches, some of whom who had candles lit them at his horn, in order to hold them at a mock service of the mass, which was one of the devil's ceremonies. He had also, sometimes, a kind of cap or hat over his horns. " He has before him his member hanging out, which he exhibits always a cubit in length; and he has a great tail behind, with a form of a face under it, with which face he does not utter a word, but it serves only to offer to kiss to those he likes, honouring certain witches of either sex more than the others." The devil, it will be observed, is here represented with the symbol of Priapus. Marie d'Aspilecute, aged nineteen years, who lived at Handaye, deposed that the first time she was presented to the devil she kissed him on this face behind, beneath a great tail, and that she repeated the kiss three times, adding that this face was made like the muzzle of a goat. Others said that he was shaped like a great man, " enveloped in a cloudiness, because he would not be seen clearly," and that he was all "flamboyant," and had a face red like an iron coming out of the furnace. Corneille Brolic, a lad of twelve years of age, said that when he was first introduced to him he had the human form, with four horns on his head, and without arms. He was seated in a pulpit, with some of the women, who were his favourites, always near him. "And they are all agreed that it is a great pulpit, which seems to be gilt and very pompous." Janette d'Abadie, of Siboro, sixteen years old, said that Satan had a face before and another behind his head, as they represent the god Janus. De Lancre had also heard him described as a great black dog, as a large ox of brass lying down, and as a natural ox in repose.

Although it was stated that in former times the devil had usually appeared in the form of a serpent,—another coincidence with the priapic worship,—it appears certain that in the time of De Lancre his favourite form of showing himself was that of a goat. At the opening of the Sabbath the witches, male or female, presented formally to the devil those who had never been at the Sabbath before, and the women especially brought to him the children whom they allured to him. The new converts, the novices, were made to renounce Christ, the Virgin Mary, and the saints, and they were then re-baptized with mock ceremonies. They next performed their worship to the devil by kissing him on the face under the tail, or otherwise. The young children were taken to the edge of a stream—for the scene was generally chosen on the banks of a stream—and white wands were placed in their hands, and they were entrusted with the care of the toads which were kept there, and which were of importance in the subsequent operations of the witches. The renunciation was frequently renewed, and in some cases it was required every time the witch attended the Sabbath. Janette d'Abadie, a girl of sixteen, said that he made her repeatedly go through the ceremony of kissing him on the face, and afterwards on the navel, then on the virile member, and then on the posteriors. After rebaptism, he put his mark on the body of his victim, in some covered part where it was not likely to be seen. In women it was often placed on or within the sexual parts.

De Lancre's account of the proceedings at the Sabbath is very full and curious. He says that it "resembled a fair of merchants mingled together, furious and in transports, arriving from all parts—a meeting and mingling of a hundred thousand subjects, sudden and transitory, novel, it is true, but of a frightful novelty, which offends the eye and sickens you. Among these same subjects some are real, and others deceitful and illusory. Some are pleasing (but very little), as are the little bells and melodious instruments of all sorts, which only tickle the ear and do not touch the heart at all, consisting more in noise which amazes and stuns than in harmony which pleases and rejoices, the others displeasing, full of deformity and horror, tending only to desolation, privation, ruin, and destruction, where the persons become brutish and transformed to beasts, losing their speech while they are in this condition, and the beasts, on the contrary, talk, and seem to have more reason than the persons, each being drawn out of his natural character."

The women, according to De Lancre, were the active agents in all this confusion, and had more employment than the men. They rushed about with their hair hanging loose, and their bodies naked; some rubbed with the magical ointment, others not. They arrived at the Sabbath, or went from it, on their errands of mischief, perched on a stick or besom, or carried upon a goat or other animal, with an infant or two behind, and guided or driven on by the devil himself. "And when Satan will transport them into the air (which is an indulgence only to the most superior), he sets them off and launches them up like fired rockets, and they repair to and dart down upon the said place a hundred times more rapidly than an eagle or a kite could dart upon its prey."

These women, on their arrival, reported to Satan all the mischief they had perpetrated. Poison, of all kinds and for all purposes, was there the article most in vogue. Toads were said to form one of its ingredients, and the charge of these animals, while alive, was given to the children whom the witches brought with them to the Sabbath, and to whom, as a sort of ensign of office, little white rods were given, " just such as they give to persons infected with the plague as a mark of their contagion."

The devil was the sovereign master of the assembly, and appeared at it sometimes in the form of a stinking and bearded goat, as one, De Lancre says, which was especially repulsive to mankind. The goat, we know, was dedicated to Priapus. Sometimes he assumed a form, if we clearly understand De Lancre, which presented a confused idea of something between a tree and a man, which is compared, for he becomes rather poetical, to the old decayed cypresses on the summit of a high mountain, or to aged oaks whose heads already bear the marks of approaching decay.

When the devil appeared in human form, that form was horribly ugly and repulsive, with a hoarse voice and an imperious manner. He was seated in a pulpit, which glittered like gold; and at his side sat the queen of the Sabbath, one of the witches whom he had debauched, to whom he chose to give greater honour than to the others, and whom he decked in gay robes, with a crown on her head, to serve as a bait to the ambition of the rest. Candles of pitch, or torches, yielded a false light, which gave people in appearance monstrous forms and frightful faces.

Here you see false fires, through which some of the demons were first passed, and afterwards the witches, without suffering any pain, which, as explained by De Lancre, was intended to teach them not to fear the fire of hell. But we see in these the need-fires, which formed a part of the priapic orgies, and of which we have spoken before (p. 94). There women are presenting to him children, whom they have initiated in sorcery, and he shows them a deep pit, into which he threatens to throw them if they refuse to renounce God and to adore Satan.

In other parts are seen great cauldrons, full of toads and vipers, hearts of unbaptized children, flesh of criminals who had been hanged, and other disgusting ingredients, of which they make pots of ointments, &c. and poisons, the ordinary articles of commerce in this "fair." Of such objects, also, were composed the dishes served at the Sabbath tables, at which no salt was allowed, because Satan wished everything to be insipid, musty, and bad-tasted.

Here we see people "dancing, either 'in long,' in couples, turned back to back, or sometimes 'in round,' all turning their backs towards the centre of the dance, the girls and women each holding by the hand their demons, who teach them movements and gestures so lascivious and indecent that they would horrify the most shameless woman in the world; with songs of a composition so brutal, and in terms and words of such license and lubricity, that the eyes become troubled, the ears confounded, and the understanding bewitched, at the appearance of so many monstrous things all crowded together."

"The women and girls with whom the demons choose to have connection are covered with a cloud, to conceal the execrations and ordures attached to these scenes, and to prevent the compassion which others might have on the screams and sufferings of these poor wretches." In order to "mix impiety with the other abominations," they pretended to perform religious rites, which were a wild and contemptuous parody on the catholic mass. An altar was raised, and a priest consecrated and administered the host, but it was made of some disgusting substance, and the priest stood with his head downwards and his legs in the air, and with his back turned to the altar.

Thus all things were performed in monstrous or disgusting forms, so that Satan himself appeared almost ashamed of them.

De Lancre acknowledges that there was some diversity in the manner of the proceedings of the Sabbath in different countries, arising from difference in the character of the locality, in the "master" who presided, and in the various humours of those who attended. "But all well considered, there is a general agreement on the principal and most important of the more serious ceremonies. Wherefore, I will relate what we have learnt by our trials, and I will simply repeat what some notable witches deposed before us, as well as to the formalities of the Sabbath, as to all that was usually seen there, without changing or altering anything in what they deposed, in order that every one may select what he likes."

The first witness adduced by De Lancre is not one belonging to his own time, but dating back as far as the 18th of December, 1567, and he had obtained a copy of the confession. Estébene de Cambrue, of the parish of Amou, a woman twenty-five years of age, said that the great Sabbath was held four times a year, in derision of the four annual festivals of the Church. The little assemblies, which were held in the neighbourhood of the towns or parishes, were attended only by those of the locality; they were called "pastimes," and were held sometimes in one place and sometimes in another, and there they only danced and frolicked, for the devil did not come there in all his state as at the great assemblies. They were, in fact, the greater and lesser Priapeia. She said that the place of the grand convocation was generally called the " Lanne de Bouc " (the goat's heath), where they danced round a stone, which was planted in the said place, (perhaps one of the so-called Druidical monuments,) upon which was seated a great black man, whom they called "Monsieur." Each person present kissed this black man on the posteriors. She said that they were carried to that place on an animal which sometimes resembled a horse and at others a man, and they never rode on the animal more than four at a time. When arrived at the Sabbath, they denied God, the Virgin, "and the rest," and took Satan for their father and protector, and the she-devil for their mother. This witness described the making and sale of poisons. She said that she had seen at the Sabbath a notary, whose name she gave, whose business it was to denounce those who failed in attendance. When on their way to the Sabbath, however hard it might rain, they were never wet, provided they uttered the words, *Haut la coude, Quillet,* because then the tail of the beast on which they were mounted covered them so well that they were sheltered from the rain. When they had to make a long journey they said these words: *Pic suber hoeilhe, en ta la lane de bouc bien m' arrecoueille.*

A man seventy-three years of age, named Petri Daguerre, was brought before De Lancre and his fellow commissioners at Ustarits; two witnesses asserted that he held the office of master of ceremonies and governor of the Sabbath, and that the devil gave him a gilt staff, which he carried in his hand as a mark of authority, and arranged and directed the proceedings. He returned the staff to Satan at the close of the meeting.

One Leger Rivasseau confessed that he had been at the Sabbath twice without adoring the devil, or doing any of the things required from the others, because it was part of his bargain, for he had given the half of his left foot for the faculty of curing, and the right of being present at the Sabbath without further obligation. He said " that the Sabbath was held about midnight, at a meeting of cross roads, most frequently on the nights of Wednesday and Friday; that the devil chose in preference the stormiest nights, in order that the winds and troubled elements might carry their powders farther and more impetuously; that two notable devils presided at their Sabbaths, the great negro, whom they called Master Leonard, and another little devil, whom Master Leonard at times substituted in his place, and whom they called Master Jean Mullin; that they adored the grand master, and that, after having kissed his posteriors, there were about sixty of them dancing without dress, back to back, each with a great cat attached to the tail of his or her shirt, and that afterwards they danced naked; that this Master Leonard, taking the form of a black fox, hummed at the beginning a word ill articulated, after which they were all silent."

Some of the witches examined spoke of the delight with which they attended the Sabbath. Jeanne Dibasson, a woman twenty-nine years old, said that the Sabbath was the true Paradise, where there was far more pleasure than can be expressed; that those who went there found the time so short by reason of the pleasure and enjoyment, that they never left it without marvelous regret, so that they looked forward with infinite impatience to the next meeting.

Marie de la Ralde, "a very handsome woman tyenty-eight years of age," who had then abandoned her connection with the devil five or six years, gave a full account of her experience of the Sabbath. She said she had frequented the Sabbaths from the time she was ten years old, having been first taken there by Marissans, the wife of Sarrauch, and after her death the devil took her there himself. That the first time she was there she saw the devil in the shape of a trunk of a tree, without feet, but apparently sitting in a pulpit, with some form of a human face, very obscure; but since she had often seen him in man's form, sometimes red, sometimes black. That she had often seen him approach a hot iron to the children which were presented to him, but she did not know if he marked them with it. That she had never kissed him since she had arrived at the age of knowledge, and does not know whether she had kissed him before or not; but she had seen how, when one went to adore him, he presented sometimes his face to kiss, sometimes his posteriors, as it pleased him, and at his discretion. That she had a singular pleasure in going to the Sabbath, so that every time she was summoned to go there, she went as though it were to a wedding feast; not so much for the liberty and license they had there to have connection with each other (which out of modesty she said she had never done or seen done), but because the devil had so strong a hold on their hearts and wills that it hardly allowed any other desire to enter. Besides that the witches believe they are going to a place where there are a hundred thousand wonders and novelties to see, and where they hear so great a diversity of melodious instruments that they are ravished, and believe themselves to be in some terrestrial paradise. Moreover the devil persuades them that the fear of hell, which is so much apprehended, is a piece of folly, and gives them to understand that the eternal punishments will hurt them no more than a certain artificial fire which he causes them craftily to light, and then makes them pass through it and repass without hurt. And more, that they see there so many priests, their pastors, curés, vicars, and confessors, and other people of quality of all sorts, so many heads of families, and so many mistresses of the principal houses in the said country, so many people veiled, whom they considered to be grandees, because they concealed themselves and wished to be unknown, that they believed and took it for a very great honour and good fortune to be received there.

Marie d'Aspilcouëtte, a girl nineteen years old, who lived at Handaye, said that she had frequented the Sabbath ever since the age of seven, and that she was taken there the first time by Catherine de Moleres, who had since been executed to death for having caused a man's death by sorcery. She said that it was now two years since she had withdrawn from her relations with Satan. That the devil appeared in the form of a goat, having a tail and under it the face of a black man, which she was compelled to kiss, and that this posterior face has not the power of speech, but they were obliged to adore and kiss it. After-

PLATE XVI   THE WITCHES' SABB

wards the said Moleres gave her seven toads to keep. That the said Moleres transported her through the air to the Sabbath, where she saw people dancing, with violins, trumpets, and tabors, which made a very great harmony. That in the said assemblies there was an extreme pleasure and enjoyment. That they made love in full liberty before all the world. That some were employed in cutting off the heads of toads, while others made poison of them; and that they made the poison at home as well as at the Sabbath.

After describing the different sorts of poisons prepared on these occasions, De Lancre proceeds to report the testimony of other witnesses to the details of the Sabbath. Jeannette de Belloc, called Atsoua, a damsel of twenty-four years of age, said that she had been made a witch in her childhood by a woman named Oylarchahar, who took her for the first time to the Sabbath, and there presented her to the devil; and after her death, Mary Martin, lady of the house of Adamechorena, took her place. About the month of February, 1609, Jeannette confessed to a priest who was the nephew of Madame Martin, who went to his aunt and merely enjoined her not to take the girl to the Sabbath any more. Jeannette said that at the solemn festivals all kissed the devil's posteriors except the notable witches, who kissed him in the face. According to her account, the children, at the age of two or three years, or as soon as they could speak, were made to renounce Jesus Christ, the Virgin Mary, their baptism, &c. and from that moment they were taught to worship the devil. She described the Sabbath as resembling a fair, well supplied with all sorts of objects, in which some walked about in their own form, and others were transformed, she knew not how, into dogs, cats, asses, horses, pigs, and other animals. The little boys and girls kept the herds of the Sabbath, consisting of a world of toads near a stream, with small white rods, and were not allowed to approach the great mass of the witches; while others, of more advanced age, who were not objects of sufficient respect, were kept apart in a sort of apprenticeship, during which they were only allowed to look on at the proceedings of the others. Of these there were two sorts; some were veiled, to make the poorer classes believe that they were people of rank and distinction, and that they did not wish themselves to be known in such a place; others were uncovered, and openly danced, had sexual intercourse, made the poisons, and performed their other diabolical functions; and these were not allowed to approach so near "the master" as those who were veiled. The holy water used at the Sabbath was the devil's urine. She pointed out two of the accused whom she had seen at the Sabbath playing upon the tabor and the violin. She spoke of the numbers who were seen arriving and departing continually, the latter to do evil, the former to report what they had done. They went out at sea, even as far as Newfoundland, where their husbands and sons went to fish, in order to raise storms, and endanger their ships. This deponent spoke also of the fires at the Sabbath, into which the witches were thrown wtihout sustaining any hurt. She had seen the frequenters of the Sabbath make themselves appear as big as houses, but she had never seen them transform themselves into animals, although there were animals of different kinds running about at the Sabbath.

Jeanette d'Abadie, an inhabitant of Siboro, of the age of sixteen, said that she was taken for the first time to the Sabbath by a woman named Gratianne; that for the last nine months she had watched and done all she could to withdraw herself from this evil influence; that during the first three of these months, because she had watched at home by night, the devil carried her away to the Sabbath in open day; and during the other six, until the 16th of September, 1609, she had only gone to them twice, because she had watched, and still watches in the church; and that the last time she was there was the 13th of September, 1609, which she narrated in a "bizarre and very terrible manner." It appears that, having

watched in the church of Siboro during the night between Saturday and Sunday, at daybreak she went
to sleep at home, and, during the time of the grand
mass, the devil came to her and snatched from her
neck a " fig of leather which she wore there, as an
infinity of other people did; " this *higo,* or fig, she
described as " a form of hand, with the fist closed,
and the thumb passed between the two fingers, which
they believe to be, and wear as, a remedy against all
enchantment and witchcraft; and, because the devil
cannot bear this fist, she said that he did not dare to
carry it away, but left it at the threshold of the door
of the room in which she was sleeping." This Jeanette
said, that the first time she went to the Sabbath she
saw there the devil in the form of a man, black and
hideous, with six horns on his head, and sometimes
eight, and a great tail behind, one face in front and
another at the back of the head, as they paint the
god Janus. Gratianne, on presenting her, received
as her reward a handful of gold; and then the child-
victim was made to renounce her Creator, the Virgin,
the baptism, father, mother, relatives, heaven, earth,
and all that was in the world, and then she was required to kiss the fiend on the posteriors. The renunciation she was obliged to repeat every time she went
to the Sabbath. She added that the devil often made
her kiss his face, his navel, his member, and his pos-

teriors. She had often seen the children of witches baptized at the Sabbath.

Another ceremony was that of baptizing toads. These animals perform a great part in these old popular orgies. At one of the Sabbaths, a lady danced with four toads on her person, one on each shoulder, and one on each wrist, the latter perched like hawks. Jeanette d'Abadie went on further in her revelations in regard to still more objectionable parts of the proceedings. She said that, with regard to their libidinous acts, she had seen the assembly intermix incestuously, and contrary to all order of nature, accusing even herself of having been robbed of her maidenhead by Satan, and of having been known an infinite number of times by a relation of hers, and by others, whoever would ask her. She always fought to avoid the embraces of the devil, because it caused her an extreme pain, and she added that what came from him was cold, and never produced pregnancy. Nobody ever became pregnant at the Sabbath. Away from the Sabbath, she never committed a fault, but in the Sabbath she took a marvellous pleasure in these acts of sexual intercourse, which she displayed by dwelling on the description of them with a minuteness of detail, and language of such obscenity, as would have drawn a blush from the most depraved woman in the world. She described also the tables covered in appearance with provisions, which, however, proved either unsubstantial or of a disgusting nature.

This witness further declared that she had seen at the Sabbath a number of little demons without arms, who were employed in kindling a great fire, into which they threw the witches, who came out without being burnt; and she had also seen the grand master of the assembly throw himself into a fire, and remain there until he was burnt to powder, which powder was used by the witches to bewitch young children, and cause them to go willingly to the Sabbath. She had seen priests who were well-known, and gave the names of some of them, performing the service of the mass at the Sabbath, while the demons took their places on the altar in the forms of saints. Sometimes the devil pierced the left foot of a sorcerer under the little toe, and drew blood, which he sucked, and after this that individual could never be drawn to make a confession; and she named, as an example, a priest named Francois de Bideguaray, of Bordegaina, who, in fact, could not be made to confess. She named many other persons whom she had seen at the Sabbaths, and especially one named Anduitze, whose office it was to summon the witches and sorcerers to the meeting.

De Lancre says that many others, in their depositions, spoke of the extreme pleasures and enjoyments experienced in these Sabbaths, which made men and women repair to them with the greatest eagerness. "The woman indulged before the face of her husband without suspicion or jealousy, he even frequently acted the part of procurer; the father deprived his daughter of her virginity without shame; the mother acted the same part towards her son; the brother towards his sister; fathers and mothers carried thither and presented their children."

The dances at the Sabbath were mostly indecent, including the well-known Sarabande, and the women danced in them sometimes in chemise, but much more frequently quite naked. They consisted especially in violent movements; and the devil often joined in them, taking the handsomest woman or girl for his partner. De Lancre's account of these dances is so minute and curious that it may be given in his own words. "If the saying is true that never woman or girl returned from the ball as chaste as she went there, how unclean must she return who has abandoned herself to the unfortunate design of going to the ball of the demons and evil spirits, who has danced in hand with them, who has kissed them obscenely, who has yielded herself to them as a prey, has adored them, and has even copulated with them? It is to be, in good earnest, inconstant and fickle; it is to be not only lewd, or even a shameless whore, but to be stark-mad, unworthy of the favours with which God loads her in bringing her into the world, and causing her to be born a Christian. We caused in several places the boys and girls to dance in the same fashion as they danced at the Sabbath, as much to deter them from such uncleanness, by convincing them to what a degree the most modest of these movements was filthy, vile, and unbecoming in a virtuous girl, as also because, when accused, the greater part of the witches, charged with having among other things danced in hand with the devil, and sometimes led the dance, denied it all, and said that the girls were deceived, and that they could not have known how to express the forms of dance which they said they had seen at the Sabbath. They were boys and girls of a fair age, who had already been in the way of salvation before our commission. In truth some of them were already quite out of it, and had gone no more to the Sabbath for some time; others were still struggling to escape, and, held still by one foot, slept in the church, confessed and communicated, in order to withdraw themselves entirely from Satan's claws. Now it is said that they dance always with their backs turned to the centre of the dance, which is the cause that the girls are so accustomed to carry their hands behind them in this round dance,

that they draw into it the whole body, and give it a
bend curved backwards, having their arms half
turned; so that most of them have the belly commonly great, pushed forward, and swollen, and a little in-
clining in front. I know not whether this be caused by
the dance or by the ordure and wretched provisions
they are made to eat. But the fact is, they dance very
seldom one by one, that is one man alone with one
woman or girl, as we do in our galliards; so they have
told and assured us, that they only danced there three
sorts of branles, or brawls, usually turning their
shoulders to one another, and the back of each looking towards the round of the dance, and the face
turned outwards. The first is the Bohemian dance,
for the wandering Bohemians are also half devils; I
mean those long-haired people without country, who
are neither Egytians (gipsies), nor of the kingdom of
Bohemia, but are born everywhere, as they pursue
their route, and pass countries, in the fields, and under the trees, and they go about dancing and playing
conjuring tricks, as at the Sabbath. So they are
numerous in the country of Labourd, on account of
the easy passage from Navarre and Spain.

" The second is with jumping, as our working men
practise in towns and villages, along the streets and
fields; and these two are in round. The third is also
with the back turned, but all holding together in

length, and, without disengaging hands, they approach so near as to touch, and meet back to back, a man with a woman; and at a certain cadence they push and strike together immodestly their two posteriors. And it was also told us that the devil, in his strange humours, did not cause them all to be placed in order, with their backs turned towards the crown of the dance, as is commonly said by everybody; but one having the back turned, and the other not, and so on to the end of the dance. . . . They dance to the sound of the tabor and flute, and sometimes with the long instrument they carry at the neck, and thence stretching to near the girdle, which they beat with a little stick; sometimes with a violin (fiddle). But these are not the only instruments of the Sabbath, for we have learnt from many of them that all sorts of instruments are seen there, with such harmony that there is no concert in the world to be compared to it."

Nothing is more remarkable than the sort of prurient curiosity with which these honest commissioners interrogated the witnesses as to the sexual peculiarities and capabilities of the demon, and the sort of satisfaction with which De Lancre reduces all this to writing. They all tend to show the identity of these orgies with those of the ancient worship of Priapus, who is undoubtedly figured in the Satan of the Sabbath. The young witch, Jeannette d'Abadie, told how she had seen at the Sabbath men and women in promiscuous intercourse, and how the devil arranged them in couples, in the most unnatural conjunctions—the daughter with the father, the mother with her son, the sister with the brother, the daughter-in-law with the father-in-law, the penitent with her confessor, without distinction of age, quality, or relationship, so that she confessed to having been known an infinity of times at the Sabath by a cousin-german of her mother, and by an infinite number of others. After repeating much that she had said before relating to the impudicity of the Sabbath, this girl said that she had been deflowered by the devil at the age of thirteen—twelve was the common age for this—that they never became pregnant, either by him or by any of the wizards of the Sabbath; that she had never felt anything come from the devil except the first time, when it was very cold, but that with the sorcerers it was as with other men. That the devil chose the handsomest of the women and girls for himself, and one he usually made his queen for the meeting. That they suffered extremely when he had intercourse with them, in consequence of his member being covered with scales like those of a fish. That when extended it was a yard long, but that it was usually twisted. Marie d'Aspilcuette, a girl between nineteen and twenty years of age, who also confesesd to having had frequent connection with Satan, described his member as about half a yard long, and moderately large. Marguerite, a girl of Sare, between sixteen and seventeen, described it as resembling that of a mule, and as being as long and thick as one's arm. More on this subject the reader will find in De Lancre's own text. The devil, we are further told, preferred married women to girls, because there was more sin in the connection, adultery being a greater crime than simple fornication.

In order to give still more truthfulness to his account of the Sabbath, De Lancre caused all the facts gathered from the confessions of his victims to be embodied in a picture which illustrates the second edition of his book, and which places the whole scene before us so vividly that we have had it re-engraved in facsimile as an illustration to the present essay.[1] The different groups are, as will be seen, indicated by capital letters. At A we have Satan in his gilt pulpit, with five horns, the one in the middle lighted, for the purpose of giving light to all the candles and fires at the Sabbath. B is the queen of the Sabbath, seated at his right hand, while another favorite, though in less degree, sits on the other side. C, a witch presenting a child which she has seduced. D,

---

[1] See our plate xvi.

the witches, each with her demon, seated at table. E, a party of four witches and sorcerers, who are only admitted as spectators, and are not allowed to approach the great ceremonies. F, " according to the old proverb, *Après la pance, vient la dance,"* the witches and their demons have risen from table, and are here engaged in one of the descriptions of dances mentioned above. G, the players on instruments, who furnish the music to which the witches dance. H, a troop of women and girls, who dance with their faces turned outwards from the round of the dance. I, the cauldron on the fire, to make all sorts of poisons and noxious compounds. K, during these proceedings, many witches are seen arriving at the Sabbath on staffs and broomsticks, and others on goats, bringing with them children to offer to Satan; others are departing from the Sabbath, carried through the air to the sea and distant parts, where they will raise storms and tempests. L, " the great lords and ladies and other rich and powerful people, who treat on the grand affairs of the Sabbath, where they appear veiled, and the women with masks, that they may remain always concealed and unknown." Lastly, at M, we see the young children, at some distance from the busy part of the ceremonies, taking charge of the toads.

In reviewing the extraordinary scenes which are

developed in these witch-depositions, we are struck
not only with their general resemblance among themselves, although told in different countries, but also
with the striking points of identity between the proceedings of the Sabbath. and the secret assemblies
with which the Templars were charged. We have in
both the initiatory presentation, the denial of Christ,
and the homage to the new master, sealed by the obscene kiss. This is just what might be expected. In
preserving secretly a religious worship after the open
practice of it had been proscribed, it would be natural, if not necessary, to require of the initiated a
strong denial of the new and intrusive faith, with
acts as well as words which compromised him entirely in what he was doing. The mass and weight
of the evidence certainly goes to prove that such
secret rites did prevail among the Templars, though it
is not equally evident that they prevailed throughout
the order; and the similarity of the revelations of
the witch-confessions, in all countries where they
were taken, seems to show that there was in them
also a foundation in truth. We look upon it as not
admitting of doubt, that the Priapic orgies and the
other periodical assemblies for worship of this description, which we have described in an earlier part
of this essay, were continued long after the fall of the
Roman power and the introduction of the Christian

religion. The rustic population, mostly servile, whose morals or private practices were little heeded by the other classes of society, might, in a country so thinly peopled, assemble by night in retired places without any fear of observation. There they perhaps indulged in Priapic rites, followed by the old Priapic orgies, which would become more and more debased in form, but through the effects of exciting potions, as described by Michelet,[1] would have become wilder than ever. They became, as Michelet describes them, the Saturnalia of the serf. The state of mind produced by these excitements would lead those who partook in them to believe easily in the actual presence of the beings they worshipped, who, according to the Church doctrines, were only so many devils. Hence arose the diabolical agency in the scene. Thus we easily obtain all the materials and all the incidents of the witches' Sabbath. Where this older worship was preserved among the middle or more elevated classes of society, who had other means of secrecy at their command, it would take a less vulgar form, and would show itself in the formation of concealed sects and societies, such as those of the different forms of Gnosticism, of the Stadingers, of the Templars, and

---

[1] See Michelet, *La Sorcière*, liv. i, c. 9, on the use and the effects of the Solaneæ, to which he attributes much of the delusions of the Sabbath.

of other less important secret clubs, of a more or less immoral character, which continued no doubt to exist long after what we call the middle ages had passed away. As we have before intimated, these mediæval practices prevailed most in Gaul and the South, where the influence of Roman manners and superstitions was greatest.

The worship of the reproductive organs as representing the fertilizing, protecting, and saving powers of nature, apart from these secret rites, prevailed universally, as we have traced it fully in the preceding pages, and we only recur to that part of the subject to state that perhaps the last traces of it now to be found in our islands is met with on the western shores of Ireland. Off the coast of Mayo, there is a small island named Inniskea, the inhabitants of which are a very primitive and uncultivated race, and which, although it takes its name from a female saint (it is the *insular sanctæ Geidhe* of the Hibernian hagiographers), does not contain a single Catholic priest. Its inhabitants, indeed, as we learn from an interesting communication to *Notes and Queries* by Sir J. Emerson Tennent,[1] are mere idolaters, and their idol, no doubt the representative of Priapus, is a long cylindrical stone, which they call *Neevougee*. This idol is kept wrapped in flannel, and is entrusted to

---

[1] *Notes and Queries,* for 1852, vol. v, p. 121.

the care of an old woman, who acts as the priestess. It is brought out and worshipped at certain periods, when storms disturb the fishing, by which chiefly the population of the island obtain a living, or at other times it is exposed for the purpose of raising storms which may cause wrecks to be thrown on the coast of the island. I am informed that the Name *Neevougee* is merely the plural of a word signifying a canoe, and it may perhaps have some reference to the calling of fishermen.